Creative Problem Solving

Creative Problem Solving

Total Systems Intervention

Robert L. Flood

and

Michael C. Jackson

Department of Management Systems and Sciences
University of Hull, UK

JOHN WILEY & SONS

Chichester · New York · Brisbane · Toronto · Singapore

Other Wiley Editorial Offices

John Wiley & Sons, Inc., 605 Third Avenue,
New York, NY 10158–0012, USA

Jacaranda Wiley Ltd, G.P.O. Box 859, Brisbane,
Queensland 4001, Australia

John Wiley & Sons (Canada) Ltd, 5353 Dundas Road West,
Etobicoke, Ontario M9B 6H8, Canada

John Wiley & Sons (SEA) Pte Ltd, 37 Jalan Pemimpin #05–04,
Block B, Union Industrial Building, Singapore 2057

Library of Congress Cataloging-in-Publication Data:

Flood, Robert L.
    Creative problem solving : total systems intervention / Robert L.
Flood and Michael C. Jackson.
        p.   cm.
    Includes bibliographical references and index.
    ISBN 0-471-93052-0 (ppc)
    1. Management Science.   2. System analysis.   I. Jackson, Michael
C., *1951–* .II. Title.
T57.6.F59   1991
658.4′03—dc20   91–11559
                                                                          CIP

British Library Cataloguing in Publication Data:

A catalogue record for this book
is available from the British Library.

ISBN   0-471-93052-0

Typeset in 10/12 pt Palatino by Photo·graphics, Honiton, Devon
Printed and bound in Great Britain by Biddles Ltd, Guildford, Surrey

Contents

Preface   xi

CHAPTER 1
The Nature of Systems Thinking   1
1.1   Introduction   1
1.2   The Concept "System"   2
1.3   The Development of Systems Thinking   3
1.4   A General Conception of "System"   5
1.5   Machine Metaphor or "Closed System" View   8
1.6   Organic Metaphor or "Open System" View   9
1.7   Neurocybernetic Metaphor or "Viable System" View   10
1.8   Culture Metaphor   11
1.9   Political Metaphor   12
1.10 Remarks on Metaphor   14
1.11 Total Quality Management (TQM): An Example of the
      Use of Systemic Metaphor   15
      1.11.1 Introduction   15
      1.11.2 Philosophy, Principles and Methodology of TQM   16
      1.11.3 Creative Thinking about TQM   18
1.12 Summary   21
1.13 Case Study   22
      1.13.1 Introduction   22
      1.13.2 Your Task   22
      1.13.3 The Construction Industry in Singapore and the
             Role of the Board   23
1.14 Further Reading   28

CHAPTER 2
A System of Systems Methodologies   31
2.1   Introduction   31

2.2   Grouping Problem-Contexts   32
2.3   Grouping Types of Systems Methodology   35
2.4   A System of Systems Methodologies   41
2.5   Summary   41
2.6   Case Study   43
2.7   Further Reading   43

CHAPTER 3
The Logic and Process of Total Systems Intervention (TSI)   **45**
3.1   Introduction   45
3.2   Philosophy of TSI   46
      3.2.1   Introduction   46
      3.2.2   Complementarism   47
      3.2.3   Sociological Awareness   48
      3.2.4   Human Well-Being and Emancipation   49
3.3. Principles of TSI   50
3.4   The Three Phases of TSI   50
      3.4.1   Creativity   50
      3.4.2   Choice   51
      3.4.3   Implementation   52
3.5   TSI in Action: A Total Quality Management Example   54
3.6   Conclusion   59
3.7   Further Reading   60

CHAPTER 4
System Dynamics (SD)   **61**
4.1   Introduction   61
4.2   Philosophy of SD   62
4.3   Principles of SD   63
4.4   Model and Methodology   64
4.5   Using the Models   73
4.6   SD in Action: A Simple Expansion of the
      Stock/Inventory Model   75
4.7   Critique of SD   78
4.8   Case Study: A Project Manager's Dilemma   83
      4.8.1   Introduction   83
      4.8.2   Your Task   83
4.9   Further Reading   85

CHAPTER 5
Viable System Diagnosis (VSD)   **87**
5.1   Introduction   87

5.2 Philosophy of VSD   89
5.3 Principles of VSD   89
5.4 The Viable System Model   90
5.5 Using the Viable System Model   93
    5.5.1 Introduction   93
    5.5.2 System Identification   94
    5.5.3 System Diagnosis   94
    5.5.4 Frequent Faults   95
5.6 VSD in Action: The Example of a Major Tourism
    Services Group   96
    5.6.1 Background   96
    5.6.2 Diagnosis and Redesign   98
    5.6.3 Conclusion   109
5.7 Critique of VSD   110
5.8 Case Study: XY Entertainments   113
    5.8.1 Introduction   114
    5.8.2 Your Task   114
    5.8.3 Further Information   114
5.9 Further Reading   117

CHAPTER 6
Strategic Assumption Surfacing and Testing (SAST)   **119**
6.1 Introduction   119
6.2 Philosophy of SAST   120
    6.2.1 Churchman's Philosophy as the Inspiration of
          SAST   121
    6.2.2 The Specific Philosophy of SAST   122
6.3 Principles of SAST   123
6.4 SAST Methodology   124
    6.4.1 Introduction   124
    6.4.2 Group Formation *   124
    6.4.3 Assumption Surfacing   125
    6.4.4 Dialectical Debate   127
    6.4.5 Synthesis   127
6.5 SAST in Action: The Example of Winterton Co-
    operative Development Agency   128
6.6 Critique of SAST   133
6.7 Case Study: Thornton Printing Company   136
    6.7.1 Your Task   136
    6.7.2 Description of the Situation   137
    6.7.3 Proposed Response   139
6.8 Further Reading   141

CHAPTER 7
Interactive Planning (IP)   **143**
7.1   Introduction   143
7.2   Philosophy of IP   144
7.3   Principles of IP   148
7.4   IP Methodology   150
      7.4.1   Introduction   150
      7.4.2   Formulating the Mess   150
      7.4.3   Ends Planning   150
      7.4.4   Means Planning   152
      7.4.5   Resource Planning   153
      7.4.6   Design of Implementation and Control   153
7.5   IP in Action: The Example of Super Fresh   153
      7.5.1   Introduction   153
      7.5.2   Super Fresh   154
7.6   Critique of IP   157
7.7   Case Study: A Coffee Selling Organisation   162
      7.7.1   Introduction   162
      7.7.2   Your Task   162
      7.7.3   A Coffee Selling Organisation   162
7.8   Further Reading   165

CHAPTER 8
Soft Systems Methodology (SSM)   **167**
8.1   Introduction   167
8.2   Philosophy of SSM   168
8.3   Principles of SSM   171
8.4   Soft Systems Methodology   172
      8.4.1   Introduction   172
      8.4.2   Stages 1 and 2: Finding Out   172
      8.4.3   Stage 3: Formulating Root Definitions   175
      8.4.4   Stage 4: Building Conceptual Models   176
      8.4.5   Stage 5: Comparing Models and "Reality"   176
      8.4.6   Stage 6: Defining Changes   177
      8.4.7   Stage 7: Taking Action   177
      8.4.8   Conclusion   177
8.5   SSM in Action: The Example of Winterton Co-operative
      Development Agency   178
      8.5.1   Introduction   178
      8.5.2   Description of the Situation   179
      8.5.3   Application of SSM   180
      8.5.4   Conclusion   186

8.6	Critique of SSM	186
8.7	Case Study: Electronic Components Distributors	190
	8.7.1 Introduction	190
	8.7.2 Your Task	190
	8.7.3 Background Information	191
8.8	Further Reading	194

CHAPTER 9

Critical Systems Heuristics (CSH)   **197**

9.1	Introduction	197
9.2	Philosophy of CSH	199
9.3	Principles of CSH	202
9.4	CSH Methodology	204
	9.4.1 Introduction	204
	9.4.2 The 12 Critically Heuristic Categories	204
	9.4.3 The Polemical Employment of Boundary Judgements	207
9.5	CSH in Action: The Example of Police Strategy Towards the Carrying of Offensive Weapons	208
	9.5.1 Introduction	208
	9.5.2 Background	209
	9.5.3 Applying the 12 Critically Heuristic Categories	213
9.6	Critique of CSH	217
9.7	Case Study: A Continuation of the Offensive Weapons Example	220
	9.7.1 Introduction	220
	9.7.2 Your Task	220
	9.7.3 Further Task	221
9.8	Further Reading	221

CHAPTER 10

Total Systems Intervention (TSI) Revisited   **223**

10.1	A Brief Note on TSI	223
10.2	TSI in Action: The Example of a Council for Voluntary Service	224
	10.2.1 Introduction	224
	10.2.2 Description of the Situation	224
	10.2.3 TSI Analysis	229
	10.2.4 The Project Itself	230
	10.2.5 Recommendations	238
10.3	Critique of TSI	241
10.4	Conclusion	245

10.5 Case Study   245
10.6 Further Reading   245

Index   **247**

Preface

In the modern world we are faced with innumerable and multifaceted difficulties and issues which cannot be captured in the minds of a few experts and solved with the aid of some super-method. We are faced with "messes", sets of interacting problems, which range from the technical and the organisational to the social and political, and embrace concerns about the environment, the framework of society, the role of corporations and the motivation of individuals. It is the argument of this book that the search for some super-method that can address all these problems is mistaken and must quickly lead to disenchantment. It would be equally wrong, however, to revert to an heuristic, trial and error approach and seek to solve problems in that way. We need to retain rigorous and formalised thinking, while admitting the need for a range of "problem-solving" methodologies, and accepting the challenge which that brings. The future prospects of management science will be much enhanced if (a) the diversity of the "messes" confronting managers is accepted, (b) work on developing a rich variety of methodologies is undertaken, and (c) we continually ask the question: "What kind of problem situation can be 'managed' with which sort of methodology?"

"Total Systems Intervention" offers an approach to creative "problem solving" which will enrich the way managers, decision makers and their advisers perceive the diversity of difficulties they face. Currently existing systems-based methodologies are considered and organised according to the "ideal-type" problem situations to which they are most relevant. The key to the successful use of the "Total Systems Intervention" (TSI) approach, as will emerge, is to choose an appropriate methodology for tackling the problem situation as it is perceived, but always to recognise that other possible perceptions of that problem situation are possible. In deciding to view a problem situation in a certain way, one is making a partial representation of it. And in employing a methodology which is congruent with that partial representation, one is addressing only certain aspects of "interacting problems". It follows that alternative perceptions of the problem situation need constantly to be kept under review, and alternative approaches to problem management retained in case the character ascribed to the problem situation should change in the opinion of concerned individuals. Sophisticated users of TSI will, indeed, operate simultaneously with different views of the problem situation and with "dominant" and "supportive" methodologies to "sweep in" both the main issue of concern as well as significant side issues.

Let us now rehearse these arguments again, but this time in the context of explaining the structure of the book.

Consider the following tasks:

- Optimising the number and arrangement of supermarket check-out points to reduce waiting time to a minimum, given certain cost constraints.
- Designing a petrochemical plant.
- Pollution control for water authorities.
- Structuring an organisation which exists in a business environment of rapid technological and market change.
- Assisting decision making in a workers' co-operative.
- Making decisions on police resource allocation in dealing with vice in a major city.
- Helping debate among adherents of different doctrinal positions in the Anglican Church.
- Assisting one side or the other in an industrial dispute between managers and workers.

These represent only a handful of management problems which, we would argue, require more than common sense to resolve. They take us beyond our limited, everyday human information processing capabilities, and demand treatment using appropriately designed formal procedures. Our contention is that systems thinking (a broad term which encompasses many systems-based activities) can provide an insightful way of understanding and dealing with such "messes". Systems thinking offers numerous powerful ways of tackling problem situations, while employing a set of concepts that can comfortably be understood by practising managers and decision makers. This is part of the argument of Chapter 1.

The other thing to notice about the tasks set out above is, as previously suggested, their diversity. Intervention to help with these tasks must, therefore, recognise them as diverse and contrasting. Now, it may be thought that the systems approach itself can be accused of hiding that diversity because it sees everything as a "system". The other part of the argument of Chapter 1, however, demonstrates that an alternative use of systems concepts is possible, which retains the richness of the systems idea, and its power as a means of organising our thoughts, while filling it with different types of content each of which yields a differing interpretation of problem situations. This use of the systems idea assists us in developing novel and insightful appreciations of problematic situations rather than encouraging us to see them as all the same.

Management tasks and difficulties often assume sufficient complexity to require well worked-out methodological approaches to aid their resolution, and they are also very diverse in character. The logic leads us to suggest that managers must demand from management scientists equally diverse and contrasting systems-based methodologies for "problem management". Clearly, without access to a diversity of methods, managers would be faced with a high variety of differing "messes" without a sufficiently rich variety in available systems approaches. Fortunately, there is a diversity of systems-based "problem solving" approaches available. Each of these has been developed, implicitly or explicitly, with a particular view on the nature of modern-day complexities and how to manage them. What is needed is an overview of these various systems methods which enables them to be related to the type of problem situation each serves best. The purpose of Chapter 2 is to develop some guidelines that point to the respective strengths of different systems methods and suggest when a situation favours the use of one rather than another. We will group the most important systems approaches in a "system of systems methodologies", which is constituted from the underlying assumptions different systems approaches make about the "systems" with which they deal and about the relationship between the individuals concerned with the problem situation.

The "system of systems methodologies" stands as a rebuke to those who see the diversity of systems-based approaches as representing a fragmentation and weakening of management science as a discipline and profession. It organises tried, tested and proven systems methodologies and shows why each works well in some situations but not in others. It reveals the strengths and the inevitable limitations of each approach. It enables an informed choice of systems methodology to be made in the light of how the problem situation is perceived and what the manager, decision maker or those affected want to achieve.

Chapter 1 explains how the systems idea can be used to generate insightful perspectives on problem situations. Chapter 2 groups the most important of the available systems methodologies in a manner which reveals what problem situations each will tackle best. Chapter 3 has the task of combining the lessons of these two chapters into a unified "Total Systems Intervention" (TSI) approach to "creative problem solving". The essence of TSI is to encourage highly creative thinking about the nature of any problem situation before a decision is taken about the character of the main difficulties to be addressed. Once that decision has been taken, TSI will steer the manager or analyst towards the type of systems methodology most appropriate for dealing with the kind of difficulties identified as being most significant. As the intervention proceeds, using TSI, so the nature of the problem situation will be continually reviewed, as will the choice of appropriate systems methodology. In highly complex problem situations it is advisable to address at the same time different aspects revealed by taking different perspectives on it. This involves employing a number of systems methodologies in combination. In these circumstances it is necessary to nominate one methodology as "dominant" and others as "supportive", although these relationships may change as the study progresses.

Having, in Chapters 1 and 2, developed an understanding of the richness of systems thinking and the strength that comes from the diversity of systems methodologies, and having, in Chapter 3, harnessed the two together in the TSI methodology, the task for Chapters 4 to 9 inclusive is to make sure that the reader has access to what we consider to be to the most important methodologies. Our style of presentation is crucial in this respect. For each methodology we first of all develop a broad understanding of the philosophy and main principles that underpin it. Following on from this, the methodology itself is described. We then provide a worked example, usually drawn from our own consultancy experience, which shows the application of the methodology in a practical situation. We have already suggested above that each methodology has particular strengths and limitations, and we take advantage of the theory and methodology that we have put together, and the worked example, to highlight these in terms of

- the specific consultancy example provided, and
- more general observations.

A case study is then given for the reader to consider and work on. In this way we deal comprehensively with systems-based "problem solving".

In Chapter 10 we put the last piece of our argument in place by presenting an application and then by carrying out a critique of TSI itself.

In essence, we believe that it is vital for managers, planners and decision makers to accept the challenge of facing up to developing a quite sophisticated, although very accessible, means of dealing with the complexities of their working (or indeed social) lives. It is no longer any good simply to assume that a few tasks and techniques learnt in an *ad hoc* way are all that is required in modern-day organisational life. We offer a challenge to the reader to learn and think in detail about management issues and not simply skate over them. Our philosophy is that we wish to educate managers and not simply train monkeys.

In this preface we have pointed to the complexity and diversity of the difficulties that modern-day managers, decision makers and "problem solvers" face. We have also outlined a systems-based approach to creative problem solving called "Total Systems Intervention" (TSI), as a means of facing up to this challenge. Along the way we have described the structure of the book. For the sake of clarity, the following summary is provided.

Chapter 1

THE NATURE OF SYSTEMS THINKING

- concepts
- adding content and practical relevance to the concepts

Chapter 2

A SYSTEM OF SYSTEMS METHODOLOGY

- a diversity of systems methods and methodologies
- constitution of an ideal-type grid of problem contexts

Chapter 3

THE LOGIC AND PROCESS OF TOTAL SYSTEMS INTERVENTION

- relating perceptions of problem situations to choice of appropriate methodology
- guiding the intervention process

Chapters 4–9

SYSTEMS METHODOLOGIES (for each one separately)

- philosophy
- principles

- methodology
- worked example
- critique
- case study

Chapter 10

CRITIQUE OF TSI

- worked example
- critique

The methodologies chosen for Chapters 4–9 are an ordered selection from available systems-based "problem solving" approaches. This reflects our commitment to systems ideas as the most adequate means of managing "messes".

We have written the book without putting references in the text. The aim is to prevent the flow of ideas and argument from being interrupted. The sources for particular chapters are detailed in further reading sections at the end of each chapter. It is necessary for us to acknowledge here, however, the contributions of the ideas of G. Morgan to Chapter 1 and of P. Keys to Chapter 2.

We are grateful to British Telecom plc for their initiative in setting up a core course for their senior managers along the lines of this book. We gained many useful insights, during presentations, about how this material is best structured and put across. In particular we acknowledge the contribution of S. Hicklin, R. Batty, S. Farr, C. White and B. Wilkins, as well as the managers who have been through the course so far. Also thanks to P.A. Consulting Group in London and particularly J. Dexter who made possible the use of our ideas in their own activities. Acknowledgement should also be given to the London Metropolitan Police Force (particularly to Chief Superintendent P. Gaisford and Chief Superintendent T. Brydges), and to organisations (and individuals connected with them) whose anonymity is to be respected, but include a major tourism services group, an entertainments group, a printing firm, a high street bank, a co-operative development agency and a council for voluntary service. We also recognise the useful contribution of Chow Kok Fong to Chapter 1, C. Stevens to Chapter 4, S. Zambuni to Chapter 5, J. K. Ho to Chapter 6, INTERACT (particularly A. Barstow) to Chapter 7, C. E. Chung to Chapter 8, M. Ashton to Chapter 10. We are grateful to all of these. They have helped us understand even more clearly the practical relevance of TSI.

Ken Bowen read parts of the manuscript and provided useful comment. Christopher Stevens made a major contribution to the preparation of the figures, and Linda Saddington made a huge contribution in the preparation of the manuscript.

Most important in this whole venture are Christopher, Mandy, Pauline, Richard and Ross.

Robert L. Flood
Michael C. Jackson
December 1990

Consultancy services using Total Systems Intervention can be obtained through Systems Intervention Ltd. Contact R. L. Flood or M. C. Jackson at the Department of Management Systems and Sciences, University of Hull, Hull, HU6 7RX, N. Humberside, United Kingdom, Telephone (0482) 466309 or (0482) 465731 or fax (0482) 449776. Management consultancy or training seminars are offered.

Chapter 1

The Nature of Systems Thinking

With his death (i.e., that of P'an Ku) the details of creation began. His breath became the wind; his voice, the thunder; his left eye the sun; his right eye the moon; his blood flowed in rivers; his hair grew into trees and plants; his flesh became the soil; his sweat descended as rain; while the parasites which infested his body were the origin of the human race.
H. A. Giles, *Religion of Ancient China*, "The Ancient Faith."

1.1 INTRODUCTION

There is a whole literature discussing the meaning of the term "system" and the advantages of systemic over reductionist thinking. The main purpose of this chapter, however, is to introduce systems ideas in a way which is directly relevant to the practical concerns of managers, decision makers and "problem solvers". This is done in two ways. First, by presenting systems concepts as such and second by adding content and practical relevance to the concepts. What we succeed in building is a range of alternative systemic metaphors which can be used as a vehicle for creative and organised thought about problem situations. Each of these metaphors, as filters, can be tried as a means of viewing a problem context at hand. If one of the metaphors is dominant in bringing issues clearly into focus, then use of a systems methodology, which operates in a manner complementary to that metaphor, can obviously be recommended. This is discussed in Chapter 2.

The method suggested here, of viewing organisational "problems" using different systemic metaphors in order to see which best captures salient features, is a novel one. It admits that organisations are too complex to understand using just one model, but this is just being realistic. It is the failure to admit this fact which causes difficulties for traditional management thinking, with each theory—whether it be scientific management, human relations or whichever—claiming to provide a full account of what is important to the effectiveness and efficiency of organisations. In fact, management theories offer only partial visions of what organisations are like. This can be revealed by looking at the particular metaphors different management theories concentrate upon. Attention will be drawn to these in what follows, in the belief that this will help the novel approach of this book to link with knowledge that readers may already possess of management theory. To turn this the other way around, we could argue that our systemic metaphors allow us to draw upon the main visions of management and organisation theory, as different and yet potentially insightful ways of thinking about our focus of interest—socio-technical organisation. To illustrate these points further, we analyse the popular management philosophy of Total Quality Management (TQM) in terms of the creative use of systemic metaphors. A case study is then provided which readers can use to test their understanding of the way we employ systemic metaphors.

1.2 THE CONCEPT "SYSTEM"

"System" is a term that is widely used in contemporary Western society. This is so much the case that it has effectively been rendered meaningless in everyday use (or should it be misuse?). It seems that virtually everything that is advertised and sold has the label "system" appended to it. This, we suggest, is the everyday contentless use of "system" as merely a generalised label. Our concern is not with this shallow approach; rather we wish to enhance the richness of the concept "system" and therefore enhance practical relevance. This we achieve below in two complementary ways. We first look at the development of systems thinking, stressing that, in the modern systems approach, the concept "system" is used not to refer to things in the world but to a particular way of organising our thoughts about the world. Second, we consider the notion of "system" as an organising concept, before going on to look in detail at various systemic metaphors that may be used as a basis for structuring thinking abour organisations and problem situations.

1.3 THE DEVELOPMENT OF SYSTEMS THINKING

Pre-systems thinking was characterised by disputes between mechanists who believed that everything that occurred was completely determined by something which preceded it, and vitalists who believed that a mysterious force inhabited complex entities such as organisms. The difficulty was that, prior to systems thinking, no very satisfactory concepts existed for understanding phenomena except those employed by physicists, and their concepts seemed unable to explain the behaviour of complex phenomena. Thus space existed for the metaphysical doctrines of vitalism to flourish. However, when vitalism was effectively refuted in biology, by scientific developments that led to explanations of some hitherto inexplicable experimental results in terms of causal relationships, it looked as though the way was open for the triumph of mechanism.

Mechanistic thinking adheres to analysis and reductionism, claiming that all objects and events, and their properties, can be understood in terms of ultimate elements. This leads to the view that the Universe is constructed of building blocks arranged in a hierarchy, making up a giant machine. This idea could easily be applied to organisations. Indeed the "classical" or "rational" view of organisations sees them as made up of parts, each of which can be optimised independently in pursuit of some goal. Unfortunately for mechanism, the same difficulties which enabled vitalism to survive as a plausible doctrine for so long continued to resist its solutions. Difficulties of "organisation", whether in the biological or social realm, would not yield to reductionism. For example, organisations failed to perform well as a whole when the parts were all independently optimised. The need for systems thinking was thus established (i.e. thinking at least about the interdependence of the parts).

Systems thinking is traditionally accepted as emerging in the 1940s, as a response to the failure of mechanistic thinking to explain biological phenomena. Organisms were now to be treated as whole entities, or systems, whose identity and integrity had to be respected. They had "emergent" properties peculiar to themselves which could not be derived from their parts. They were "open" rather than "closed" to their environments. This thinking was soon transferred to the study of other "systems" such as organisations. However, since the systems view was originally born in biology it tended to rely on biological analogies, introducing ideas such as survival, adaptability, development, growth, flexibility and stability.

Such a shift, from mechanistic to systems thinking, is characterised by changes in our way of looking at certain phenomena. Consider the examples of "relationship" and "system". Relationship, in the machine world view, was analysed in terms of the interactions between two and only two elements. It was felt that more complex situations, where there were many joined elements, could always be broken down and looked at in terms of pairs. From the systems point of view, however, any situation that could be so analysed would not be deemed "complex". The systems perspective recognises multifarious interactions between all the elements making up a complex situation. A related change overtook the idea of "system". In mechanistic thinking a "system" is an aggregate of parts in which the whole is *equal* to the sum of the parts. In systems thinking, a "system" is a complex and highly interlinked network of parts exhibiting synergistic properties—the whole is *greater than* the sum of its parts. For example, it would be argued, by systems thinkers, that a human being, let us say you, as a walking, talking, conscious organism, must be evidently more than the sum of the parts of which you are comprised. If this were not so then you could hardly love, hate, be clever, be stupid, etc., since none of these properties is present in the parts themselves.

Other elaborations were added as the systems view developed. For example, a key idea in machine thinking is the Second Law of Thermodynamics, an equilibrium theory that suggests everything is moving towards disorder inside a "closed system" (wherein a set of interacting elements has zero contact with anything that may lie outside the network). A broader view was necessary, to deal with organismic behaviour since evidently:

- organisms are open systems with energy and material entering and leaving them;
- organisms are not "at rest" within their immediate environments.

Thus the equilibrium idea from physics was abandoned in biology and replaced by homeostasis, a concept that refers to the maintenance of a steady state, a kind of continuity, in a changing environment.

Although the early adherents of systemic thought used systems concepts to refer to situations in the world as if they were real systems, we have since learnt that this view is not satisfactory, particularly when considering social situations such as encountered in business, government and international relations. In these circumstances the "real world" is simply too complex to capture using systems models. We are better off, therefore, self-consciously using systems models as abstract structures for organising our thoughts about problem situations. This is done by constructing various systemic metaphors which can be used to interrogate the "real world" providing insights and promoting creative decision making and "problem solving". There should be no risk of confusing these systemic metaphors, each of which explicitly emphasises only certain important characteristics or issues in problem situations, with the "real world" in which the intervention is taking place. Thus the familiar danger of mistaking the model for the reality is avoided.

Systems thinking developed, therefore, as an alternative to mechanistic thinking, and proved itself more satisfactory for explaining not only complex biological but also social phenomena. As mentioned above, a recent and important shift in the use of the systems idea has seen it being employed not to refer to things in the world, but to systemically organised conceptions of the world. This is how the term "system" in this book should be read. We now present a general conception of "system" which can be used to think about the phenomena of the world, before moving on to giving that general conception differing contents, as a way of arriving at our range of systemic metaphors.

1.4 A GENERAL CONCEPTION OF "SYSTEM"

As already stated, systems ideas were first developed, in their modern form, in the biological sciences, and this is how we have introduced them and understood them to date in this text. We want in this section, however, to present the concept of "system" free, as far as possible, of any biological flavouring. We want to develop a general conception of system which we can, in the next section, fill with any kind of content (including content from the social sciences) to provide the different flavourings making up our range of systemic metaphors.

The central concepts of a generalised conception of system are shown in Figure 1.1. The terms used in this figure are: element, relationship, boundary, input and output, environment and feedback. We need some further notions to describe the complete conception, these are: attributes, transformation, purpose, open system, homeostasis, emergence, communication, control, identity and hierarchy. Let us expand on these ideas.

A system consists of a number of elements and the relationships between the elements. A richly interactive group of elements can be separated from those in which few and/or weak interactions occur. This can be achieved by drawing a boundary around the richly interactive group. The system identified by a boundary will have inputs and outputs, which may be physical or abstract. The system does the work of transforming inputs into outputs. The processes in the system are characterised by feedback, whereby the behaviour of one element may feed back, either directly from another element by way of their relationship, or indirectly via a series of connected elements, to influence the element that initiated the behaviour. We give attributes to elements and relationships according to how we measure them (e.g. for an element we might use size, weight, colour, number, volume; and, for relationships,

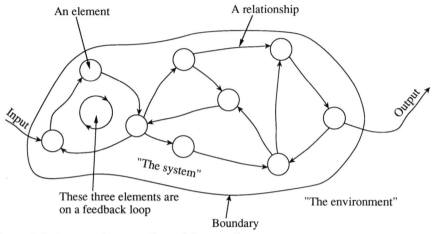

Figure 1.1 A general conception of "system"

measurements might be in terms of intensity, flow, strength).

A system so described is separated by its designated boundary from its environment. It is termed an open system if the boundary is permeable and allows inputs from and outputs to the environment. A system is able to sustain an identity by maintaining itself in a dynamic steady state in the face of and using its changeable environment (we label this homeostasis). That does not mean that nothing is happening in the system; all the constituent parts may themselves have to adapt and/or change in the process of continuing essential transformation processes. A system that maintains an identity and stable transformation processes over time, in changing circumstances, is said to be exhibiting some form of control. Essential to this is the communication of information between the elements. A system can be said to be purposive if it is carrying out a transformation, and is termed purposeful if its purpose is internally generated.

A system stabilised by its control mechanisms, and possessing an identity, can be further understood through its emergent properties. These are properties relating to the whole system but not necessarily present in any of the parts. The term "synergy" refers to the increased value of parts working together as a whole. Emergent properties similarly arise where a complex interconnected network exhibits synergy such that "the whole is greater than the sum of the parts".

Systems are generally understood to occur in hierarchies, so that a system we are considering may also be considered as a sub-system of a wider system. And, if we "blow up" any of the parts of the system of concern, we may usefully conceive of them as sub-systems which exhibit all the characteristics of a system as set out above. We say that these sub-systems are identifiable at a higher level of resolution than the system of which they are part. Sub-systems may themselves be considered in terms of parts, or sub-subsystems, at an even higher resolution level. Since the concept of hierarchy is very significant for a number of the systems methodologies we consider later, let us try to illustrate it further.

Imagine we have a microscope. It is in fact a very special microscope. An ordinary traditional scientific microscope helps us to see things in an ever more detailed reductionist way, as things physically are. Our microscope, however, is a systemic scientific microscope that has the inbuilt capability of discriminating between the richly and poorly interacting features under view and hence displays "systems". It is selective and leaves out aggregates. It can be used with numerous magnifications that lead us to various "levels of resolution". This we can term systemic reduction.

This illustration helps us to picture the concept of hierarchy, but there is a danger that we must be wary of. The illustration suggests that systems are of the "real world", which we have already said is not the case. We can overcome this by extending our thinking to include filters which can be placed over the lenses at any level of resolution (Figure 1.2). These filters are equivalent to the systemic metaphors that we are about to study. The danger is now largely overcome because, through these filters, we necessarily consider systems as abstractions.

We have our general conception of "system" in place, broadly in terms of complex networks. To this must be added content in the form of different "flavourings". This will provide the systemic metaphors which we shall employ as filters for looking at problem situations. We call these "systemic" because each one amounts to some kind of complex interactive network, whether it be for example a "system of functional units" or a "system of social rules and practices". In what follows we will consider five metaphors in some detail. These five capture, at a general level, the insights of almost all management and organisation theory. They are:

- machine metaphor, or "closed system" view;
- organic metaphor, or "open system" view;
- neurocybernetic metaphor, or "viable system" view;
- cultural metaphor; and
- political metaphor.

The first of those listed can be considered a pre-systems metaphor, while the others are more clearly systemic metaphors. In each case we suggest when it might be useful to look at a problem situation using the metaphor, and what difficulties might arise from doing so.

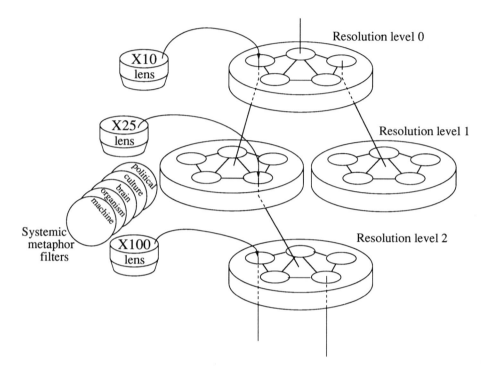

Figure 1.2 Lens and filter metaphor as a way of understanding hierarchy, and the notion of systemic metaphor as a means of organising our thoughts about messes

1.5 MACHINE METAPHOR OR "CLOSED SYSTEM" VIEW

Much has been written on the machine view. In management and organisation theory, the machine view is typified by theories of bureaucracy (Weber) and scientific management (Taylor). A machine is recognised as a technical apparatus that has several (often standardised) parts each with a definite function. Much emphasis is placed on the efficiency of the parts. The machine operates in a routine and repetitive fashion and performs predetermined sets of activities, seeking the rational and efficient means of reaching preset goals and objectives. More generally, much emphasis is placed on control while little emphasis is placed on environment. This view of problem situations has both strengths and weaknesses as outlined above.

When or why is the machine view useful in practice?

- When the task to be performed is straightforward.
- For repetitive production of a single product.
- When the "human parts" fit into the design and are prepared to follow machine-like commands.
- In a stable environment.
- Examples are the armed forces and large franchises such as fast food chains.

When or why does the machine view break down in practice?

- It reduces the adaptability of the organisation (i.e. a machine-like organisation is vulnerable in a volatile environment).
- It requires a mindless contribution that is difficult to maintain with mindful parts (i.e. it will either dehumanise or will lead to conflicting aims between machine and minds).

1.6 ORGANIC METAPHOR OR "OPEN SYSTEM" VIEW

The machine view was, as we have seen, strongly challenged by the emergence of systems thinking. Complex phenomena began to be considered as "systems". Because modern systems thinking was born in the biological sciences, this initially took the form of organic analogies.

In management and organisation theory the first challenge to the machine view came from human relations theory. It was perceived that attention had to be given to the human aspect of organisations, since individuals operated most effectively when their social and psychological needs were catered for. Issues of motivation (e.g. Maslow's hierarchy of needs), leadership style (e.g. McGregor's Theory X and Theory Y), participation, democracy and various job enrichment strategies emerged out of this view. Later, other needs were added to the list of those that organisations had to meet if they were going to "survive"—they needed particular structures according to their technology and their size, they needed particular management systems. It became commonplace to treat organisations as if they were like organisms. Their primary aim was seen as being survival rather than goal seeking (compare the machine metaphor). Various theorists (e.g. Parsons, Katz and Kahn) provided lists of "needs" which had to be met if organisations were to survive and be effective.

The organic metaphor nowadays incorporates ideas drawn from studying phenomena from several levels of resolution: from the cell, to the single organism, to ecology and thoughts about evolution. The central idea remains, however, that of the organism or organisation as an "open system". This, in abstract, holds to the idea of a system as a complex network of elements and relationships that interact forming highly organised feedback loops, existing in an environment from which it draws inputs and to which it dispenses outputs. An "open system" is homeostatic in that there is self-regulation (i.e. where a machine—a closed system—suffers from wear and tear, an open system is able to offset much of that degradation by importation of energy, allowing it to maintain a steady state). Survival and adaptability are other concepts that complement the "open system" idea within the framework of the organic metaphor.

When or why is the organic view useful in practice?

- When there is an open relationship with a changing environment.
- When there are needs to be satisfied in order to promote survival.
- To promote responsiveness and change.
- When the environment itself is complex, containing a variety of competitors and so on.
- Examples are most industrial firms in today's turbulent environments.

When or why does the organic view break down in practice?

- It neglects to recognise that organisations are socially constructed phenomena which, arguably, must be understood from the point of view of the people within them.
- It emphasises harmonious relations between the parts, when in organisations they are often conflictual and/or coercive.
- It sees change as being generated externally, as the system adapts to its environment, and does not provide for proactive development.

1.7 NEUROCYBERNETIC METAPHOR OR "VIABLE SYSTEM" VIEW

Another strand of systems thinking that developed in parallel with the "open system" view is the neurocybernetic perspective. This metaphor emphasises active learning and control rather than the passive adaptability that characterises the "open system" view. In management and organisation theory it has led to attention being focused on information processing and viability.

The neurocybernetic view looks to the brain as a well tried and tested control system that depends upon an ability to communicate and learn. It builds upon the standard cybernetic model which has a transformation process (that which is being controlled), an information system (that relays information about the controlled process to a control unit), a control unit (that compares the actual to a desired state of the controlled process) and an activating unit (that brings about changes in the controlled process according to instructions from the control unit). Control can only be successful if the variety of the controller is equal to or greater than that which is being controlled. The neurocybernetic metaphor or "viable system" view adds to this the importance of "learning to learn" (i.e. accepting dynamic rather than static aims and objectives, and self-questioning rather than merely self-regulating). A so-called holographic brain metaphor stresses getting the whole into the parts, creating connectivity and redundancy, and simultaneous specialisation and generalisation.

When or why is the neurocybernetic view useful in practice?

- It promotes self-enquiry and self-criticism and therefore the possibility of dynamic goal seeking based on learning.
- When there is a high degree of uncertainty.
- It encourages creativity.
- Examples are to be found in autonomous work groups, innovative industrial firms, consultancy firms and in R and D work.

When or why does the neurocybernetic view break down in practice?

- It tends to forget that the purposes of the parts may not always be the same as the purposes of the whole.
- Adopting recommendations based on this metaphor would require most extant organisations to undergo significant changes that would threaten those that are favoured by the status quo; so they will be resisted.
- It neglects to recognise that organisations are socially constructed phenomena.

1.8 CULTURE METAPHOR

Culture is a powerful metaphor through which we can consider any organisation or problem situation. It can be understood as the often unspoken but familar ways of thinking and acting that exist in all firms and enterprises. In organisation and management theory, "engineering" corporate culture has been recognised as a useful way of promoting the organisation as a collectivity with employees who have, and accept, a collaborative and community-like spirit. There will, of course, be both official and unofficial corporate cultures as well as sub-cultures in any organisation.

In a broad sense a culture refers to various nebulous, shared characteristics at all levels of organisation: societal, corporate, group, etc.

Studies in international relations suggest that typical features of culture, at the national level, are shared language, religion and history, and in general a mutual sense of belonging. At the level of the firm a culture is a shared reality, or a socially constructed reality (of values and beliefs), that deems certain social practices to be normal, acceptable and desirable. Culture is extremely important in all organisations because it determines how organisations react, for example, to change and what changes are perceived to be feasible. Culture can act as a conservative restraining force or can generate innovation. The need to manage culture is becoming increasingly recognised as in various Quality Management theories.

When or why is the cultural view useful in practice?

- When it shows that "rational" aspects of organisational life are only rational in terms of the "installed" culture and that there are other values with which any official culture can be contrasted.
- It highlights the fact that the cohesion generated by shared social and organisational practices can both inhibit and encourage organisational development and this has to be recognised and managed.
- It offers a new perspective on organisational change (i.e. instead of focusing exclusively on technology and structure, a cultural perspective would also emphasise changing the perceptions and values of employees).
- Examples exist in high technology Japanese firms and in the competitive individualism exhibited in many American companies, but the ideas are equally applicable to machine-like military set-ups.

When or why does the cultural view break down in practice?

- It may lead to explicit ideological control that will generate feelings of manipulation, resentment and mistrust (except, perhaps, in very small firms).
- Culture is something that takes time to evolve and cannot be swept into established groups overnight.
- When political in-fighting characterises organisational life.
- It does not tell managers how to structure complex organisations.

1.9 POLITICAL METAPHOR

The political metaphor applied to problem situations looks at relationships between individuals and groups as competitive and involving the pursuit of power. In the industrial relations literature there are three contrasting views on the character of any political situation. These are labelled unitary, pluralist and coercive. We use these distinctions here, as we do in the next chapter, to distinguish types of relationship between participants in a problematic situation. The politcal metaphor focuses on issues of interests, conflict and power. It is through these three issues that the political character of a situation may be assessed (as either unitary, pluralist or coercive, see Table 1.1). Using the political metaphor sensitises us, particularly, to the possibility of conflict in organisations.

When or why is the political view useful in practice?

- It highlights all organisational activity as interest based and emphasises the key role of power in determining political outcomes, thus it places power at the centre of all organisational analysis.
- It emphasises that goals may be rational for some actors while not so for others—"Whose rationality is being pursued?"
- It proposes disintegrative strains and tensions and thus balances the more usual systems emphasis on functionality and order (such as in the "open system" metaphor).
- It encourages recognition of the organisational actor as political for both motivational and structural reasons.
- It reminds us that all organisations show examples of political activity.

When or why does the political view breakdown in practice?

- When explicit recognition of the politics of the situation leads to further politicisation and generates mistrust.

Table 1.1 Political characteristics of situations in terms of the issues of interest, conflict and power

	Unitary	Pluralist	Coercive
Interest	Common objectives—a well integrated team	Diverging group interests with the organisation as a mutual focal point—loose coalition	Oppositional and contradictory interests—rival forces
Conflict	Rare and transient	Inherent, but may well have positive aspects	Inevitible and likely to lead to radical change of whole structure
Power	Replaced by conceptions such as leadership and control	Medium through which conflict of interest may be resolved	Unequally distributed thus allowing domination, subjugation and so on

- It may over-emphasise the need to handle political issues at the expense of other factors which are essential to organisational health—proper organisational structures, responding to market changes, etc.

As we have seen the political metaphor, at a higher level of resolution, contains three different perspectives—unitary, pluralist and coercive. These perspectives themselves can be seen as resting upon metaphor; the unitary upon a "team" metaphor, the pluralist upon a "coalition" metaphor, and the coercive upon a "prison" metaphor. We shall make further use of this in later sections and chapters.

1.10 REMARKS ON METAPHOR

The use of the idea of "likeness", as it is employed through metaphor, helps us to gain insight into difficult-to-understand phenomena or issues in terms of things that we are familiar with. In the quotation that heads this chapter, for example, we see how the ancient Chinese attempted to explain the creation of the earth in terms of the familiar human form. The process of thought involved is not that dissimilar from the way modern, Western, scientific thinking works. For example, the theory of waves in water (frequency, amplitude, energy, etc.) was used as a way of helping to explain the phenomenon of light. What, it was asked, would be the insights gained by considering light as waves. The outcome of this is documented in every standard physics book, but it should be noted that this explanation was only partial and subsequent additional analogical reasoning has led to a complementary particle theory of light.

Managers too use ideas of likeness much of the time. For example, we often hear about "mechanisms of accounting", "company evolution", "fighting for survival", "company culture". Our aim in this chapter is both to recognise this and to maximise the positive benefits that can be gained from it. Combining the general conception of system set down earlier with each of the five "flavourings", just discussed, yields five systems metaphors which can be used by managers and their advisers to view problem situations in a coherent way. This set reflects, at a general level, the knowledge base of management and organisation theory, but powerfully it also covers the basic assumptions underpinning the range of systems-based "problem-solving" methodologies presented in Chapter 2. The argument is that any of these metaphors might highlight significant difficulties or issues which an enterprise faces. If one of the metaphors brings difficult issues into focus particularly clearly, then we shall argue (as you will find in Chapters 2 and 3) that it is sensible to use a systems methodology, to tackle the issues, which is consistent in its approach with the metaphor employed. For example, if looking at an organisation as an organism best informs us of the issues in question (opportunities and constraints, difficulties and problems, organisational and environmental, etc.) then a methodology which assumes and operates as though organisations are like organisms should be chosen.

We are arguing for the disciplined and systematic use of metaphor. The knowledge base from which we have drawn our metaphors is that of most relevance to managers and their advisers. Of course, many other ideas of likeness can be used and we certainly do not want to discourage this interest. We only suggest that what is done is understood in terms of the logic and process of Total Systems Intervention (see Chapter 3), and considered through the various frameworks developed and presented in this book.

Before we pass on to Chapters 2 and 3 we want to explicate further the ideas of this chapter by examining the popular management philosophy called Total Quality Management (TQM) as an articulation of systemic metaphor. We demonstrate that, implicit in TQM (as with any management philosophy or indeed systems methodology), are different accounts of what an organisation is like and that the practice of TQM attempts to respond to each of these accounts. This will help illuminate our Total Systems Intervention (TSI) approach. We believe that managers should entertain different visions of what their enterprise is or could be like (by using different metaphors) and then address the issues thrown up by each vision using an appropriate systems methodology. We believe that because TSI makes this process explicit, it has significant advantages over TQM for promoting learning.

1.11 TOTAL QUALITY MANAGEMENT (TQM): AN EXAMPLE OF THE USE OF SYSTEMIC METAPHOR

1.11.1 Introduction

Total Quality Management (TQM), in essence, is about increasing customer service, improving the quality of goods and services, and involving people in their work. This management philosophy has been promoted extensively in the literature and has been adopted widely in industry and commerce. A short article by Thorn published in the *Industrial Society Magazine* in September 1988 will largely be our focus, since it very nicely sums up the main principles of TQM. These will be summarised below and then reviewed in terms of systemic metaphor.

1.11.2 Philosophy, Principles and Methodology of TQM

There are two distinct but interlinked processes at work in TQM: to improve the quality of manufacturing and other business processes, and to develop the view that all employees have an individual responsibility for quality. The crucial concern for achieving quality focuses on improving customer service—both internally and externally. The advice from a finance to a sales department, for example, should be treated as a service to be considered (in terms of quality) in the same way that sales should deal with (as traditionally viewed) external customer services.

This broad philosophy splits into two action areas of communication and control.

(1) Communication has to be dealt with both externally and internally.
   (a) External communication with customers must be improved and maintained, so an organisation must raise the skills of those who deal with customers and improve their understanding of customer perceptions, and improve the skills of those with first-line supervisory responsibility for staff who deal directly with the customer.
   (b) Internal communication with other departments (in fact, now considered customers) must be improved and maintained; it is highly problematic to raise external standards without having carried out a similar internal programme. It is argued that three types of internal communication need to be recognised and dealt with:
      (i) down-the-line communication through the regular drill of team briefings on desired and actual quality standards (emphasis on local achievements, difficulties and targets);
      (ii) consultation, which may improve working methods by calling on the widest possible expertise in an organisation, and can as a start be improved simply by encouraging managers and supervisors to listen to their staff; and
      (iii) lateral communication, for example, involving marketeers, designers, accountants, and production engineers in the development of a new product at an early stage, thus reducing difficulties later.
(2) Control is a sister idea to that of communication. In TQM it is argued that people should be organised into small manageable teams (four to fifteen) in order to promote effective control. There are three points to be made.
   (a) Accountability has to be properly established and principal lines of control decided upon, in particular the issue of project versus departmental lines of control must be resolved.

(b) Quality Control must report to the line manager whose responsibilities must include monitoring standards.

(c) Management information systems may have to be changed in order that verifiable results on quality (and quantities) can be realised.

The ethos in which communication and control are established must incorporate participation. Everyone must feel that they have a share in the "quality problem". Each person must also have clear and unambiguous targets for quality improvement. It is important to remove divisions and reduce some differentials, for example by harmonising terms and conditions.

Elsewhere in the literature we find ideas about realising a quality company. Implementation of TQM should be systematic, proceeding as follows for the company and for each department.

- Set mission.
- Develop plans to improve quality.
- Carry out an analysis of the purpose of the company and the departments.
- Define initial projects to introduce TQM.
- Carry out training and education.

Set mission means that a quality statement is produced which gives an "identity" to the organization as a whole and the departments at all levels in the quality programme.

Develop plans to improve quality broadly follows Juran's trilogy:

- Quality planning: set goals, develop means to meet goals and summarise into a quality plan.
- Quality control: evaluate actual performance in terms of meeting standard customer requirements.
- Quality improvement: improve on the past (e.g. competitiveness, customer satisfaction, etc.).

These clearly imply the need for a "quality management system" to plan, control and improve. The main feature of this, typically, is a structure of Quality Councils. This structure is normally based on the hierarchical company tree; and hence slips back into a fundamentally mechanical conception.

Analysis of the purpose of the (company and) departments amounts to a number of tasks:

- To define clearly the purpose and align it with the business strategy and goals.

- To define requirements, measurements and working relationships between the department and its customers.
- To identify the necessary activities of the department, to realise what is being done and why, and to assess whether each activity adds value to the product.

Define projects means the department identifying projects that reflect the quality improvement plan. The projects must also sit within the organisation's mission or quality vision.

Education and training then aims to develop an awareness and an understanding of quality through workshops at which the ideas are discussed and disseminated.

The philosophy, principles and methodology of TQM, outlined above, are summarised in Figure 1.3. We shall now use our systemic metaphors, and the knowledge gained of their various strengths and weaknesses, to interrogate the TQM approach.

1.11.3 Creative Thinking about TQM

We have been involved in specific consultancies working with Total Quality Management, and enhancing our understanding of its philosophy and process through creative use of the systems metaphors has proved to be extremely beneficial. To get the most out of these differing experiences, and to maintain the anonymity of our clients, we present here the general case for TQM. This is done by going through the main points of the philosophy and principles of TQM in a reorganised form and suggesting (in parenthesis) what systems metaphor is being invoked by each point. We will then consider the methodology of implementation.

(1) There is an emphasis on communication:
    (a) within each part, functional, local homeostasis (a living cell, organic);
    (b) between parts, functional, overall internal homeostasis (an organism, organic); and
    (c) between relevant parts and an environment, open homeostasis, even symbiosis (an organism or perhaps ecological, organic).
(2) There is an emphasis on control:
    (a) set clear targets (machine, mechanical);
    (b) drill of team briefing (machine, mechanical);
    (c) consultation for organisation—wide expertise (learning, neurocybernetic).

    There are hints, therefore, of mechanical and neurocybernetic thinking in TQM. There are clearer signs of the organic metaphor, drawn from ideas about the cell, the organism and ecology.

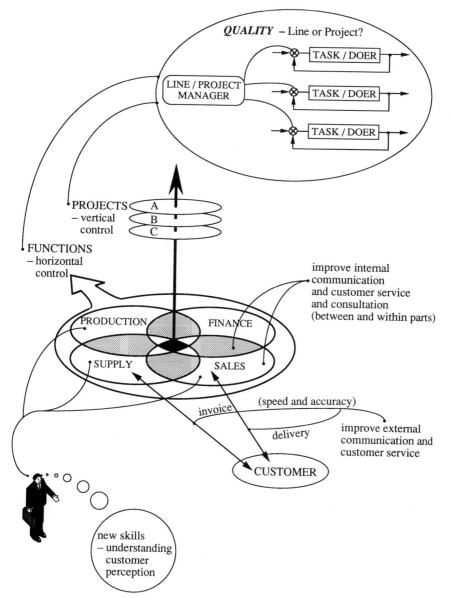

Figure 1.3 A summary of Total Quality Management

What is even more striking, however, is the emphasis placed on developing cohesion and a common culture. The cultural metaphor is invoked for the possibilities it offers for generating commitment among employees to quality.

(3) There is an emphasis on collaboration, and on all employees "owning" quality (culture). TQM encourages:
  (a) greater harmonisation of terms and conditions, thus creating a sense of belonging;
  (b) a collaborative community-like spirit, an emphasis on customer service between departments;
  (c) a collectivity, project teams pursuing a "company-wide policy";
  (d) a mutual sense of belonging, all employees are part of the quality culture;
  (e) certain practices to be deemed normal and desirable; and
  (f) a shared language, the "total quality language".

It is now possible to consider TQM and the metaphors it employs to understand and intervene in organisations, and to ask what possible difficulties might be encountered with TQM. This is done by looking at the limitations of the two major systems metaphors it implicitly uses (the organic and the cultural). In fact we have encountered all these problems in our consultancy practice.

(1) An organic view may lead to:
  (a) an emphasis on harmonious relations with no way of dealing with issues of conflict/coercion—we have encountered divergences of opinion among those involved in a TQM programme on matters such as "Who owns and controls quality?"; and
  (b) too little attention being paid to the issue that organisations are socially constructed phenomena and to internally generated change—which in TQM practice are largely overcome by simultaneous use of the cultural perspective.

(2) A cultural view may lead to:
  (a) feelings of ideological control, manipulation and mistrust—which, in one large organisation with which we had dealings, did prevail in some localities;
  (b) difficulties with installation—we found that, in some cases, attempts were made to sweep TQM in overnight, but a culture takes time to evolve;
  (c) prevention of instalment if political forces prevail and are ignored; and
  (d) lack of guidance on how to structure an organisation—overcome in the TQM case by simultaneous use of organic thinking.

Turning to the methodology of implementation of TQM, implicit reference to the various metaphors can also be found. The nature of the relationship between participants is assumed to be unitary and this implies no difficulty in setting a clear and generally acceptable mission. This unitary or "team" setting of the political metaphor is usually found accompanying the machine, organism and brain metaphors. The idea of spreading the quality mission by giving each department an "identity" in the quality programme hints at further neurocybernetic thinking. There is much emphasis on control and measurement, to be realised through the usual structure of the hierarchical company tree. This reflects machine thinking based on Taylorist and Weberian organisation theory and introduces the power element of the political metaphor. Finally, education and training is evidently all about establishing a quality culture in the company.

The account and analysis provided above show how TQM implicitly draws upon a number of metaphors. The cultural metaphor is dominant, but the organic and machine are also strongly present, and there are elements of neurocybernetic thinking. TQM draws much of its strength from this mixing of metaphors and the consequent range of strategies that it employs. Its weaknesses tend to arise because the "coalition" and "prison" aspects of the political metaphor, and the lessons that could be learnt from using these, are ignored. Obviously it is highly illuminating of TQM to consider it in this creative way using the systemic metaphors, part of the TSI armoury. Hopefully it helps to suggest the power of TSI itself, which is able consciously and explicitly to draw on all the metaphors, and a full range of systems methodologies equipped to respond to the lessons learnt from employing any of the metaphors to examine problem situations.

The analysis of the methodological ideas of TQM sketched out above could be more thoroughly dealt with following Chapter 2. Readers are invited to consider in more detail the method of implementation for TQM, discussed by several gurus such as Juran, Deming and Crosby, after completing that chapter, when they can make a more comprehensive enquiry into the implications of the approach.

1.12 SUMMARY

In this chapter we have considered the nature of the concept "system" and looked at the development of modern systems thinking. It was noted that the idea "system" has become contentless in everyday language, but we were able quickly to re-establish our interest by thoroughly considering a general conception of system and showing how this could be filled with content, and provided with different "flavourings", to produce a number of systems metaphors. It should be noted that these metaphors are not mutually exclusive; for example the military can be seen through both a machine and a culture "filter" with revealing results.

There are several advantages in using such metaphors to help us get to grips with messy situations and, if nothing else, they remind us that many so-called organisational "problems" are only consequences of the way we choose to conceptualise the situation. The contribution that we shall concern ourselves with now, however, is the use of metaphors in highlighting aspects of problem situations and the help they can thus give in guiding us to appropriate systems "problem-solving" methods. Consciously looking at a problem situation using different metaphors should help a manager in creative thinking. Hopefully it will help readers to make creative use of whatever knowledge they already possess of management theory in terms of the new systems ideas. Once it has been decided which metaphor best captures the essence of the issues of concern, it is a short step to identifying the perceived nature of the problem context in terms of the classification of systems methodologies presented in the next chapter. Using the "system of systems methodologies", a relevant systems approach can then be chosen. We must work out this system of systems methodologies, but first we offer a case study for you to experiment on with the new systems ideas that you have acquired.

1.13   CASE STUDY

1.13.1 Introduction

Documented below is an account of the construction industry in Singapore, provided by the Chief Executive of the Construction Industry Development Board, Chow Kok Fong. The report is written in a style sympathetic to the subject matter of Chapter 1, being produced by the Chief Executive after exposure to the idea of systemic metaphors and following some discussion with us. The article has been edited so that the explicit metaphor analysis has been removed, allowing readers to undertake an open-ended case study for themselves.

1.13.2 Your Task

Your task is to look at the situation facing the construction industry in Singapore and its Board in terms of systemic metaphors. Which metaphors highlight best the situation in which the industry and the Board find themselves? You should also consider the Board's strategies in terms of systemic metaphor and review the strengths and weaknesses of these strategies.

1.13.3 The Construction Industry in Singapore and the Role of the Board

The industry is an important component of the national economy. It accounts for between 6% and 10% of Singapore's Gross Domestic Product. The sector as a whole employs 95 000 people, or roughly 9% of the total workforce. Because of the small labour pool in Singapore, one half of these workers come from neighbouring countries such as Malaysia and Thailand.

A Government agency called the Construction Industry Development Board was set up under an Act of Parliament to improve the competitiveness and quality delivery capability of the construction sector in Singapore and to support the export of the country's construction services.

The Board's policy formulation function involves much hard bargaining. To begin with, all policy proposals initiated by the Board have to be reviewed against the interests of various sectors in the construction industry and in terms of political impact on the population. The principal interest groups are the contractors, the developers, the other public sector construction procurement agencies (such as the Housing and Development Board, the Public Works Department, and the Port Authority), the professional bodies representing architects and engineers, and the unions. These groups represent the principal actors in any construction project and their support is usually considered vital for the success of any measure which relates to the industry as a whole.

An example would be the policy relating to the admission of foreign workers into the country. Singapore has a small population. Each year the economy grows at two and half times the rate of growth of the working population. Consequently, there tends to be conflict between:

- the suppliers of services and products in the sector who want the government to increase the inflow of foreign workers;
- the public who fear that an unrestrained increase in foreign workers will bring in its wake a host of social problems; and
- the trade unions who have to be seen to protect the jobs and wages of indigenous workers against low-wage imported workers.

In the construction industry, the problem is even more acute simply because there is a dearth of Singaporeans who wish to take up construction careers: construction careers are perceived to be dangerous, to carry low social status and to be unpleasant.

To resolve the labour shortage issue, the Board formulated and implemented an ambitious strategy. Attention was given to improving the efficiency of the construction process. This has to be tackled across a wide front, including improved design practices and improved construction methods. The Board has to compel architects and engineers to develop more "buildable" designs so that the work can be more easily tackled by increasing numbers of relatively less skilled foreign workers. Professional bodies such as the Singapore Institute of Architects and the Institute of Engineers fear that such practices inhibit the creativity and freedom of the professions they represent. In turn, building-material suppliers and manufacturers express concern that such measures will require extensive changes to manufacturing and distribution processes. Occasionally major developers and building owners may be led by the other interest groups to the view that these measures will prevent their projects from adopting a unique design and character. There is a mixture of fact, fiction and hyperbole in all these views. The Board has to use the mechanisms available to it to study, assess and then make explanations to the affected interest groups.

At the same time construction practices have to become more efficient. They should become more capital intensive and less labour intensive. An example will be to use prefabricated components or to use more mechanisation so that there will be less need for supporting labourers. Contractors become concerned that investments in these construction approaches may not be justified in view of the fluctuations in construction demand, although to some extent these concerns are mitigated by the provision of tax incentives. Trade unions fear that once these methods take root, jobs may be structurally displaced. This is balanced against the following considerations:

- In the absence of these changes, their members will be anchored for a long time in low-paying low-skilled jobs. The Board was able to persuade the pivotal trade union leaders that, in the long term, these measures will upgrade the productivity and the quality of work undertaken by their members and hence lead them to earn more.
- The government through the Board makes available generous training grants and support facilities to enable Singapore workers to upgrade their skills.

It is simply not possible to reconcile all the interests of the various factions. While the Board attempts to take a position on an objective analysis of the various issues, it is inevitable that a certain interest group with more political muscle at a particular point in time can introduce an inevitable bias in decisions. The reality is that the decisions and programmes formulated by the Board have to be pragmatic and require the Chief Executive to appreciate the kind of strategic allies which are necessary to support key areas of a major proposal affecting a large cross-section of the industry.

The Board's own clout in relation to these issues stems from its authority in determining public sector construction procurement policies. As a means of last resort, the Board can bring the collective public sector procurement clout to bear to provide a security that the policies it advocates take root in the industry. The specifications of Government construction contracts, for instance, can be used to incorporate certain policy requirements so that the pace of change can be accelerated. This procurement clout is considerable because public sector agencies account for about 60% and 75% of all construction orders. However, it is used only when the Board is convinced that the long-term benefits of a proposed policy justify short-term unpleasant effects in some quarters.

It will be readily apparent that an unfortunate aspect of all this is that on occasions policy compromises are forged which are incompatible with the technical merits of the project concerned. This problem surfaces most visibly when a new policy has to be shown to succeed quickly and, in order to do so, concessions are made which undermine some of the long-term benefits which the programme was designed to achieve. To reduce this possibility, it has been found useful to set out in unequivocal terms the criteria by which a particular policy would be considered to have succeeded at the outset before it is fully developed. Whenever the acceptance of the policy demands concessions, which will cause the particular policy proposal to fail to achieve these criteria of success, this will trigger the need for the entire policy proposal to be reconsidered.

Another view of the Board can be usefully gained by considering its corporate environment and operational ethos. The Board's operations are dictated to a large extent by the socio-economic forces which shape the construction sector. Prevailing economic expectations and sentiments and the performance of economic sectors such as manufacturing and trade all impact on construction demand. A steep increase in tourist arrival expectations, for instance, has recently (1990) revitalised the hotel construction sector.

Similarly, the state of the US economy exercises an important bearing on Singapore's manufacturing capacity and hence on the level of factory construction. This constant change in the environment means that the Board's strategies have to be frequently reassessed. It is necessary that the responsible operational unit develops a capacity to conduct a quick assessment of each problematic context and formulates a strategic approach from which a potential solution may be derived. The pace of work and the control of the work have, therefore, to reside with the operational unit to a large extent so that a high level of responsiveness is achieved. This places considerable responsibility on to the shoulders of the Board's officers at the operational level.

Most of the Board's officers are aged between 25 and 40. They are selected from among the cream of the graduates in architecture, building, engineering and economics each year. Of the 60 graduate level officers, 92% possess the equivalent of a first class or upper second from some of the leading universities in Britain, Australia, Canada, the United States and Singapore: 40% of these are schooled at Oxford, Cambridge, MIT and Imperial College. Almost 85% have at least five years of experience in the construction sector before joining the Board. Most opt to join the Board because of the Board's reputation for fast track career development in the construction sector. This is because the Board provides young graduates with opportunities to be exposed to a wide range of disciplines and access to leaders of the industry both in Singapore and in the region.

The Board's success depends critically on the extent to which these ambitious officers can be mobilised as a team and be made to feel they have personal stakes in the Board's mission. They must also be able to react to external changes. This is because it is easy for any institutionalised development approach to become extremely rigid and structured over time and be driven into obsolescence by a changing environment. An atmosphere is nurtured wherein each officer appreciates that while it is legitimate for him/her to pursue a personal career agenda aggressively, career advancement within the Board is determined equally by the way an individual works as a member of a larger group, pursuing group-oriented objectives. Many in the private sector perceive the Board's mission, to raise construction cost competitiveness and construction quality, as a distant, long-term desirable. Consequently, it is necessary for each officer to be completely convinced of the Board's mission in this area. The Board has to work out career advancement plans with each individual officer, and to conduct training and staff induction programmes to generate this commitment.

To sustain the appetite for situations which challenge the whole person, the Board's ethos is carefully cultivated. Incoming officers undergo a concentrated induction programme during which they take part in simulation exercises and undergo training in public administration. They are expected to understand clearly the Board's mission and the strategic context within which the Board operates. At the end of these two-month programmes, they are generally sufficiently competent to deliver presentations to gatherings of industry leaders and senior executives. The message of responsiveness is constantly drilled into all Board officers. They have to be conscious of the extensive ramifications which may result from a wrong diagnosis or an inadequate response, and yet appreciate that in many situations the adage "no decision is worse than a bad decision" applies. There is an overrriding sense that Singapore has a tradition of administrative will at every level to ensure right decisions are implemented, however difficult or unpopular they may be. Yet the whole must be balanced carefully with political realism and with an appreciation of the environment within which the sector operates.

Resident corporate planning meetings involving all operational officers are held which serve to:

- determine the extent to which the Board's mission is being achieved;
- examine ways through which the Board's mission may be advanced; and
- set targets for particular units in the coming period.

The Board requires officers to be assessed in terms of both quantitative and qualitative results. This involves tiered assessment criteria. When the project provides services which are more than paid for by project revenue, then that project satisfies the condition of market need. When it is not clear as to whether it satisfies the market need, then it is necessary to consider either the quantifiable benefits of a project in terms of improving construction productivity or quality (usually in terms of savings) or the quantifiable benefits of a project in terms of expanding the Board's impact on the industry (media impact score). The qualitative assessment applies especially to officers who are considered to have high career potential within the Board and are hence likely to be selected for top management positions. This group of officers are assessed on what has been termed their "helicopter" ability, that is the ability to look at problems from beyond the narrow confines of their immediate operational responsibility and adopt an holistic world view. It is reflected by the way their decisions allow for changes in basic parameters against the context of environmental uncertainty.

The final result is an intense, self-driven but collegial atmosphere which demands the very best personal qualities of an officer. Officers are encouraged to internalise achievements in a group context. Lateral job rotations are also planned as a matter of course, so that within the first four years of service, an officer would have the benefit of having worked in at least two different operational units.

New sets of radically different economic factors are expected to bear on the construction sector in Singapore over the next few years. The first is the increasing economic clout of Japan and the other Asia Pacific economies. The second is the possibility that the opening up of Eastern Europe may prompt some European multinationals and competitors to shift some of their strategic focus away from this region. Both sets of factors have important implications for domestic construction and design firms. They suggest that Singapore firms need to be even more competitive and quality conscious, but also hold out more opportunities for the expansion of Singapore corporations.

At the management level, the kind of linear extrapolation advocated by the traditional principles of scientific management thought are likely to be insufficient to enable the new managers in the industry to cope with these changes. Problematic contexts will thus need to be increasingly defined in other terms. It is not easy for some managers to do this, mainly because in the Singapore situation most leaders of the industry have come from technology-oriented backgrounds which make them more at home in situations described in machine terms.

The Board will continue to play a pivotal role only if it can continue to retain within its ranks the best professional officers. To do this, its ethos must be compatible with the demands made on the organisation so that it can continue to function as a responsive policy formulation and developmental agency.

1.14 FURTHER READING

• For an introduction to systems thinking:

Flood, R. L. and Carson, E. R. (1992). *Dealing with Complexity: An Introduction to the Theory and Application of Systems Science*, 2nd edition, Plenum, New York.

• For a comprehensive overview of the ideas of metaphor applied to thinking about organizations:

Morgan, G. (1986). *Images of Organization*, Sage, Beverley Hills.

• For some of the background management and organization theory feeding into our metaphors:

Gerth, H. H. and Mills, C. W. (eds.) (1970). *From Max Weber*, Routledge and Kegan Paul, London.
Katz, D. and Kahn, R. L. (1978). *The Social Psychology of Organizations*, 2nd edition, Wiley, New York.
Maslow, A. H. (1954). *Motivation and Personality*, Harper and Row, New York.
McGregor, D. (1960). *The Human Side of Enterprise*, McGraw-Hill, New York.
Parsons, T. (1956). Suggestions for a sociological approach to the theory of organizations—1, *Administrative Science Quarterly*, **1**, 63–85.
Peters, T. J. and Waterman, R. H., Jr. (1982). *In Search of Excellence*, Harper and Row, New York.
Simon, H. A. (1947). *Administrative Behaviour*, Macmillan, New York.
Taylor, F. W. (1947). *Scientific Management*, Harper and Row, London.

- For material on Total Quality Management:

Crosby, P. B. (1980). *Quality is Free*, Mentor, New York.
Deming, W. Edwards (1982). *Out of the Crisis*, MIT Press, Mass.
Juran, J. M. (1988). *Juran on Planning for Quality*, Free Press, New York.
Thorn, J. (1988). Zeroing in on total quality, *Industrial Society Magazine*, September, pp. 20–21.

Chapter 2

A System of Systems Methodologies

We shouldn't read too many books . . . It will be enough to read a dozen or so. If we read too many, we can move towards our opposite, become bookworms, dogmatists, revisionists.
Mao Tse-Tung in S. Schram (ed.) *Mao Tse-Tung Unrehearsed.*

2.1 INTRODUCTION

A major difficulty for managers and management scientists seeking to use systems thinking is knowing how to employ the range of different systems approaches available. Suppose a manager faces some major organisational issues and is convinced that using a systems approach can help alleviate the difficulties, should he or she choose:

- operational research
- systems analysis
- systems engineering
- system dynamics
- viable system diagnosis
- general system theory
- socio-technical systems thinking
- contingency theory
- social systems design
- strategic assumption surfacing and testing
- interactive planning
- soft systems methodology

• critical systems heuristics?

Each approach has been tried and tested and works well in some circumstances. But how is a manager supposed to know which will be the most suitable in the situation facing him or her? Unless advice can be provided on the strengths of the different approaches and guidelines given on the circumstances in which each may be best employed, confusion is likely to result.

Fortunately, it is possible to provide guidelines that point to the respective strengths of different systems approaches and suggest when a situation favours the use of one rather than another. Thus, an apparent weakness of systems thinking—the range of different approaches—turns into a strength. The diversity of approaches should not yield confusion but signal competence and effectiveness in a variety of problem situations.

We shall now logically group together what we believe are the most important systems methods and methodologies into a "system of systems methodologies". We do this by looking at the underlying assumptions they make about problem situations or problem contexts in terms of the metaphors we have already discussed, and by presenting two new dimensions which give us a clearer understanding of those metaphors and their interrelatedness, and how they can aid in relevant methodology choice(s) and intervention.

Systems approaches are based upon different metaphorical understandings, different views of reality and this conditions the way each advises seeking to intervene in and change organisations. This idea is explained in detail in the next section. Our purpose now is to uncover the basic assumptions underpinning the different systems approaches, to see what view of problem contexts each methodology takes.

2.2 GROUPING PROBLEM CONTEXTS

The following categorisation of problem contexts is made with the aim of grouping the different systems methodologies and is constructed with that end in mind. It is not meant as a grid into which different problem situations in the "real world" can be easily fitted. This would be a simplistic and naive view of our efforts. Obviously there can always be argument and dispute about how any actual "real world" problem context should best be classified. One of the points about the classification is that it should inform just such a debate. In sociological terms, therefore, this is an "ideal type" classification which draws out some key features of different problem contexts, but which does not expect any "real world" appreciation of a problem context to fit exactly any one box (i.e. just as situations can be usefully viewed through several metaphorical "lenses").

That said, it has been found useful to group problem contexts according to two dimensions:

- systems
- participants.

The systems dimension refers to relative complexity in terms of the "system" or "systems" that make up the problem situation, and within which other difficult pluralistic or coercive issues of concern may be located.

The participants dimension refers to the relationship (of agreement or disagreement) between the individuals or parties who stand to gain (or lose) from a systems intervention. It thus allows us to build pluralistic and coercive appreciations of problem situations into any understanding of complexity that is promoted through the systems dimension.

The argument is that these two aspects of problem contexts (systems and participants) seem to have a particularly important way of casting light on the nature of the "problems" found within them and, therefore, offer a fruitful way of characterising problem situations.

Let us now proceed by considering the two dimensions in turn. The overall grouping of problem contexts will then result from bringing the two together again.

Systems can be classified or categorised in a variety of ways. Very generally, we suggest, a continuum of "system types" may be usefully identified. At one end of our continuum are relatively simple "systems". At the other end are "systems" which are highly complex.

Simple "systems" have the following characteristics:

- a small number of elements;
- few interactions between the elements;
- attributes of the elements are predetermined;
- interaction between elements is highly organised;
- well-defined laws govern behaviour;
- the "system" does not evolve over time;
- "sub-systems" do not pursue their own goals;
- the "system" is unaffected by behavioural influences;
- the "system" is largely closed to the environment.

Complex "systems" have the following characteristics:

- a large number of elements;
- many interactions between the elements;
- attributes of the elements are not predetermined;
- interaction between elements is loosely organised;
- they are probabilistic in their behaviour;
- the "system" evolves over time;

- "sub-systems" are purposeful and generate their own goals;
- the "system" is subject to behavioural influences;
- the "system" is largely open to the environment.

In what follows, reference will be made to simple problem contexts which contain relatively "simple systems" manifesting "easy" problems and complex problem contexts which contain relatively "complex systems" manifesting "difficult" problems. We will have to be careful, however, not to be fooled by either superficial simplicity or superficial complexity. For example, if we consider an aeroplane that has many parts and interrelations we might mistakenly label this complex. Mistaken it would be, because characteristically such technological realisations are operated according to "well-defined" laws of behaviour and are not evolutionary, and on these grounds should be labelled relatively simple. On the other hand a superficially simple system, say the organisation of two people in interaction, is often non-deterministic and evolutionary (it may be a learning system) and hence should be labelled relatively complex.

To classify participants we adopt terminology from the industrial relations literature which we have already met in the last chapter when considering the political metaphor. Unitary, pluralist and coercive relationships between participants are seen as possible. For our purposes, these will be defined as follows:

Unitary

- they share common interests;
- their values and beliefs are highly compatible;
- they largely agree upon ends and means;
- they all participate in decision making;
- they act in accordance with agreed objectives.

Pluralist

- they have a basic compatibility of interest;
- their values and beliefs diverge to some extent;
- they do not necessarily agree upon ends and means, but compromise is possible;
- they all participate in decision making;
- they act in accordance with agreed objectives.

Coercive

- they do not share common interests;
- their values and beliefs are likely to conflict;
- they do not agree upon ends and means and "genuine" compromise is not possible;
- some coerce others to accept decisions;

- no agreement over objectives is possible given present systemic arrangements.

A problem context is, therefore, called unitary if the set of participants is unitary, pluralist if the set is pluralist and coercive if the relationships exhibit coercion. In general, problem contexts become more difficult to handle as they cease to be unitary since issues of "system" and organisation become confounded by misunderstanding, or even worse, any attempt to promote understanding is confounded by political–coercive forces.

If the dimensions of systems and participants are now combined to yield what we will call a six-celled matrix, problem contexts can be seen to fall into the following ideal-type categories (see also Figure 2.1):

- SIMPLE–UNITARY
- COMPLEX–UNITARY
- SIMPLE–PLURALIST
- COMPLEX–PLURALIST
- SIMPLE–COERCIVE
- COMPLEX–COERCIVE

Each of these problem contexts differs in a meaningful way from the others and its integrated characteristics are found usefully to reflect types of "problem issue". The charting of these six "ideal type" problem contexts implies the need for six types of "problem-solving" methodology. This provides a very convenient means of grouping available systems approaches.

2.3 GROUPING TYPES OF SYSTEMS METHODOLOGY

The purpose of this section is to see how the assumptions underpinning existing systems approaches reflect the problem contexts identified in

	UNITARY	PLURALIST	COERCIVE
SIMPLE	Simple–Unitary	Simple–Pluralist	Simple–Coercive
COMPLEX	Complex–Unitary	Complex–Pluralist	Complex–Coercive

Figure 2.1 An "ideal type" grouping of problem contexts

the previous section. This, of course, will be somewhat underdeveloped, amounting to an ideal-type guide with which we can hardly do justice to the methodologies under discussion. A number of these methodologies naturally transcend the matrix cells which, if taken too literally, would seem to have created unnecessarily artificial barriers between simple and complex, and between unitary, pluralist and coercive (e.g. systems engineering, which we label simple–unitary, but which tackles some aspects of "complexity"). It is arguable that the assumptions of others do not preclude their inclusion in more than one cell (critical systems heuristics, perhaps, could be included as complex–pluralist, although we choose to highlight its unique recognition of coercion). Further, we are not always dealing with fully explicit systems methodologies. System dynamics and viable system diagnosis, concentrate primarily on modelling systems in particular ways. How these models are then used is open to interpretation. In these cases we have done our best logically to infer a methodology from the nature of the modelling, or whatever other evidence is available. This is bound to be controversial, but it does not matter for our purpose, which is to present a comprehensive yet diverse view of systems-based "problem solving".

What we try to do below is to focus upon the essence of very different systems approaches. A much more sophisticated treatment of representative methodologies is, of course, provided in Chapters 4–9. To adherents of methodologies that we necessarily treat in passing in this section, and do not have space to deal with more fully later, we acknowledge that they may well have further value to offer. In compensation for this omission, we hope that the service we are attempting to provide to systems thinking as a whole, by showing the complementarity of existing approaches, is sufficient.

Further details of where to find out more about many of the approaches and ideas mentioned, and where to find discussion of them, are included in the relevant "further reading" sections in later chapters. For now we will concentrate on grouping types of systems methodology according to our six ideal-type problem contexts.

Simple–Unitary

By simple–unitary we refer to methodologies that assume problem contexts are simple–unitary. Examples are:

- operational research;
- systems analysis;
- systems engineering;
- system dynamics.

These methodologies assume that the "problem solver" can easily establish objectives in terms of a system(s) in which it is assumed a problem resides. It is also taken for granted that there is little or no dispute about these (a unitary situation). The "system" of concern can often be represented in a quantitative or highly structured model which will simulate performance scenarios under different operational conditions (these models in terms of our first continuum are very often simple). Obviously such methods should only be used when these assumptions hold in relation to "real world" circumstances or needs.

Systems analysis, as an example, is usually portrayed as having the following sequence of steps:

- set an objective or objectives to accomplish;
- undertake assessment of alternative routes by which the objective may be accomplished;
- make an assessment of the costs or resources required by each route;
- develop a mathematical model or models to simulate alternatives;
- select a criterion, relating objectives and costs or resources, for choosing the preferred or optimal alternative;
- simulate, optimise and make a choice.

Important metaphors implicitly guiding these "hard" systems approaches are the organisation as a "machine" and as a "team". We can observe, therefore, that this part of the system of systems methodologies is characterised or even constituted by these metaphors.

Complex–Unitary

This category includes:

- viable system diagnosis;
- general system theory;
- socio-technical systems thinking;
- contingency theory.

The "systems" of concern are found to exhibit many, if not all, of the features at the complex end of our first continuum (i.e. they are complex). They have many elements in close interrelationship, exhibit probabilistic behaviour which is difficult to predict, are open to the environment and include purposeful parts. There is, however, assumed to be general agreement about the goals to be pursued (a unitary situation). This is inferred because these systems approaches do not include steps which are designed to facilitate debate about overall objectives and purposes.

Viable system diagnosis (which is treated in detail in Chapter 5), for example, requires that we:

- determine the purpose to be pursued and the relevant system for achieving this purpose (the "system in focus", that portion of the model where the main issues and actors are assumed to reside);
- specify sub-systems and wider systems;
- detail the environment, operations and management of each sub-system;
- study the co-ordination of the "system in focus";
- study the control of the "system in focus";
- study the development function of the "system in focus";
- study the policy-making function of the "system in focus";
- check that all information channels, transducers and control loops are properly designed.

Two important metaphors underpinning these "cybernetic" (because they concentrate on communication and control) systems approaches are those of the organisation as an "organism" (organic) and as a "brain" (neurocybernetic metaphor). Implicit also is the idea of a "team". These metaphors therefore characterise or constitute the complex–unitary area of the system of systems methodologies.

Simple–Pluralist

- Social systems design (Churchman's approach—see Chapter 6).
- Strategic assumption surfacing and testing.

These methodologies assume that issues are difficult to handle primarily because of disagreements among participants about the goals to be served through the "system" of concern (relationships between participants are pluralist). It is assumed that, once the conflict on issues is dissolved (a unitary position is realised), any "problems" remaining will be relatively simple to deal with using simple–unitary methods. The argument of the system of systems methodologies is that methodologies which we would relate to the simple–pluralist cell assume that organisations can be properly understood and dealt with as machines through machine-type approaches once we have resolved the pluralism. Methodologies related to the complex–pluralist cell assume that organizations have to be treated like organisms and brains, and the task is, therefore, more difficult. In each case the issues relating to the participants are integrated with a particular vision of the organization (i.e. as a machine, an organism, or a brain). Strategic assumption surfacing and testing (presented in detail in Chapter 6 and summarised below) combines attention to pluralism with a machine vision of the organization. It pays little attention to any structural or organisational principles that might underpin successful systems design. There is no attempt to deal with organisational systemicity:

- group formation;
- assumption surfacing
  - stakeholder analysis
  - assumption rating;
- dialectical debate;
- synthesis.

An important metaphor underpinning these softer systems approaches is the organisation as a "culture". This tends to work in tandem with the "coalition" setting of the political metaphor and characterises or constitutes this area of the grid.

Complex–Pluralist

- Interactive planning;
- Soft systems methodology.

These methodologies are designed to tackle contexts in which there is a lack of agreement about goals and objectives among the participants concerned, but where some genuine compromise is achievable (a pluralist situation). They also give advice on how to deal with difficulties stemming from the perceived complexity of contexts (which are assumed to be "complex"). For example, they offer guidelines in one form or another for the design of whatever "systems" we might wish to bring into existence.

Soft systems methodology (which is dealt with in detail in Chapter 8), for example, has the following "stages":

- "start" with a problem situation unstructured;
- work towards a problem situation expressed and name some relevant human activity systems;
- formulate root definitions of relevant human activity systems;
- develop conceptual models of the systems named in the root definitions;
- undertake comparison of conceptual models with the expression of the problem situation;
- discuss culturally feasible and systemically desirable changes;
- take action to improve the problem situation.

An important metaphor underpinning these soft systems approaches is, again, that of the organisation as a "culture". This extends the area that is constituted by this metaphor. The "coalition" setting of the political metaphor is almost equally significant. Also used in a supporting role are ideas stemming from the organisation as an "organism" (organic metaphor) and as a "brain" (neurocybernetic metaphor), but this only reiterates the point we made earlier, that pluralistic issues are seen as integral with particular perspectives (i.e. complex) on the nature of organizations.

Simple–Coercive

- Critical systems heuristics.

This approach can reveal the "politics" of problem contexts, where real differences of interest as well as of values and beliefs may exist, and where different groups seek to use whatever power they have to impose their favoured strategy upon others (the relationship between participants is coercive). It suggests how properly organised debate on the resolution of conflicts can be set up and assumes that this task is relatively clear cut. Critical systems heuristics (dealt with in Chapter 9) assumes, therefore, that the sources of power of the different participants will be relatively easy to identify. That is why we say it makes simple rather than complex–coercive assumptions. It advises that power can be considered through the following questions:

- What interests are being served by a proposed system design?
  - Who is the actual client of the system (S)?
  - What is the actual purpose of S (including consequences as well as declared intentions)?
  - What is S's inbuilt measure of success?
  - Who is actually the decision taker?
  - What does the decision taker control?
  - What is not controlled by the decision taker?
  - Who is actually involved as planner?
  - Who is involved as expert?
  - Where do those involved in planning seek the guarantee that their planning will be successful?
  - Who is, or may be, affected by the planning but is not involved in it?
  - To what extent are the affected, but not involved, being encouraged to take over planning?
  - Is the world view underlying the design of S the world view of (some of) the involved or (some of) the affected?
- How can a genuine debate be organised between those involved in the system design and those who have to live with/in the design?

The "prison" metaphor from the political perspective is important for this approach and characterises or constitutes this area of the system of systems methodologies.

Complex–Coercive

In complex–coercive contexts, complexity characterising the situations of concern hides the true sources of power of the various participants. No systems methodology currently bases itself upon the assumptions that problem contexts are complex and coercive. We do not yet, therefore, possess the tools to tackle such contexts when they arise in the "real world". It is clear that a methodology based upon such assumptions would have to consider:

- the various sources of power in organisations;
- the organisation's culture and the way this determines what changes are feasible;
- the mobilisation of bias in organisations;
- the relationship of hierarchies in organisations to class, sex, race and status divisions in the wider society.

Again, the "prison" metaphor from the political perspective is important for understanding such problem contexts.

2.4 A SYSTEM OF SYSTEMS METHODOLOGIES

Putting the findings of Section 2.3 into our earlier matrix we arrive at Figure 2.2. We can further summarise our argument, in terms of the relationship of dominant metaphors to methodologies, in Figure 2.3.

These figures highlight the areas of strength of the different systems approaches and confirm our earlier hope that the variety of approaches available to decision makers would provide competence and effectiveness in different problem contexts. Rather than a single methodology being offered for all situations, we have put together an informed approach that recognises the partial nature of each methodology and works out how these partialities can be brought together to form a much more comprehensive view of systems-based "problem solving".

2.5 SUMMARY

In this chapter we have logically grouped together what is otherwise a bewildering array of systems methodologies. We have considered, schematically, what each methodology assumes about the nature of

	UNITARY	PLURALIST	COERCIVE
SIMPLE	S–U • OR • SA • SE • SD	S–P • SSD • SAST	S–C • Critical systems heuristics
COMPLEX	C–U • VSD • GST • Socio-tech. • Contingency theory	C–P • Interactive planning • SSM	C–C ?

Figure 2.2 A grouping of systems metholodogies based upon the assumptions they make about problem contexts

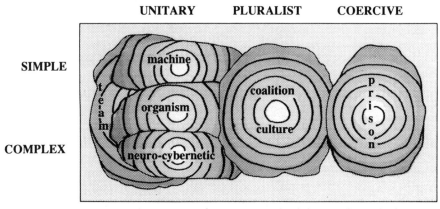

Figure 2.3 Constituting the system of systems methodologies through dominant metaphors

problem contexts (in terms of the "systems" from which "problems" or issues emerge) and the "participants". We must reiterate, however, that it must remain a matter of careful debate how any "real world" issues or "problems" should be described and, therefore, how the grid of problem contexts can be drawn upon to reflect and organise our ideas about these issues in a meaningful way. It follows also that the choice of systems methodology *should be informed* by the "system of systems methodologies", *it should not be determined* by it. The "system of systems methodologies" is not a short cut to, but rather an enrichment of, Total Systems Intervention (TSI). For example, the whole point of using systemic metaphors in the process of TSI, is to avoid the drawing of premature or narrow conclusions about the issues being faced.

Total Systems Intervention combines creative thinking about the nature of problem situations, using the systems metaphors, with informed choice of systems methodology, based upon knowledge of the strengths and weaknesses of different methodologies gained from the "system of systems methodologies". We believe that a rewarding route to the successful treatment of the most significant "problems" or issues facing an organisation is to follow the full logic and process of TSI, as set out in the next chapter.

2.6 CASE STUDY

The interested reader could make a useful diversion before moving on to Chapter 3, by returning to the methodology for implementing TQM that was touched upon in Chapter 1, and using knowledge gained so far, to undertake a "system of systems methodologies" assessment. What assumptions does TQM make about problem contexts? The reader might also like to consider methodologies or techniques currently used in the organisation in which he/she is employed, or those that are familiar from other experiences, as another way of trying out the ideas of this chapter.

2.7 FURTHER READING

- For an overview of the development of the "system of systems methodologies" argument, consult the original papers by:

Jackson, M. C. (1990). Beyond a system of systems methodologies, *Journal of the Operational Research Society*, **41**, 657–68.

Jackson, M. C. (1987). New directions in management science, in *New Directions in Management Science* (eds. M.C. Jackson and P. Keys), pp. 133–64, Gower, Aldershot.

Jackson, M. C. and Keys, P. (1984). Towards a system of systems methodologies, *Journal of the Operational Research Society*, **35**, 473–86.

Chapter 3

The Logic and Process of Total Systems Intervention (TSI)

I am a dreamer. I am, indeed, a practical dreamer. My dreams are not airy things. I want to convert my dreams into realities.

Throughout my life I have gained more from my critic friends than from my admirers, especially when the criticism was made in courteous and friendly language.

I am a lover of my own liberty and so I would do nothing to restrict yours.

Mahatma Gandhi

3.1 INTRODUCTION

Total Systems Intervention (TSI) represents a new approach to planning, designing, "problem solving" and evaluation. The process employs a range of systems metaphors to encourage creative thinking about organisations and the difficult issues that managers have to confront. These metaphors are linked through a framework, the "system of systems methodologies", to various systems approaches, so that once informed agreement is reached about which metaphors most thoroughly expose an organisation's concerns, an appropriate systems-based intervention methodology (or set of methodologies) can be employed. Choice of an appropriate systems methodology will guide "problem solving" in a way that ensures that it addresses what are found to be the main concerns of the particular organisation involved.

From this account it can be seen that we already have in place two of the three main building blocks of TSI. An appropriately rich array of systems metaphors was developed in Chapter 1 and the "system of systems methodologies" was constructed in the last chapter. It remains to detail and analyse the different systems methodologies themselves and this, of course, is the job of the later chapters of the book.

TSI is itself, however, a methodology (or perhaps meta-methodology) in that it advocates combining the three building blocks (these three aspects of systems thinking) in an interactive manner which is deemed to be particularly powerful and fruitful. In this chapter the logic of the combination, and hence the TSI methodology or process itself, is explored theoretically. This is done in the same way as we intend looking at all the other methodologies. First the philosophy of TSI is unearthed, then the principles embedded in the approach (seven in this case) are set out, finally the phases of the methodology (three in TSI) are described. To bring further clarity to this theoretical exposition a short example is provided in this chapter of a consultancy intervention in an organization, using TSI to improve quality management. A much larger example is given in Chapter 10, by which time the reader will have gained sufficient background in the use of different systems methodologies.

Other demonstrations of TSI at work can be found in Chapters 4–9. Although, as suggested, we will concentrate on different systems methodologies in turn (as "dominant" methodologies), the worked examples that we provide often reflect the logic of TSI and not the logic of the individual methodologies. They employ all of the three building blocks of TSI according to the meta-methodology of TSI. Similarly, it is hoped, readers will employ TSI to tackle the case studies provided and not simply use the particular methodology that is the focus of the chapter they happen to be on. Attentive readers will recognise that TSI is being put through exactly the same demonstrative process in the book that individual methodologies receive in respective chapters—but that there is one thing missing. That thing is a "critique" of TSI which will, in fact, be provided in Chapter 10.

3.2 PHILOSOPHY OF TSI

3.2.1 Introduction

The philosophy underpinning TSI is "critical systems thinking". This is a new development in the systems movement which is described more fully in the works of the authors listed in this chapter's "further reading" section. Briefly, and for our purposes here, critical systems thinking can be seen as making its stand on three positions. These are "complementarism", "sociological awareness" and the promotion of "human well-being and emancipation".

3.2.2 Complementarism

The complementarist position in systems thinking is best set out in comparison to the prevailing "pragmatist" and "isolationist" arguments.

Pragmatists argue that management scientists should not concern themselves with "airy-fairy" theoretical issues but concentrate on building up a "tool-kit" of techniques which have been shown to work in practice. This is a popular position among, for example, management consultants anxious to get the job done and keep the client happy. It neglects however to consider whether better results might be obtained if more theoretically guided interventions were made. It fails to recognise that learning can take place only if practice (successful or otherwise) can be related back to a set of theoretical presuppositions which are being consciously tested through that practice. In elevating "what works in practice" to the position of deciding between "good" and "bad" interventions, the possibility that factors other than "proper" method or methodology choice (e.g. simply serving the powerful) might be the reason behind success is excluded. Finally, it follows that pragmatism abandons the hope of developing management science as an intellectual discipline, the main tenets of which can be passed on to "apprentices".

Isolationism in its most primitive form implies sticking to one method or methodology only, because the analyst knows and wants to know no other approach. More sophisticated isolationists engage in a kind of "imperialism", adhering stolidly to one well worked out theoretical position and linked methodology, but adapting other methods and methodologies for use under the tutelage of the preferred theoretical position. This has the inevitable effect of distorting the methods or methodologies chosen for incorporation, with a consequent loss of the force they command when properly used in the service of their more appropriate theoretical rationalities. Isolationism divides management science and the systems community unto warring factions, each arguing for the primacy of its favoured approach—whether it be hard (approaches based on means–end), soft (approaches based on interpretations and their interrelations) or cybernetic (approaches based on laws of organisation)—and its ability to tackle all (or the great majority) of "problem types".

Complementarism is steadfastly opposed to the "pick and mix" strategy of the pragmatists. Different methodologies express different rationalities stemming from alternative theoretical positions which they reflect. These alternative positions must be respected, and methodologies and their appropriate theoretical underpinnings developed in partnership. Further, the claim of any one theoretical rationality to be the sole legitimate one (isolationism) or to absorb all others (imperialism) must be resisted. This should not lead the management science community to fragment into independent groups. As the discussion of systems metaphors and the "system of systems methodologies" has shown, the existence of a range of systems methodologies, each driven by a different theoretical position, can be seen as a strength rather than as a weakness of the systems movement. All that is required is the guidance offered by complementarism so that each methodology is put to work only on the kinds of issues or "problems" for which it is the most suitable.

3.2.3 Sociological Awareness

The sociological awareness of critical systems thinking, which is necessarily incorporated into TSI, recognises that there are organisational and societal pressures which have led to certain systems methodologies being popular for guiding interventions at particular times. For example, it was inconceivable that soft systems thinking could ever have become popular in Eastern European countries dominated by the Stalinist bureaucratic dictates of the one party system. With the move towards free-market capitalism and political pluralism, however, one can expect that the circumstances which allowed "hard" and "cybernetic" approaches to "succeed" will change, and that softer approaches will become more acceptable. From another angle we could point to a dominant or institutionalised view of knowledge, such as the traditional rational scientific approach, dictating which methodologies are legitimate. These are examples which suggest why it is important to enquire into the popularity or otherwise of certain systems approaches in given circumstances, and to "liberate" those which are illegitimately suppressed.

It is the same sociological awareness which should make users of TSI contemplate the social consequences of using particular methodologies. For example, the choice of a "hard" or cybernetic methodology implies that one goal or objective is being privileged at the expense of other possibilities. Is this goal or objective general to all organisational stakeholders, or is it simply that of the most powerful? Similarly, the use of "soft" systems methodologies, which are dependent upon open and free debate for the justification of their results, might have deleterious social consequences if the conditions for such debate were absent.

3.2.4 Human Well-Being and Emancipation

Critical systems thinking, and the thrust of TSI therefore, is emancipatory in that it seeks to achieve for all individuals, working through organisations and in society, the maximum development of their potential. This indeed is the basis on which "complementarism" discussed above can be grounded and guided. As Jürgen Habermas has argued, there are two fundamental conditions underpinning the socio-cultural form of life in the human species. These he calls "work" and "interaction". "Work" enables human beings to achieve goals and to bring about material well-being through social labour. Its success depends upon achieving technical mastery over natural and social processes. The importance of work leads human beings to have a "technical interest" in the prediction and control of natural and social affairs. This is one of two anthropologically based cognitive interests which Habermas believes the human species possesses. The other is linked to "interaction" and is labelled the "practical interest". Its concern is with securing and expanding the possibilities for mutual understanding among all those involved in social systems. Disagreement between different groups can be just as much a threat to the reproduction of the socio-cultural form of life as a failure to predict and control natural and social processes.

While work and interaction have for Habermas pre-eminent anthropological status, the analysis of "power" and the way it is exercised is equally important, Habermas argues, if we are to understand past and present social arrangements. The exercise of power in the social process can prevent the open and free discussion necessary for the success of interaction. Human beings have, therefore, an "emancipatory interest" in freeing themselves from constraints imposed by power relations and in learning, through a process of genuine participatory democracy, involving discursive will-formation, to control their own destiny.

Now, if we all have a technical, a practical and an emancipatory interest in the functioning of organisations and society, then a management science which can support all these various interests has an important role to play in human well-being and emancipation. But this is exactly what complementarism and sociologically aware systems thinking can provide. It is clear that "hard" and cybernetic systems approaches can support the technical interest, soft methodologies the practical interest, and critical systems heuristics can aid the emancipatory interest.

So much for the philosophy of TSI, which comes through in the principles and practice, and should be known and respected by all who would use this approach.

3.3 PRINCIPLES OF TSI

There are seven principles embedded in the three phases of TSI. These are:

- organisations are too complicated to understand using one management "model" and their problems too complex to tackle with the "quick fix";
- organisations, their strategies and the difficulties they face should be investigated using a range of systems metaphors;
- systems metaphors, which seem appropriate for highlighting organisational strategies and problems, can be linked to appropriate systems methodologies to guide intervention;
- different systems metaphors and methodologies can be used in a complementary way to address different aspects of organisations and the difficulties they confront;
- it is possible to appreciate the strengths and weaknesses of different systems methodologies and to relate each to organisational and business concerns;
- TSI sets out a systemic cycle of enquiry with iteration back and forth between the three phases;
- facilitators, clients and others are engaged at all stages of the TSI process.

3.4 THE THREE PHASES OF TSI

The three phases of TSI are labelled "creativity", "choice" and "implementation". We shall consider these in turn, looking in each case at the task to be accomplished during that phase, the tools provided by TSI to realise that task, and the outcome or results expected from the phase.

3.4.1 Creativity

The *task* during the creativity phase is to use systems metaphors as organising structures to help managers think creatively about their enterprises.

The sorts of question it would be pertinent to ask are:

- "Which metaphors reflect current thinking about organisational strategies, structures, and control and information systems (including past, present and future concerns)?"
- "Which alternative metaphors might capture better what more desirably could be achieved with this organisation?"

- "Which metaphors make sense of this organisation's difficulties and concerns?"

The *tools* provided by TSI to assist this process are the systems metaphors set out in Chapter 1. Different metaphors focus attention on different aspects of an organisation's functioning, as we have seen. Some concentrate on organisational structure, others highlight human and political aspects of an organisation. Some examples are:

- the organisation as a "machine" (closed system view);
- the organisation as an "organism" (open system view);
- the organisation as a "brain" (learning system view);
- the organisation as a "culture" (emphasis on norms and values);
- the organisation as a "team" (unitary political system);
- the organisation as a "coalition" (pluralist political system);
- the organisation as a "prison" (coercive political system).

The main aspects of organisations highlighted, and those aspects neglected, by each metaphor will be disclosed in order to enhance discussion and debate.

The *outcome* (what is expected to emerge) from the creativity phase is a "dominant" metaphor which highlights the main interests and concerns and can become the basis for a choice of an appropriate intervention methodology. There may be other metaphors which it is also sensible to pursue into the next phase. The relative position of dominant and these "dependent" metaphors may indeed be altered by later work. If all the metaphors reveal serious problems then the organisation is obviously in a crisis state.

An example of "creativity" at work on an existing organisational strategy is the dissection of TQM, provided in Chapter 1, to find out what metaphors it embraces and therefore upon which features of the organisation it concentrates.

3.4.2 Choice

The *task* during the "choice" phase is to choose an appropriate systems-based intervention methodology (or set of methodologies) to suit particular characteristics of the organisation's situation as revealed by the examination conducted in the creativity phase.

The *tools* provided by TSI to help with this stage are the guidelines of the "system of systems methodologies" (as set out in Figure 2.2), and, derived from that, knowledge of the underlying metaphors employed by systems methodologies (expressed in Figure 2.3).

Although it would be possible to link systems methodologies and systems metaphors directly, the pattern in the variety of systems methodologies is best discerned if the link is made through the "system of systems methodologies". As was demonstrated in Chapter 2, the "system of systems methodologies" neatly unearths the assumptions that each methodology makes about the "system(s)" with which it deals and about the relationship between the "actors" concerned with that "system". Putting these points together in the matrix of Figure 2.2, it is apparent that systems methodologies can be grouped according to whether they assume problem contexts to be simple–unitary, simple–pluralist, simple–coercive, complex–unitary, complex–pluralist or complex–coercive. Combining the information gained about the problem context during the creativity phase, and the knowledge provided by the "system of systems methodologies" about the assumptions underlying different systems approaches, it is possible to move towards an appropriate choice of systems intervention methodology. For example, if the problem context is characterised by there being clear and agreed objectives (unitary) and by being transparent enough so that it can be captured in a mathematical model (simple), then a methodology based upon simple–unitary assumptions can be used with every hope of success.

On the basis of the "system of systems methodologies" it is possible to relate individual methodologies to the systems metaphors previously described, as in Table 3.1. Bearing in mind the metaphors which came out as "dominant" and "dependent" during the "creativity" phase and the conclusions of the "system of systems methodologies", appropriate choice of systems methodology (systems methodologies) to guide intervention and change can now be made.

The most probable *outcome* of the "choice" phase is that there will be a "dominant" methodology chosen, to be tempered in use by the imperatives highlighted by "dependent" methodologies.

3.4.3 Implementation

The *task* during the implementation phase is to employ a particular systems methodology (systems methodologies) to translate the dominant vision of the organisation, its structure, and the general orientation adopted to concerns and problems, into specific proposals for change.

The *tools* provided by TSI are the specific systems methodologies used according to the logic of TSI. The dominant methodology operationalises the vision of the organisation contained in the dominant metaphor. The logic of TSI demands, however, that consideration continues to be given to the imperatives of other methodologies. For example, the key difficulties in an organisation suffering from structural collapse may be best highlighted using the metaphors of "organism" and "brain" (see the application reported in Chapter 5) but the "cultural" metaphor might

Table 3.1 Systems methodologies related to systems metaphors (S is Simple, C is Complex, U is Unitary, P is Pluralist, C is Coercive)

Systems methodology (examples)	Assumptions Problem Contexts	Underlying metaphors
System dynamics	S–U	Machine Team
Viable system diagnosis	C–U	Organism Brain Team
SAST (strategic assumption surfacing and testing)	S–P	Machine Coalition Culture
Interactive planning	C–P	Brain Coalition Culture
SSM (soft systems methodology)	C–P	Organism Coalition Culture
Critical Systems Heuristics	S–C	Machine/Organism Prison

also appear illuminating, if in a subordinate way given the immediate crisis. In these circumstances a cybernetic methodology would be chosen to guide the intervention, but perhaps tempered by some ideas from soft systems methodology. Managers in another organisation might wish to redesign their information system but be held back by conflicting views about where the organisation should be going, exacerbated by some political in-fighting. This situation might usefully be understood with the "coalition" metaphor as dominant, but with the "brain" and "prison" metaphors also being illuminating. In this case soft systems methodology might guide the intervention but with aspects of cybernetics and critical systems heuristics also being used.

The *outcome* of the implementation stage is co-ordinated change brought about in those aspects of the organization currently most vital for its effective and efficient functioning.

The three stage methodology of TSI is set out in Table 3.2. It is important to stress, however, that TSI is a systemic and iterative methodology. It asks, during each phase, that continual reference be made, back or forth, to the likely conclusions of other phases. So, for example, during phase 1, "creativity", attempts are made to anticipate the likely consequences of particular visions of the organisation's structure, and information and control requirements. This idea is reflected in the circular representation of TSI shown in Figure 3.1.

To add further "real world" content to the logic and process of TSI described so far, and by again drawing upon consultancy experiences as we do throughout, we now consider how an organisation thought its way towards implementation of a total quality programme using TSI.

3.5 TSI IN ACTION: A TOTAL QUALITY MANAGEMENT EXAMPLE

For the purpose of capitalising on understandings that the reader has already developed, we will put together an example based on how TQM was introduced into an organisation. The intervention went broadly along the following lines.

The problem situation initially confronted was a "mess", one that had not been tackled through any rigorous means of enquiry but just left to take its own course. The organisation, which we will label "Gek Mui Enterprises" (it was a South East Asian company), was suffering from decreasing orders and loss of market share in a buoyant market. The Sales Director detested the Company Secretary. This conflict came to a head when new credit control rulings were introduced which were very strict, and amounted to a drastic change in policy for a company that

Table 3.2 The three phase TSI methodology

CREATIVITY	
Task	– to highlight aims, concerns and problems
Tools	– systems metaphors
Outcome	– "dominant" and "dependent" metaphors highlighting the major issues
CHOICE	
Task	– to choose an appropriate systems-based intervention methodology (methodologies)
Tools	– the "system of systems methodologies"; the relationship between metaphors and methodologies
Outcome	– "dominant" and "dependent" methodologies chosen for use
IMPLEMENTATION	
Task	– to arrive at and implement specific change proposals
Tools	– systems methodologies employed according to the logic of TSI
Outcome	– highly relevant and co-ordinated intervention

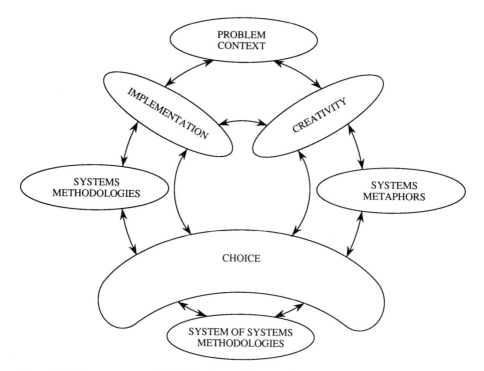

Figure 3.1 The process of Total Systems Intervention

had traditionally been sales oriented (i.e. customers paid as and when they chose, some debtors frequently running to 60 or even 90 days). The Company Secretary's concern for cash flow seemed understandable, but the poor relationship between him and the Sales Director prevented there being a coherent Board view. The customers, not being used to strict credit control, frequently rang the Sales Director complaining bitterly. This antagonised the Sales Director even more. Accentuating these difficulties, the Managing Director was clearly sales oriented too.

Morale in the Accounting and Finance Department was at an all time low for several reasons. As a consequence of the sales orientation of the company, accountants and finance clerks were seen as the "poor people" doing a low grade job. Members of staff in this service function were consequently subjected to various jibes and were quite prepared to believe them to be true. Even worse, these groups had experienced an unusually high turnover of staff, particularly in management functions, and it was, therefore, impossible to achieve continuity in relations within or externally to the organisation. A related difficulty concerned the Management Information Systems (MIS) group. MIS were closely linked to the finance and accounting groupings. The theory was that data would therefore be readily accessible. The MIS group consisted of mathematicians and statisticians, whose job it was to convert the data into specified information. Speed and accuracy were vital but missing, and the feeling was that if Sales were so superior then they undoubtedly could manage as an autonomous function—"let them do their own dirty work". In order to promote access to information, a "hot line" between the MIS manageress and the Managing and Sales Directors was installed. The MIS manageress was expected always to be available and she resented this. She was seen as a stooge for the sales group by her own staff. Another problem with the MIS was that the only information analysed was that which arose naturally within the organisation. External information gathering had never been carried out.

Although these emerged as the main features of the situation, the organisation more generally suffered from poor internal communications and lack of motivation among staff.

Systems metaphors were used (see Chapter 1) in a direct yet *invisible* way to develop an appreciation and understanding of the situation. It was the ideas underpinning the metaphors rather than the metaphors themselves which were exposed to those involved in the intervention. Rather than adopting the straightforward style of asking employees, etc., whether they considered the organisation could or should be considered like a brain, we would look for certain features like volatility of environment, clear organisational mission (i.e. identity) and examine issues relating to control, co-ordination, commitment, measures of performance, etc. Rather than posing questions such as "Is the organisation like, or ought it be like a machine?", we would consider issues of hierarchy, division of labour, standardised parts, non-adaptability, etc.

The process of creative thinking can be prompted not only through ideas of "likeness" but also by adopting a dialectical approach: asking when particular metaphors break down in practice and comparing and contrasting the different visions provided by alternative metaphors. The critical process we undertook went as follows:

(1) Use metaphors to help enrich perceptions. Ask, "When would metaphor 'x' be useful in practice?" (likeness).
(2) Use metaphors to challenge perceptions. Ask, "When would metaphor 'x' break down in practice?" (challenge).
(3) Carry out (1) and (2) for other metaphors.
(4) Mix and enrich—mix metaphors to seek further likeness and make further challenges.
(5) Remix metaphors to enrich perceptions further.

(6) By synthesis and resynthesis, move towards appreciation of a dominant and some support metaphors.

Using the findings that emerged from the logic and process above, we drew upon the "system of systems methodologies" (described in Chapter 2) to guide choice of a "relevant problem-solving" approach. This was carried out while recognising that TSI emphasises the possibility of a shifting dominance in metaphor and methodology, and the continual need to keep an eye open for this.

Exploring with metaphors led us to believe that there was a desperate need to promote a shared culture in the organization, particularly because of the fragmentation in the "coalition". In addition, the nature of the business context pointed to the need for substantial evolutionary developments in the firm, the whole situation being characterised by many of the features of complexity discussed in Chapter 2. With further guidance from the ideals of the "system of systems methodologies", we chose soft systems methodology, SSM (see Chapter 8), which assumed that the nature of social and organisational reality was "complex" as well as "cultural" (i.e. SSM was chosen to be dominant at the outset). SSM undeniably can help in pluralistic contexts and would lead to further clarification of what could be done in the future (beyond perhaps any ideas yet conceived) while maintaining some sympathy for organic needs.

The soft systems analysis led us to conclude that there was a need for a "customer satisfaction system", or perhaps more ambitiously a "Total Quality Management" system. This should lead to greater cohesion and help to convince lost customers to place their business with Gek Mui Enterprises once again. That was a good starting point and a coalition genuinely formed and agreed upon the need for quality issues to be addressed. But there was some substantial dispute about the nature of the implementation that would be required.

The Managing Director and a large part of the normal decision-making body believed that implementation should be "top-down" and that this implied nothing by way of changes in organisation (a major selling point promoted by traditionalist TQM gurus such as Crosby). It was felt that TQM was simply a matter of attitude change and that all efforts should be directed to this end. Some representatives, mainly from "operations", were, however, unhappy about the top-down approach and felt that there were more immediate difficulties to face up to, in terms of organisation in the short term, and that the introduction of TQM did imply organisational change as well as attitudinal change.

At this stage strategic assumption surfacing and testing (SAST—see Chapter 6) was drawn upon to look closely into the assumptions implied by each of the two views. This was certainly logical because the notion of pluralism and culture remained dominant, but now the issues were much more clear cut. We needed to consider the two interdependent "solutions" and, in particular, to challenge seriously the accepted top-down way of doing TQM. One policy option that diverged considerably from the traditional top-down view had emerged. If we could dialectically resolve these issues by testing strategic assumptions, then we might be ready to change dominant metaphor and methodology again by moving from a "what" methodology (pluralist) to a "how" methodology (unitary). This is consistent with the philosophy of SAST, that once we have dealt with pluralism then we can relatively easily deal with the remaining technical matters through appropriate methods.

At the same time and to enhance the SAST process, systems metaphors were drawn upon to critique TQM (along the lines of the case study in Chapter 1, Section 1.11.3). This effort highlighted the mechanical viewpoint that the Managing Director and other "top-down" supporters assumed. They were considering, as dialectical debate revealed, that Quality Councils should be organised according to the standard bureaucratic organisational tree. This is precisely what TQM gurus suggest. Alternative styles of implementation were brought out by the SAST debate. The principles of TQM (see Chapter 1) were found to be open to metaphorical reinterpretation. It was decided that if quality were to be ensured in this organisation, subject to a volatile environment, then viability would have to become a major consideration.

If we remind ourselves of the philosophy, principles, methodology and critique of TQM in Chapter 1, then we will remember that a neurocybernetic view, although present, was not dominant. In this case, however, we decided to use the viable system model (see Chapter 5) to reinterpret some of the ideas of TQM as traditionally conceived. For example, why implement an "identity" down a company hierarchical tree when the VSM has an exceptional contribution to make through recursivity? Also, if we are thinking about continuous learning and improvement then the VSM again shows its strength. This is also the case with auditing of quality and the idea of measures of performance. More generally, can we honestly claim to have a "quality system", or expect to realise the ongoing benefits of one, if we cannot guarantee viability? In short, the principles of TQM and a viable system approach, as we interpreted them, were seen to be highly compatible for Gek Mui Enterprises.

The rest of this diary would amount to technical description and is not included because the purpose of this case study is only to examine the logic and process of TSI in action. What we hope has emerged from this account is the highly iterative and systemic nature of TSI, and the realisation by readers that any kind of systematised use of TSI would be unacceptable, and will lack in main emphasis that which we wish to promote, that is, creativity.

3.6 CONCLUSION

This chapter has sought to demonstrate the way that the logic and process of TSI can be used to support and enrich organisational planning, decision-making and "problem-solving" capabilities. It cannot do full justice to TSI itself. It is difficult at this stage of the book, without having experienced in detail interventions with the most important methodologies, to capture the iterative nature of TSI and the details of each phase in prose. First, TSI is a three phase, systemic approach in which each phase contains also the other two. There is at each phase a pass through "creativity", "choice" and "implementation", it is simply the emphasis on each that changes as the moment for action approaches. This means that events during each phase can change the relationship between dominant and dependent metaphors and dominant and dependent methodologies. The second reason why it cannot do justice to TSI at the moment, is because it is in the detailed working out of the meaning and implications of different metaphors, and in the precise understanding of the nature, strengths and weaknesses of different systems methodologies, that the rich content of TSI lies. We will show all this in Chapter 10 after considering the case studies emphasising particular methodologies in Chapters 4 to 9. Real appreciation, however, will be derived from actually using TSI to guide intervention.

We pass on now, to give detailed consideration to some specific systems methodologies, thereby providing readers with the third building block of TSI. Our choice of methodologies has been guided by two assumptions. First, that systems approaches offer the surest source of theoretical guidance for implementing an intervention and change strategy. Therefore, we have chosen only systems-based methodologies. Second, that it would be most useful to readers to demonstrate applications of as wide a range of systems methodologies as possible. Hence we have employed the "system of systems methodologies" to help us make what is the broadest possible coverage of systems methodologies according to their underlying assumptions, without missing out any of the most powerful approaches that the reader should know about. In fact we have chosen to concentrate upon:

- system dynamics
- viable system diagnosis
- strategic assumption surfacing and testing
- interactive planning
- soft systems methodology
- critical systems heuristics.

In each case we will consider philosophy, principles and methodology.

We then present an example application, normally based on our consultancy efforts, which illustrates use of the particular methodology of concern as the "dominant" methodology within the TSI framework. A critique, setting out the strengths and weaknesses of the methodology follows that.

Our task in each critique is to craft an intertwining of lines of argument, to manufacture a meta-paradigmatic net with which we can assess the legitimacies and limitations of the various systems methodologies at different levels (paradigm being a general term that represents the pulling together of issues relating to ideology, epistemology, ontology, methodology and method). In fact each systems methodology is assessed in terms of its theoretical presuppositions, the methodological guidelines it offers, its ideological biases and its utility. This hopefully comprehensive critique is followed in each chapter by a case study that summarises a problem situation with which we have been faced but this time without discussion of our own intervention efforts, so that readers can try out the methodology they have been considering and the logic and process of TSI, assuming, at least initially, that the methodology examined in that chapter is the dominant methodology.

3.7 FURTHER READING

- For the critical systems thinking which underpins TSI the main references are:

Flood, R. L. (1990). *Liberating Systems Theory*, Plenum, New York.
Flood, R. L. and Jackson, M. C. (eds.) (1991) *Critical Systems Thinking: Directed Readings*, Wiley, Chichester
Jackson, M. C. (1991). *Systems Methodology for the Management Sciences*, Plenum, New York.
Oliga, J. C. (1992). *Power, Ideology and Control: A Critical Systems Perspective*, Plenum, New York.

- For the critical theory that underpins critical systems thinking see:

Habermas, J. (1972). *Knowledge and Human Interests*, Heinemann, London.
Habermas, J. (1974). *Theory and Practice*, Heinemann, London.
Habermas, J. (1984). *Reason and the Rationalization of Society*, Beacon Press, Boston.

- You might also like to consult the learned journal *Systems Practice* where issues of a critical systems nature are discussed.

Chapter 4

System Dynamics (SD)

Nothing puzzles me more than time and space; and yet nothing troubles me less, as I never think about them.
Charles Lamb in a letter to T. Manning, 2 January 1810.

4.1. INTRODUCTION

The seminal ideas of system dynamics (SD), originally known as industrial dynamics, can be attributed to Jay Forrester and his work at the Massachusetts Institute of Technology. He developed a theory of information feedback and control as a means of evaluating business and other organisational and social contexts. This also involved developing an analytical modelling methodology.

The essential ideas are very basic. It is argued that any situation can be considered as complex, but mainly in terms of elements and "flows" ; flows being the relationships between the elements (in terms of Chapter 2 this is superficially complex). All influential elements must be included within a boundary. Connecting elements may form loops and hence feedback analysis is considered very important. In fact, a SD model could look very similar in diagrammatic form to the general conception of system that can be found in Chapter 1, particularly in Figure 1.1 (although inputs and outputs transcending the boundary are restricted in a SD model). It is a simple use of standard traditional systems ideas, called systems theory, that have been developed into the elegant mathematics of linear control theory and the much more troublesome non-linear control theory in other domains, such as control engineering. Its accessibility, however, makes SD an approach that can be understood and/or drawn upon by those in organisations involved in decision making. On analysis, SD is found to assume that social reality is best considered simple and unitary. The type of model developed in SD dictates this. Although there may be many elements and relationships, the model structures developed are normally deterministic and do not evolve over time (the parameters are time-invariant), and the model is largely closed to the environment (all influential factors are contained within, the main inputs being in the form of perturbations to the model). Analysis is, therefore, along a closed sequence of causes and effects, a closed path of action and information. The model also implies some underlying taken-for-granted purpose, the unitary position expressed in terms of the transformation being performed by the system (the model).

We will now look at SD in more detail, considering sequentially its philosophy, principles, model and methodology.

4.2 PHILOSOPHY OF SD

A system dynamics (SD) view is one that places emphasis on structure, and the processes within that structure, assuming that this is how dynamic behaviour in the "real world" can best be characterised. SD, then, considers behaviour as being principally caused by structure, it is a theory of the structure of systems and dynamic behaviour. Structure includes not only the physical aspects of plant and production processes, it also importantly refers to the policies and traditions, both tangible and intangible, that dominate decision making.

Building on this general view, SD assumes that analysis of a situation can be undertaken from an external objective viewpoint and that the structure and dynamic processes of the "real world" can be re-created in both systems diagrams and mathematical models. In this sense, our vital interest is assumed to be in understanding how the generative mechanisms of a SD model can be used to represent, predict and to some extent explain some portion of reality, and how this information can be used to help bring about some appropriate beneficial control. This reflects very well Habermas' idea of human technical interests.

In an organisational context these ideas translate as follows. Many businesses and social situations can be characterised by the complexity of their element structure and the multi-causal feedback loops that exist between the elements. The output of an element will become the input to another element and hence to a large extent the complex of these exchanges can explain the phenomenon of change. Now, representing this in a SD model is a step towards coding into computers, which can then rapidly simulate the mass of interactions and the interconnectedness of loops, thus creating for us future business scenarios. This, it is argued, is an effective means of enhancing human intuition.

Since we can determine structural changes to the model and control the inputs (model perturbations), as if we had this capability over the real business situation, we are able to test out our ideas and plans to simulate what future outcomes these may lead to. We then apply ideas of feedforward control. Given desirable outcomes we will want to steer towards them by introducing the plans that gave rise to the simulated success, but given undesirable outcomes we will prefer to avoid these plans.

4.3. PRINCIPLES OF SD

The philosophy of system dynamics (SD) emphasises model structure, which supports an interest in prediction and control, and so these will be our main principles of analysis.

Structure is seen as having four significant characteristics, which amount to the focal concerns of any SD analysis. These are order, direction of feedback, non-linearity and loop multiplicity.

- *Order* A key issue in the development of a SD model concerns the number of "levels" that are used to represent the structure (i.e. those variables which represent amounts of something, such as stock levels or surplus levels). The number of levels determines the order of the system. Many managerial contexts are represented by twentieth order, and in some cases in excess of one-hundredth order systems. Levels will be discussed in the next section when we describe the SD model in some detail.
- *Direction of feedback* We noted in Chapter 1 that feedback is where the behaviour of one element may feed back, either directly from another element by way of their relationship, or indirectly via a series of connected elements, to influence the element that initiated the behaviour. This feedback, through loops, may be either negative or positive. Negative is an inhibiting or controlling influence. Positive is augmenting, creating either growth or decline. Positive and negative are the directions of feedback and are a central concern in the analysis of structure.
- *Non-linearity* Systems influenced by positive feedback produce exponential growth or decline from a set point. Unlike linear systems, such feedback is not necessarily detrimental in non-linear systems, since non-linear coupling of positive and negative loops can lead to dominance shifts between them, thus allowing for controlled growth. Also, positive loops can control other positive loops.

- *Loop multiplicity* Very few managerial, economic, or social situations can be adequately represented by a single-loop structure. Several loops, both positive and negative, are invariably involved. The number and degree of interactions between these loops lead to difficulties in identifying key variables, predicting outcomes and hence are difficult to comprehend without computer simulation. Without the help of simulation and subsequent analyses, behaviour appears to be counter-intuitive.

Given sound reasoning and understanding of structure in the development of a SD model, it is assumed that high quality prediction and control can be achieved.

Prediction is all about using whatever means we may have to look into the future. The aim with SD is to simulate possible scenarios for businesses, firms and other organisations which, it is assumed, substantially decreases uncertainty and gives us greater confidence about implementing decisions. Time-based mathematical models, as used in SD, have been found to perform the task of prediction well where "real world" behaviour is relatively deterministic. The quality of prediction is obviously contingent on the quality of the model, and that is largely determined by the soundness of the analytical modelling methodology employed. Given that we can achieve reliable prediction, we may then focus our attention on introducing control policies.

The kind of control that we are concerned with when formulating policies is feedforward control. This contrasts with feedback control which in SD is about maintaining internal system stability. Feedforward control relies on prediction, derived from how a system responds to structural change or other disturbing stimuli and highlights how desirable or undesirable future states can be realised or avoided. The control aspect is implementing redesign of system structure and/or decision policies so that predicted desirable states can be achieved.

The whole focus of SD-based prediction and control is on the model. The model cannot be adequately considered outside the methodology through which it is formulated and it is, therefore, to the model and methodology that we now turn our attention.

4.4 MODEL AND METHODOLOGY

There are many versions of how a quality model can be formulated. Most of these concentrate on formulation and simulation, but forget to deal explicitly with issues of pragmatic utility, and hence run the risk of achieving scientifically superb yet practically useless white elephants. For this reason we have decided to present, albeit briefly, a comprehensive modelling methodology developed from our own work. Embedded in this methodology is the core formulation component that we will concentrate on a little later.

The modelling methodology of concern is shown in Figure 4.1. We will first of all provide an overview of this iterative methodology.

Initially there is some organisational problem situation that focuses the attention of those involved in decision making, and leads to their purposeful activity. It is essential at the outset to carry out task formulation, which helps us to consider what might be an appropriate way forward. Within the logic and process of TSI this has already been catered for and so, now assuming SD is the most relevant approach, we need to set about identifying modelling purposes. These determine in unitary fashion the essential characteristics of the model to be formulated. A potentially worthwhile investigation at this stage is to undertake a critical review of extant models. In some cases particular difficulties may already have been rigorously addressed and the findings reported in journals or other forms of literature. For example, many difficulties in the health services have already been addressed through operations research techniques and simulation methods. By carrying out such a review, investigators may be able to incorporate a pragmatic element into their studies according to previous findings.

Although we have discussed using models as ways of working out predictions, this does not exclude the idea that model structure may itself represent proposed organisational design, and so a thorough assessment of "users" (i.e. those affected by the design) may be necessary so that "relevant" design is undertaken. This is not a matter of questioning the purposes, which is dealt with through the logic and process of TSI, but amounts to raising questions about practicability and usability. The design must help the people to achieve the set purposes.

The review of extant models and user analysis are important precursors to model formulation.

Model construction begins by drawing upon a model development submethodology (a part of the overall scheme of Figure 4.1). There are a number of key concerns that have to be reflected upon, importantly including the availability of data, significant theories in the area of concern, and any laws which may have been derived to explain particular phenomena. Also, with any modelling effort, a whole range of assumptions will be made. These must be declared in order to increase model transparency and hence falsifiability. The number, importance and controversy of these assumptions will be related to the quality and availability of data, theories and laws.

A validation submethodology needs to be introduced. Validation needs to be an explicit part of the whole modelling process, however, there is

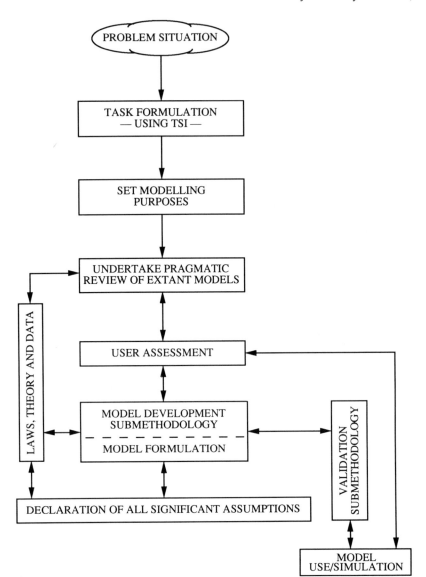

Figure 4.1 Modelling methodology that integrates into the logic and process of Total Systems Intervention

real value in detailing the main validatory concerns. These are empirical, theoretical and pragmatic validity.

Empirical validation proceeds by way of adaptive fitting, comparing model response to available data over a range of dynamic tests, involving structural changes and other model perturbations. This should involve quantitative and qualitative feature testing and sensitivity analysis, normally by simulation. Theoretical validation involves the comparison of any theories that are assumed in the model with those available in the scientific literature. The model does not necessarily have to conform to generally accepted theories, but comparison can prove to be insightful and thus valuable. Pragmatic validity amounts to continuous assessment about the value of any proposed design in terms of the people and the purposes to be met.

When some satisfactory correspondence has been attained between that which is being modelled, the model, and the modelling purposes, then the model can be used for prediction and control in policy analysis. Even at this stage, however, our interest in formulation and validation will continue.

We will now turn our attention to model formulation, and in this will take a closer look at what a SD model looks like. Our main concern will be with conceptualisation, formulation and simulation.

When conceptualising, SD style, we must recall that the main focus is on structure. The first issue that we need to deal with is deciding upon the "order of the system" to be developed, which is equivalent to the "age-old" systems concern of boundary setting. The general advice offered is that all elements that are likely to generate an influence in the problem situation must be included. So we now have a criterion for inclusion in and exclusion from the model. This internal closed view creates a drastically different "problem focus" from any other of the "problem-solving" approaches dealt with in this book. It leads to a unique conceptualisation process.

Conceptualisation proceeds by identification and description of that which should be within the boundary. An aid to this process is the "signed digraph" approach, which is a causal loop diagram that expresses the "direction of feedback" (a simple example is shown in Figure 4.2). A signed digraph is an expression of how elements influence and interact with other elements. This helps us to an understanding of "loop multiplicity" as explained later.

After the system structure has been clearly declared through a signed digraph representation, this is converted to a SD flow diagram prior to mathematisation. We achieve this by assuming the relationships are flows, termed "rates", that connect the main elements, which are termed "levels" of any SD model. We therefore have "levels" and "rates".

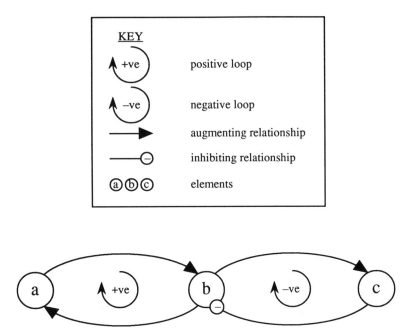

Figure 4.2 An example of a signed digraph showing both +ve (positive) and −ve (negative) loops

A level is a quantity that dynamically changes over time, and a rate is a flow which contributes to that change per unit of time. Imagine the dynamics of stock control, where the quantity of any single product in store changes over time according to manufacturing rate in and delivery rate out. A SD diagrammatic or symbolic representation of rate (like a valve) and level (like a vessel) is shown in Figure 4.3. The stock control idea is shown in Figure 4.4 where manufacturing adds to and delivery subtracts from the stock level. Now, if this business is properly controlled, then delivery rate (which could represent demand rate) would positively feed back to manufacturing rate, as indicated in Figure 4.5. Here we see

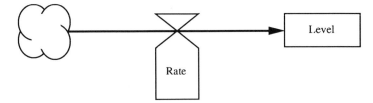

Figure 4.3 System dynamics diagrammatic representation of rates and levels

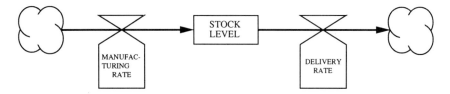

Figure 4.4 System dynamics diagrammatic representation of stock level, 1

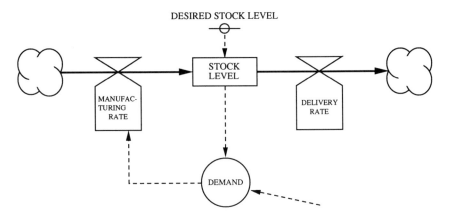

Figure 4.5 System dynamics diagrammatic representation of stock level, 2

the addition of an auxiliary (symbolised by a circle), a "source" or "sink" (symbolised by a cloud) and a constant (a small flying saucer). The whole diagram reads: there is a stock level which is increased by supply of manufacturing output and decreased by delivery to customers. If the level begins to decrease then this indicates an increase in demand and hence should lead to an increase in manufacturing rate. This allows the stock level to return to a desired level.

The logic of all this can be summarised as follows (see Figure 4.6). *R* is a rate, the amount of something that flows in a given time period (per unit time); *L* is a level, the accumulation of rates added to an initial condition; *A* is an auxiliary variable. Levels and rates are necessary to describe a situation. Auxiliaries are used to break down rate equations into manageable parts, to convert flows from one type to another and to provide information to change/control rates, which is particularly useful when we come to writing sets of equations from the SD diagram. Rules of this logic, captured in Figure 4.6, are as follows.

• A level in a loop can only be preceded by a rate.

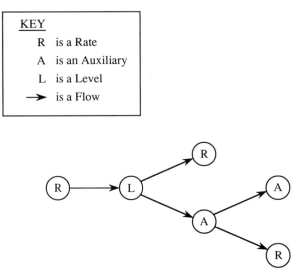

Figure 4.6 Logic of flows according to the rules of system dynamics modelling

- A level may be followed by an auxiliary or rate.
- An auxiliary may be followed by another auxiliary or by a rate.
- A rate must be followed by a level.
- A level may not directly affect another level.

Now all the symbols of SD diagrams have been introduced, and are consolidated in Figure 4.7, so we need only to show how this symbolic expression can be translated into a mathematical representation. By using a simple code (with DYNAMO) or use of symbols (with STELLA) we can then enter the model into SD software that does all the rest of the work on the user's command. We will pursue the example of stock level control.

Let us develop equations that are in exact notation form for entry into a DYNAMO (DYNAmic MOdelling) computer simulation program. DYNAMO is helpful, not only because it carries out simulation, but also because it presents results in either tabular or graphical form. This software has been developed further into the more versatile Professional DYNAMO.

We will assume that we have a stock level of 1000, say of a particular model of car, and that over a month we expect to sell 800 of them, and because of that we have planned to manufacture 800. This can be represented as

$$SL(1) = SL(0) + 800 - 800 = 1000 \tag{4.1}$$

The stock level at the end of the month $SL(1)$ is calculated from the stock

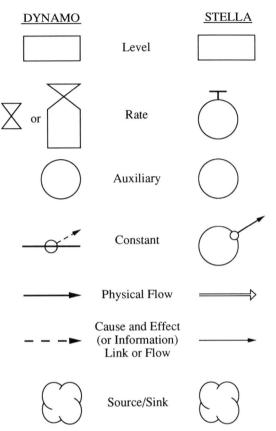

Figure 4.7 Symbols used in a system dynamics diagrammatic representation with either DYNAMO or STELLA for use with the Apple Macintosh

level at the start of the month $SL(0)$ (the initial condition), plus the manufacturing input and minus the delivery output. If we were concerned with weekly changes (let us assume this is one-quarter (1/4) of a month) then we could write the following equation and iterate 4 times

$$SL(1) = SL(0) + 1/4(800-800) \qquad (4.2)$$

Equations 4.1 and 4.2 show that we can in fact generalise

$$SL \text{ (current)} = SL \text{ (one time interval earlier)} \qquad (4.3)$$
$$+ \text{ (length of the time interval)}*(M-D)$$

where M is manufacturing or input rate and D is delivery or output rate.

This can be simplified by using a small amount of notation shown below.

- Level K is a level calculated at the present time.
- Level J is a level calculated one time interval earlier.
- DT (delta time) is the length of the time interval between J and K.

For our stock level equation we therefore have

$$SL.K = SL.J + DT(M.JK - D.JK) \qquad (4.4)$$

So the stock level at any time (say K) is equal to the level one time interval earlier (therefore J), plus the difference between manufacturing (M) input during that time interval (JK) and the delivery (D) output over that time interval (JK).

Rates enable progress to be made in steps determined by DT. At time K the state of the levels (at time period one) will determine the rate for the next time period, that is KL (at time period two). In the next time step, what was L (the future) is now K. Therefore, the timescript representing that rate changes from $.KL$ to $.JK$ (see Figure 4.8).

Both maufacturing and delivery rates are variable. Let us assume that we have control over the manufacturing rate but that demand is outside our control (we are attributing no importance to marketing and sales). According to our diagram in Figure 4.5, manufacturing rate is influenced by stock level, so if stock level falls below a desired level, manufacturing rate will rise. We will assume that an indicator on demand (DI) can be derived from stock level and desired stock level (DSL) which is a constant

$$DI.K = DSL - SL.K \qquad (4.5)$$

Manufacturing rate can therefore be expressed in the following way

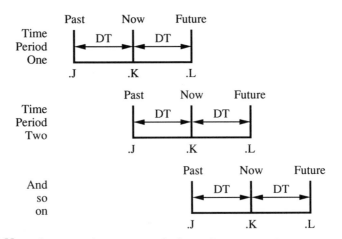

Figure 4.8 How time notations are worked out for system dynamics models

$$M.KL = DI.K/MC \qquad (4.6)$$

where MC is a manufacturing constant that recognises manufacturing cannot simply be switched on and off, experiencing in reality time delays ($M.KL \geq 0$). The set of equations that can be drawn up to represent Figure 4.5 is now summarised

MC	=	a constant relating to the manufacturing process	(4.7)
DSL	=	a constant determined by management	(4.8)
$D.KL$	=	a variable determined outside the model	(4.9)
$M.KL$	=	$DI.K/MC$	(4.10)
$DI.K$	=	$DSL - SL.K$	(4.11)
$SL.K$	=	$SL.J + DT(M.JK - D.JK)$	(4.12)

Of course, we could improve this model in many ways. For example, the demand indicator (DI) in Equation 4.11 (an auxiliary) could be some kind of weighted average over a year, to take into account seasonal variations and prevent oscillation.

In the set of coupled formulae, Equations 4.7–4.12, we have shown how constants, auxiliaries, rates and levels are represented. You may wish to check the logic of this against that contained in Figure 4.6.

Now that you have understood the ideas outlined above, you may be surprised to know that, in mathematical terms, you have learnt the basic theory of constructing and solving (by integration) first order ordinary difference equations. You will also be, as we are, pleased to know that solution of these equations need not be done by hand—a computer takes over this chore.

We have dealt with the combined matters of the SD model and methodology. Our next task is to consider how we might use the various models in planning and decision making.

4.5 USING THE MODELS

SD models may be used to redesign system structure and/or decision policies, which can then be implemented. According to Meadows, an influential writer in this area, there are three stages in a decision-making process to which SD must contribute. First, is to appreciate in a broad sense the situation of concern and to develop a non-precise understanding of the dynamics. Second, this broad understanding needs to be translated into ideas about how to improve problematic aspects (i.e. policy formation), which requires deeper investigation into the structure that underlies behaviour, although exact precision is not necessary. Third, is the need for detailed implementation where precision is vital. It is argued that the spectrum from qualitative signed digraphs through to "exact" quantitative mathematical models meets the needs of all of the three stages in decision making.

Our first interest might be a qualitative one, in the signed digraph conceptualisation that precedes mathematical model formulation. Analysis of the microstructure may offer some insight. The loops of the model can be identified and classified as either positive or negative. We can think about loop multiplicity, how the loops interact and which loops appear to be central. This better-than-intuitive analysis can be developed into a quite sophisticated loop analysis, but this is beyond the scope of the current study.

Loops can, however, be further understood by assessing the time scale (or length) associated with the operation of a loop. As a first step we might attach, say, S, M or L to each signed directed relationship (S for short, M for medium, L for long). The strength (or weighting) of the relationships (and consequently the loops) can also be analysed in a similar way, and hence the relative effect of two or more loops on a shared variable can be qualitatively assessed.

Time scale and strength analysis are useful in some circumstances such as developing broad understandings and initial policy formulation, but the main drive of a SD analysis is to develop quantitative models where possible, to help work out detailed plans for implementation of the initial policy formulations.

Once a good quality mathematical model has been formulated and entered into computer software, we will want to carry out a few preliminary simulation studies, looking for an appropriate value of DT and undertaking some steady-state analyses.

As can be seen from Equation 4.4, the value we adopt for DT will determine how many times that equation needs to be solved over each time interval simulated (i.e. $(K-J)/DT$ times). Being able to set DT so as to minimise the number of calculations, and hence substantially save on time taken to simulate, is clearly desirable. There is, however, an added complication. Without going into the technical theoretical details, we need to note that the smaller DT gets the more accurate the solution is (although this rule has its extreme limits). So we have to make a trade-off between speed of simulation and accuracy.

DT is determined by the shortest time constant used in the model (i.e. the value S assigned to our loops in the signed digraph). Once this is known, and to maintain some form of accuracy, a value of between 0.25 and 0.5 of the time constant is used. This prevents unrealistic oscillations (i.e. uncaptured variable changes).

Steady-state analysis is necessary for our initial confidence in the model and may inform us about stability in the model and therefore the "real world" situation. The idea is to set all variables at their steady-state value so that the model should run indefinitely at those values over time. Equation 4.1 shows how this can be achieved with the stock level equations. We begin to learn a lot more, however, when experimenting with the model through perturbations.

Model response to disturbances allows us to consider the effects of a range of policy options, either options concerning planning new ways forward or dealing with unexpected changes. We could consider new ways forward by (and depending on the type of model) increasing production, diversifying products, reducing/expanding the size of the workforce, increasing quality standards, introducing new marketing and sales strategies, introduction of automated machinery, changing pricing policy, etc. Alternatively, some examples of unexpected changes that can be simulated are effects of strikes, fall/rise in demand, resource scarcity, increasing competition, energy price rises, changes in corporation tax, etc. (although we must remember that we may find it difficult to simulate causes, having to be satisfied only with effects).

We can try and explain responses to disturbances by examining model structure through loop dominance and delays. For example, considering loop dominance, if there were only a single positive or negative loop we could remove this and see what effect that has on model response. There may be two loops of either direction, and we can remove one and then in a separate experiment the other, to see which loop is dominant or even just more influential, if either. We may find that at the outset one loop is dominant, but later on another loop shifts into a dominant position. A whole range of these heuristic experimentations can be carried out and much can be learnt about the multiplicity of loops.

Another angle on model use is to undertake delay analysis. Delays may be physical material (the time involved in processing physical materials) and time delays (delays resulting from the time involved in perceiving and acting upon information). The delays can easily be introduced into models and their effects observed.

In this section we have considered some of the main uses of SD models. We discovered that there are three stages in decision making that SD, in proper context, may help us with. This has prepared us for a single detailed study which expands the example of inventory control.

4.6 SD IN ACTION: A SIMPLE EXPANSION OF THE STOCK/INVENTORY MODEL

We have looked at the basic concept of a stock level (see Figure 4.5) but for us to get this simple model to work some changes need to be made (see Figure 4.9). Note that the following example has been annotated according to STELLA conventions.

Stock Level

In Figure 4.5 we put Demand as an influence on Manufacturing Rate and back to Stock Level, but in practice this is too simple and provides us, the managers, with little information from which to make any judgement. It is necessary to introduce an auxiliary equation that compares Desired Stock and the actual Stock Level, which we will call Change in Stock. This can then be used to control the Manufacturing Rate, acting positively on the Stock Level (i.e. it will tend to increase its level). In turn the Delivery Rate will be determined by the Stock Level which acts negatively on it (i.e. it will tend to reduce its level).

Sales

The Sales and Sales Rate are external influences (demand) on the Stock Level. The Sales Rate will, in some way, be determined by the Delivery

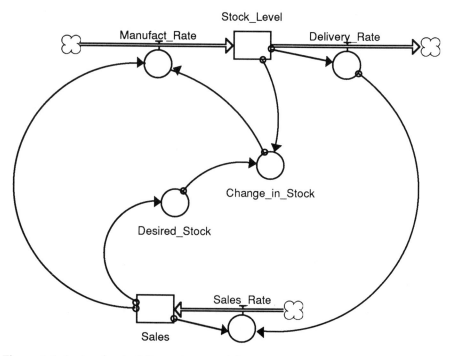

Figure 4.9 A simple stock/inventory model

Rate (stock cannot be sold if it is not available). Likewise, as Sales increase and the Delivery Rate remains the same, the Sales Rate will decrease. As Sales increase the Manufacturing Rate will also increase (with some delay), but this is influenced by the managers.

As mentioned previously, we will determine the quantity of Stock Level needed (Desired Stock) and compare this to Sales Level which determines what the Change in Stock is. This in turn will offer the greatest "leverage" (influence) on the Manufacturing Rate. This completes the loop which determines the level of stock.

The graph in Figure 4.10 is a typical output from a simple model like ours. The two variables Sales and Stock Level are almost reflective over time (i.e. as one variable increases the other decreases). The model includes a random number generator to simulate the influence of sales from a source outside the model. This enables us to see how the other model variables respond to these random demands (as might be found in the "real world"). In this case we can see that as sales increase stock decreases, but more importantly the processes of the model are under some form of control. If the sporadic changes are removed (or smoothed out) we would see that the norms for both variables are almost level.

This model remains far too simple to be of use in the real world. A considerable amount of further development is necessary. Furthermore, every organisation with an inventory control system will be different. Stock demand, manufacturing rate, delivery rate and desired stock are

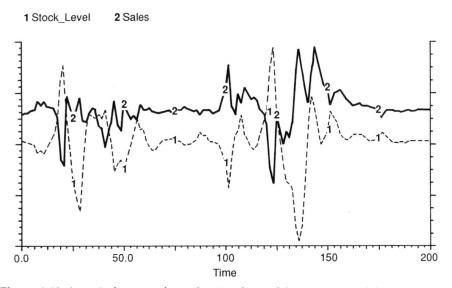

1 Stock_Level   **2** Sales

Time

Figure 4.10 A typical output from the simple stock/inventory model

either deemed to be objective and specific (manufacturing time as a response to demand) to an organisation, or subjective and judgemental according to the company's or manager's policies (the desired amount of stock to be held).

For the reader to appreciate the power of such an enquiry method, access to a computer will be needed at some stage (for most situations either the use of a Personal Computer to run equation DYNAMO or an Apple Macintosh to run the icon based STELLA—which has been used in this example). We have briefly explained how a simple computer simulation model can be constructed to enable managers to "play around" with the variables which can be directly influenced.

4.7 CRITIQUE OF SD

There are plenty of criticisms of system dynamics which have appeared in the literature since Forrester's first efforts at formulating the approach in the late 1950s and early 1960s. Our task is to try and make sense of these at the four levels of theory, methodology, ideology and utility, as outlined in the conclusion to Chapter 3. This framework, for critiquing methodologies, which we shall use in each of our chapters on specific systems approaches, should help the reader to get inside the critical discussion and draw out the main points of the argument.

Before embarking on the critique of system dynamics using this framework, however, two preliminary points should be made. First, system dynamics has not stood still since its initial conception and, in particular, there have been a number of attempts to increase its capability in dealing with more qualitative issues and less structured problem contexts. While acknowledging the progress made in this respect, our attitude to these attempts is that they have not fundamentally changed the nature of the approach. System dynamics models still centre on capturing the structure of the "real world" and rest upon some taken-for-granted purpose. Recent developments have led to real confusion about the precise nature of SD but they have left it firmly rooted in simple–unitary thought.

The second point we need to make is that SD has been attacked by critics of very different persuasions. Its attempts to loosen some of the characteristics of the scientific method in order to tackle problems of greater complexity, have left it open to the charge, from advocates of other "hard" systems approaches, of having abandoned scientific rigour. On the other hand, its failure to fully embrace "subjectivity" as a necessary part of any analysis of social systems has convinced soft systems thinkers that it remains inapproriate to deal with difficulties encountered in complex–pluralist situations. The reader will need to disentangle which of the following criticisms come from which viewpoint—a not too difficult task for which guidance will, in any case, be given.

Theory

SD has been criticised theoretically for abandoning the scientific method (point (a)), but most of the criticisms of the theory underlying the approach stem from the soft systems position (points (b) to (d)).

(a) SD diverges from the normal scientific method and is criticised by advocates of other hard systems approaches for having done so. The scientific method (as usually described) proceeds by reduction to observe and measure relevant phenomena and the relationships between them, then to formulate laws and rules, and finally by aggregation of the laws to explain overall systems behaviour. SD attempts, through its general theory of systems behaviour, to grasp the whole, even when this is difficult to model. Putting in place the feedback loops which constitute system structure and explain system behaviour is held to be more important than exact representation achieved through precise reductionist methods. Obviously this leaves SD open to charges that it lacks scientific rigour and is imprecise. It apparently jumps to conclusions about whole system behaviour before the data have been collected and the laws verified which would make such conclusions justifiable. Of course, from the SD point of view, adhering strictly to the scientific method would exclude it from addressing most of the problem types for which it was originally intended. It was in order to tackle more complex problems, on which sufficient data were difficult to obtain and about which laws were difficult to formulate, that it deviated from the scientific method in the first place.

(b) Soft systems thinkers question the underlying assumption of SD that there is an external world made up of systems the structure of which can be grasped using models built upon feedback processes. To soft systems thinkers social systems are much more complex than this. They are the creative construction of human beings whose intentions, motivations and actions play a significant part in shaping "system" behaviour. Because intentions derive from inside social systems, from the conscious human actors which constitute them, many possible appreciations of the nature and purpose of particular social systems are possible. SD simply does not deal with the innate subjectivity of human beings and the consequences of this for the study of social systems. In essence the argument is that social systems cannot be studied, in the way of system dynamics, objectively from the outside. Rather it is necessary to come to terms with human consciousness and to study the world views and actions of the individuals that continually construct and reconstruct them.

(c) It follows that the attempt of SD thinkers to model external reality is misguided. Social systems are not only too complex for this but the subjective intentions of human beings cannot be captured in such "objective" models. In particular the emphasis placed upon *structure* as the means of revealing knowledge about the optimal behaviour of systems cannot be accepted. Social systems are seen, by soft systems thinkers, to be constituted through *processes* in which different values and conceptions of reality are negotiated and renegotiated. Rather than attempting the impossible task of modelling this overall process, soft systems thinkers are content to build models which contribute to a debate about different appreciations of the situation—models which explicate the implications of particular world views. Soft systems thinkers argue that models should be designed to increase mutual understanding not seek to represent external reality.

(d) Since it is held that social reality is too complex to model, soft systems thinkers argue that SD models must be distorted, one-sided reflections of reality. They are models from one, often unstated, point of view. In each model there is embedded a taken-for-granted purpose which can often be associated with the transformation that is being undertaken but ultimately relates back to the particular prejudices of the modellers. SD provides no means of questioning the purpose underlying any model, for example, by comparing it to another model constructed on the basis of an alternative world view. The criteria for deciding upon what is the optimal behaviour of a system are similarly bound up with one model and one world view and so are hidden from examination and go unquestioned.

Methodology

(a) The hard systems critique of SD methodology is again aimed at the modelling process. From the point of view of the scientific method models should only be built when sufficient information is known about an area of concern to provide verification of the relationships embedded in the model. In its concern to be of practical use SD is not content to wait upon all the necessary data becoming available. It seeks to build its systems models based upon judgements about interdependencies even when data are uncertain or missing. For Forrester getting the structure of the model right is more important than collecting endless reams of data. Unfortunately this sometimes seems to lead SD analysts to ignore extant theories in particular areas of enquiry.

(b) Soft systems thinkers similarly derive their critique of SD methodology from what they see as the theoretical shortcomings of the approach. They argue that the methodology, or method, of SD is impoverished not because it does not adhere slavishly to the scientific method, but because it is unsuitable to the subject matter of concern. Social systems are held not to be amenable to quantitative investigation. SD attempts to use mathematics in a loose fashion on variables (rates) and states (levels) that are often far from being clearly identifiable. The richness of social reality defeats SD modellers. The way forward would be to work with an array of models each reflecting a particular world view.

Ideology

(a) Rather worrying from the ideological point of view is the manner in which SD analysts act somewhat like élite technicians. They see themselves serving decision makers, and managers, as experts providing objective and neutral guidance. There is no involvement of other "stakeholders"—SD analysts being limited to offering solutions before disappearing while the decision makers carry out implementation. Obviously, therefore, the purposes served by SD go unquestioned. Ignoring other stakeholders in this way may seem to be ideologically biased and ethically unsound. From the soft systems perspective it is also likely to detract from the attainment of "whole system improvement". Particular stakeholders pursue their own narrow interests which may be shortsighted and damage the system in the long term.

(b) SD modellers using feedforward control appear to believe that there are optimal future states that we should steer systems towards. However, these states are not made explicit. This is particularly worrying in the case of social systems which will contain different groups espousing alternative aims and intentions. SD modellers are likely implicitly to privilege the aims of some groups over others.

Utility

(a) Hard systems thinkers believe that SD models are sometimes based upon poor data, sometimes ignore extant theories and often do not undergo a rigorous enough validation regime. It follows that they cannot give very accurate predictions of future states and so are of limited usefulness to decision makers.

(b) Soft systems thinkers could forgive SD its lack of precision in areas where precision is difficult to obtain—scientific exactitude must sometimes be sacrificed for ready practical usefulness. What they cannot forgive is its attempt to present itself as an objective and neutral approach in the domain of social systems where "objectivity" (at least in the usual sense of that word) and "neutrality" are simply impossible to obtain. Only in very specific circumstances will SD be useful to tackle problem situations in socio-technical systems. First, SD is only recommended for use when particular tasks have been decided upon which require and lend themselves to a rigorous study of structure as a particular means of assessing options on policy and organisation design, that is, where there are identifiable physical flows and information links, and also where elements not considered in the model are unlikely to exert an influence in the foreseeable future—so the closed system models of SD are adequate. Essentially, these problem situations must not be too complex. Secondly, it is important that all assumptions upon which an SD model rests are surfaced and discussed. What is proper and suitably rigorous, as suggested by our modelling methodology, is that SD modellers express and highlight quality of data and what themes and/or laws have been drawn upon, and offer these in a declaration of assumptions which can be debated.

(c) A final point of soft systems criticism against SD concerns the relationship SD presupposes as existing between analysts and decision makers. The SD approach sees these functions as separate, the analyst simply presenting expert recommendations to the decision maker. According to soft systems thinkers this is not the way to get recommendations accepted and implemented. The analyst needs to be much more closely involved with the decision maker. Working together on a problem so that the decision maker comes to own the study and its results is recommended. Soft systems thinkers emphasise the need for mutual interaction between client and analyst throughout a study.

What we have found in this critical review of SD is that many points of critique arise from the approach being used in problem contexts where it does not have competence. When SD is used within the logic and framework of TSI these concerns are seen, of course, to dissolve. For example, at the outset of a TSI study all relevant stakeholders would be brought into the intervention process, alternative world views would be considered, and only after creative and careful reasoning would SD be recommended; on occasions some way into the intervention process. In appropriate cases, therefore, SD can be drawn upon and found to contribute in a most useful way. As with all approaches, we need to deal critically with the legitimacies and limitations, not make "isolationist" claims. SD can and does help with particular aspects of our technical interest in prediction of trends and testing out control policies.

4.8 CASE STUDY: A PROJECT MANAGER'S DILEMMA

4.8.1 Introduction

A project manager's main planning system is based upon a logic simulation of the work to be carried out. This helps the people who carry out the work but does not necessarily consider the needs of those who control it. Such a logic-based model does not consider all the environmental influences that affect satisfactory completion.

4.8.2 Your Task

Consider the situation where you are a project manager and there are a number of core elements which affect the performance of your team. As a project manager you have direct control over some of them.
Consider the following elements:

- Workforce size made up of:
  - skilled team size   (Both these types of labour resources have to
  - unskilled team size   work together and have equal amounts of work
                          do to. They may need to be increased or
                          decreased as progress is made through the
                          project.)
- People leaving the project and needing to be replaced.
- Amount of work to complete (measured in man-hours per week).
- Productivity.
- The amount of progress being made.
- The amount of work remaining.
- The amount of work that has to be redone due to faults.

Figure 4.11 captures the main dynamic features of the situation.
Expand Figure 4.11 with elements not initially considered so that the model of this project portrays the real situation in more detail (you may need to break up some of the elements into smaller ones).
Identify the elements that you as a project manager have direct control over. You will also need to take into account such influences as time

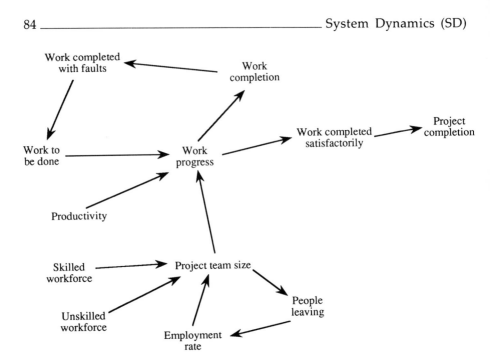

Figure 4.11 The main dynamic features of a project

delays and the influence of introducing new labour resources (remember that they may not be as productive initially as those already working on the project).

You, as a project manager (i.e. the controller) have a dilemma. After expanding the model to represent the situation, you realise that adjustments can be made to many elements. SD modelling enables a policy maker to identify the elements of greatest leverage—the ones having the greatest influence on the model's behaviour. The advantage of being able to model on a computer is that the time taken in this identification process is reduced. This process is carried out by adjusting one, some, or all of them at the same time. However, the more you adjust prior to a simulation the less chance there is of being able to identify the significant ones. These changes should be the result of careful consideration and you as a manager only need to adjust the element(s) which have the greatest influence to provide the desired change. Be careful, however. Remember, for example, that a proportional increase in the workforce size does not always produce the same proportional increase in work completion. A decrease in the overall productivity may be the result of the old workforce having to spend time showing the new members of the team what to do. Likewise, the number of faults produced could increase as a result of having new people—these faults may have to be rectified with help from experienced members of the team.

Therefore, you need to consider each element in turn and follow the influences it exerts directly and indirectly on the goal to be achieved— satisfactory completion of the project. The way to carry this out, without the aid of a computer, is to deal with each element in turn and those that it directly influences. Consider for example time delays and multiplying factors, do they have a positive or negative influence on the succeeding element(s)? The many loops in your model then have to be analysed—how do they affect each other and finally exert pressure on the achievement of the goal (in this case the completion of the project)? Once you are sure how the model works, there will probably be a need to add other elements initially left out. Finally, you should end up with a model that reflects the project situation. The model can now be used to try out various managerial policies—you can trace how an increase or decrease in an element will finally affect the completion of the project. The aim of this model is to provide you with an understandable representation with which to try out policy scenarios, and which is quicker and less costly than implementing them directly and being unsure of the consequences.

4.9 FURTHER READING

• To understand the nature of system dynamics and its methodology:

Forrester, J. W. (1961). *Industrial Dynamics*, MIT Press, Cambridge, Mass.
Forrester, J. W. (1969). *Principles of Systems*, Wright-Allen Press, Cambridge, Mass.
Meadows, D. M. (1980). The unavoidable a priori, in *Elements of the System Dynamics Method* (ed. J. Randers), pp. 23–57, MIT Press, Cambridge, Mass.
Roberts, N., Anderson, D., Deal, R., Garet, M. and Shaffer, W. (1983). *An Introduction to Computer Simulation: A System Dynamics Approach*, Addison-Wesley, Reading, Mass.

• A good range of examples of system dynamics in use is provided by:

Roberts, E. B. (ed.) (1964). *Managerial Applications of System Dynamics*, MIT Press, Cambridge, Mass.

• More recent interpretations of system dynamics can be found in:

Coyle, R. G. (1977). *Management System Dynamics*, Wiley, Chichester.
Wolstenholme, E. F. (1990). *System Enquiry: A System Dynamics Approach*, Wiley, Chichester.

• For the criticisms of system dynamics:

Keys, P. (1990). System dynamics as a systems-based problem-solving methodology, *Systems Practice*, **3**, 479–93.

- For our modelling methodology:

Flood, R. L. and Carson, E. R. (1991). *Dealing with Complexity: An Introduction to the Theory and Application of Systems Science*, 2nd edition, Plenum, New York.

Chapter 5

Viable System Diagnosis (VSD)

There are two things wrong with the role of science in our society. One is its use as a tool of power, wherever that is concentrated by economic forces. The other is its elite image. None of us wishes to be manipulated by power; and if science is the tool of power, to hell with it. None of us wishes to entrust our liberty to a man in a white laboratory coat, armed with a computer and a row of ball-point pens in his pocket, if he does not share in our humanity.

We cannot feed the starving, we cannot stop war; we are in a terrible muddle with education, transportation, the care of the sick and old; institutions are failing, and we often feel unsafe in the streets of our own cities. All this is inefficient. Then it cannot be correct to say that the way to preserve liberty is to be so damned inefficient that freedom is not even threatened. We have to become efficient in order to solve our problems; and we have to accept the threat to freedom that this entails—and handle it.

Stafford Beer, *Designing Freedom*, Canadian Broadcasting Company.
Two extracts from the 6th lecture given in 1973 called "The free man in a cybernetic world".

5.1 INTRODUCTION

The viable system model (VSM) of Stafford Beer is a thorough working out of ideas from the science of organisation, or cybernetics. There are some similarities with a system dynamics approach in that both employ techniques of systems modelling, and both types of modelling can be realised as complex networks of interrelated mathematical formulae. From our point of view, however, we shall only deal with the qualitative aspects of the VSM for social contexts, and how these portray a powerful image of a well organised business, firm or whatever.

A main difference from the kind of model usually built in system dynamics, is that the VSM focuses on organisation rather than structure, and assumes that this has an evolutionary nature. As any engineer will know, this is not meant to imply that quantitative simulation models like those of system dynamics cannot be built to represent an evolutionary process; this can be achieved by introducing time-varying parameters such that the structure of the model is itself changeable. This is all right for some purposes, and in fact we have been involved in the construction of such models. But the fact remains that these are phenomenally complicated and inaccessible articulations of certain aspects of reality, and are of no value whatsoever to the everyday manager, planner, decision maker or consultant. What is more, the techniques are capable of dealing very well with machines and even organisms, but do not model well the behaviour of less predictable "systems" containing human beings. Given the need for engineering design of machines, pass on the job to any expert engineering designer. The manager, however, can well benefit from a qualitative realisation of cybernetic conceptions that has been put together to help us deal with social organizations.

The VSM can be used for diagnosing "problems" of organisation, hence the term viable system diagnosis (VSD), particularly those arising in complex probabilistic "systems" that comprise purposeful organised parts and are open to a changing environment (what we call complex) and yet in which there is general or easily attainable agreement about the goals or objectives to be pursued (the nature of the relationship between participants has to be unitary). This is the case because the model itself assumes all these features. In terms of the argument in Chapter 2, we are saying that the underlying assumptions are complex–unitary. Of course, it would be an unwise person who boldly announced the "discovery" of a complex–unitary situation without some creative pre-investigation, and that is one of several places where the logic and process of TSI comes into play.

So, the utility of the cybernetic approach comes to the fore when, for example, issues in a business or a firm are characterised by particular defects or pathologies, possibly localised, that are resistant to or ignored by normal treatment. In such circumstances, the viable system view assumes that natural cybernetic laws are being violated—hence the need for diagnosis and the use of cybernetic findings in reorganisation.

Let us now develop these ideas further in terms of the philosophy, principles, model, and methodology for employment of the model in diagnosis.

5.2 PHILOSOPHY OF VSD

The philosophy that drives Beer's view of cybernetics concerns the kind of changes we are experiencing in the twentieth century. He thinks that new ways are needed to deal with difficulties associated with these changes. The main points are summarised below.

- Organisational and social "problems" arise because of new degrees of complexity (organisational, technological, informational and so on) and are characterised by interdependency.
- Scientifically based management taking advantage of technological advances (e.g. increased information processing capability) is vital because more traditional approaches are quite simply too trivial, and in isolation are not well worked out. Therefore, a scientific model that is based on cybernetic principles and which encompasses many ideas from management science is fundamental in our efforts to deal with modern complexities.
- Since control is the main concern, then the best approach is to replicate a well tried and tested "control system", this being evident in the neurocybernetic processes of the human brain and nervous system as it has evolved over millenia (the same control model can, however, be derived from cybernetic first principles and is applicable to all systems).
- Organisations ideally are ordered so as to achieve efficient and effective realisation of set goals, although the goals themselves have to be continually reconsidered in response to a rapidly changing environment through self-questioning, learning and by assessing future scenarios.

5.3 PRINCIPLES OF VSD

The principles that underpin this approach are all cybernetic in nature since, as highlighted in the introduction to this section, when organisations do not perform well it is assumed that cybernetic principles are being violated. Some of these principles are outlined below.

- Recommendations endorsed by the VSM do not prescribe a specific structure, rather they are concerned with the essentials of organisation and maintenance of identity. They are, therefore, relevant to all types of enterprise, whether small, medium or large, in all types of industry.
- The notion of "recursion" is fundamental so that vertical interdependence can be dealt with. Recursion means that the whole system is replicated in the parts so that the same viable system principles may

be used to model a sub-system (a division) in an organisation, that organisation and its supra-system (that of which the system is a part, or a division of).

- In any viable unit, horizontally interdependent sub-systems (divisions) are integrated and guided by the viable units' "meta-system", or "higher" management levels.
- Sources of command and control are of particular concern and in the VSM these sources are spread throughout the architecture of the "viable system", which enhances self-organisation and localised management of "problems".
- Emphasis is placed on the relationship between the viable unit and its environment in terms of influencing and being influenced by it and particularly on using this relationship to promote learning.
- There are many other cybernetic principles that make up the viable system view, from rather simple notions of feedback to important principles such as the Law of Requisite Variety, that is, the variety of the controller must be equal to or greater than that which is being controlled.

A diagnosis of the potential viability of a proposed system, or of the causes of problems arising in an actual organisation, using these cybernetic principles as captured in the VSM, is the central part of any VSM study. For this reason, we shall now concentrate on the model itself.

5.4 THE VIABLE SYSTEM MODEL

The VSM is an arrangement of five functional elements (Systems 1–5) that are interconnected through a complex of information and control loops (see Figure 5.1). Emphasis on recursion allows us to use this same basic model to represent, for example, a company and its divisions together with the wider organisations of which it may also be a functional part. We can study the five functional elements in turn:

System 1

- System 1 parts are directly concerned with implementation.
- Each part is autonomous in its own right.
- Each part must, therefore, exhibit all the features of a viable system itself, including the five functions (although in the shorthand of Figure 5.1 only Systems 1 and 2 of the parts are shown separately—Systems 3, 4 and 5 all rest in the square management boxes).
- Each part connects to its local environment and so absorbs much of the overall environmental variety.

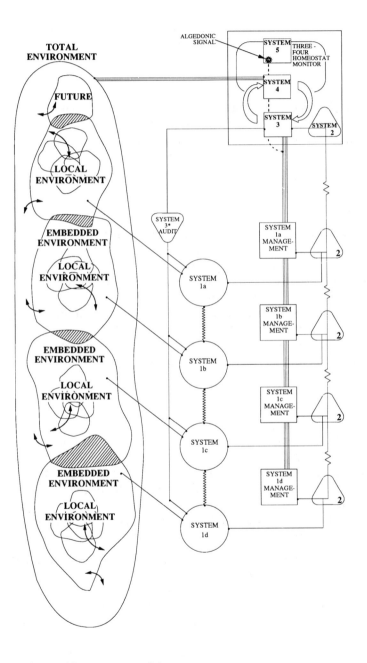

Figure 5.1 The viable system model

System 2

- Co-ordinates the parts that make up System 1 in a harmonious manner.
- Dampens uncontrolled oscillations between the parts.

System 3

- A control function that ultimately maintains internal stability.
- Interprets policy decisions of higher management.
- Allocates resources to the parts of System 1.
- Ensures effective implementation of policy.
- Carries out "audits" using the System 3* auditing channel.

System 4

- An intelligence gathering/reporting function that captures all relevant information about a system's total environment.
- Provides a model of the organisation's environment.
- Distributes environmental information upwards or downwards according to its degree of importance.
- Brings together internal and external information in an "operations room"—an environment for decision.
- Rapidly transmits urgent information from Systems 1, 2 and 3 to System 5 (alerting System 5 through the "algedonic" signal).

System 5

- Is responsible for policy.
- Responds to significant signals that pass through the various "filters" of Systems 1, 2, 3 and 4.
- Arbitrates between the sometimes antagonistic internal and external demands on the organisation as represented respectively by Systems 3 and 4.
- Represents the essential qualities of the "whole system" to any "wider system" of which it is a part.

Also important to the model are appropriate information flows and communication links. The information flowing around the various communication channels in the model is information about how the different parts of the organisation, and the organisation as a whole, are performing in relation to their respective goals. Achievement in most organisations is measured in terms of money; the criteria of success being the extent to which profits are maximised and costs minimised. This is not regarded as satisfactory by Beer. Such measurement ignores how well the organisation is doing in terms of preparing for the future, by investing in research and development for example, or in terms of more abstract resources like employee morale. Instead, Beer advises adopting three levels of achievement: actuality, capability and potentiality. Actuality refers to the current achievement with existing resources and constraints; capability is the possible achievement using existing resources within existing constraints; and potentiality is what could be achieved by developing resources and removing constraints. These levels can be combined to give three indices (productivity, latency and performance— see Figure 5.2) which can be used as comprehensive measures of performance in relation to all types of resource throughout the organisation.

Software is available which calculates the indices, registers what is of significance to managers and predicts whether trends are developing which require managerial attention. In this way the essential need for information to be delivered in real time can be satisfied.

5.5 USING THE VIABLE SYSTEM MODEL

5.5.1 Introduction

The procedure for using the model to diagnose the faults of a proposed system design or an actual organisation is quite complicated. It can, however, be roughly divided into two activities:

• System identification (according to the "organisation" of the VSM);

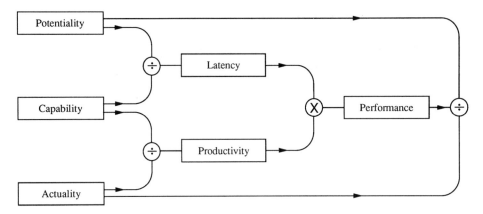

Figure 5.2 Indices of performance

- System diagnosis (reflecting on the cybernetic principles that should be obeyed according to the VSM).

Various tasks have to be undertaken in each part as described below.

5.5.2 System Identification

- As with any "unitary" methodology it is necessary initially to identify or determine the purpose(s) to be pursued.
- Taking the purpose as given, determine the relevant system for achieving the purpose. This is called the "system in focus". Remember that the purpose of a system is what it does and what the viable system does is done by System 1 (so it is System 1 that produces the "system in focus").
- Specify the viable parts of the System 1 of the system in focus.
- Specify the viable system of which the system in focus is part (wider systems, environment, etc.).

5.5.3 System Diagnosis

In general, draw upon cybernetic principles to carry out the following.

- Study the System 1 of the system in focus:
  - for each part of System 1 detail its environment, operations and localised management;
  - study what constraints are imposed upon each part of System 1 by higher management;
  - ask how accountability is exercised for each part, and what indicators of performance are taken;
  - model System 1 according to the VSM diagram.
- Study the System 2 of the system in focus:
  - list possible sources of oscillation or conflict between the various parts of System 1 and their environments and identify the elements of the system (the various System 2 elements) that have a harmonising or damping effect;
  - ask how System 2 is perceived in the organisation (as threatening or as facilitating).
- Study the System 3 of the system in focus:
  - list the System 3 components of the system in focus;
  - ask how System 3 exercises authority;
  - ask how resource bargaining with the parts of System 1 is carried out;
  - determine who is responsible for the performance of the parts of System 1;

- clarify what "audit" enquiries into aspects of System 1, System 3 conducts;
- understand the relationship between System 3 and the System 1 elements (is it perceived to be autocratic or democratic?) and find out how much freedom System 1 elements possess.
• Study the System 4 of the system in focus:
  - list all the System 4 activities of the system in focus;
  - ask how far ahead these activities consider;
  - question whether these activities guarantee adaptation to the future;
  - determine if System 4 is monitoring what is happening to the environment and assessing trends;
  - assess in what ways, if any, System 4 is open to novelty;
  - find out whether System 4 provides a management centre/operations room, bringing together external and internal information and providing an "environment for decision";
  - question if System 4 has facilities for alerting System 5 to urgent developments.
• Study the System 5 of the system in focus:
  - ask who is on "the Board" and how it acts;
  - assess whether System 5 provides a suitable identity for the system in focus;
  - ask how the "ethos" set by System 5 affects the "perception" of System 4;
  - determine how the "ethos" set by System 5 affects the System 3–System 4 homeostat (is System 3 or System 4 taken more seriously?);
  - investigate whether System 5 shares an identity with System 1 or claims to be something different.
• Check that all information channels, transducers and control loops are properly designed.

Diagnosis often leads to the discovery of violations of cybernetic principles. Some of the common faults found in organisations are presented below.

5.5.4 Frequent Faults

The following are some of the most common faults found in organisations as revealed by cybernetics.

• Mistakes are made in articulating different levels of recursion.
• The importance of certain parts of System 1 is not recognised, so they are not treated as viable systems and lack a localised management to tend to their affairs.

- The existence of additional irrelevant features of structure which hamper viability is found.
- System 2, 3, 4 or 5 of an organisation becomes "autopoietic" and seeks viability in its own right. In a viable system, Systems 2, 3, 4 and 5 should serve the whole system by promoting the implementation function and should not be allowed to function at the expense of the system as a whole—they should not become bureaucratic.
- System 2 is not fully established because local managers of System 1 resent interference from this relatively junior control echelon.
- System 4 is weak because it is regarded as a "staff" function and its recommendations are ignored—according to Beer, it should be part of "line" management.
- System 5 collapses into System 3 because System 4 is weak.
- System 3 managers are found interfering in the management process at System 1 level.
- System 5 is not creating an identity and is not representing the essential qualities of the whole system to the wider system of which it is part.
- The communication channels in the organisation and between the organisation and the environment do not correspond to the information flows said to be necessary in any viable system.
- Transmission of the indices of performance is not rapid enough.

Having considered the model, the model in use, and some common faults that may be uncovered through diagnosis, we are now in a position to look in detail at an application of the viable system ideas.

5.6 VSD IN ACTION: THE EXAMPLE OF A MAJOR TOURISM SERVICES GROUP

5.6.1 Background

Initially we shall consider the general background of the situation, some of the specific issues that needed to be addressed, and the rationale behind the choice of a viable system approach.

Tourism in the country Zania, where this example is set, is the single largest foreign exchange earner. Such earnings are vital for the growth of the economy of this developing country and for stability. Political stability is reciprocally a key guarantor of continuity and growth in the tourism industry. Instability leads to market collapse which can be devastating to tourism companies that inevitably have large overheads such as fixed assets and staff costs. A period of stability in Zania has led to recent rapid growth of the tourism industry.

Another important issue bearing on the tourism industry in Zania is that the standard of education of the majority of citizens is rather basic. This has an impact on the capabilities of those working at the lower levels in organizations. An almost inevitable result is that management styles in Zania tend to be autocratic. A challenge, we perceived, was to seek to introduce a more liberated democratic style for lower staff levels.

To complicate these business issues even further, Zanian society has to deal with significant amounts of corruption. This runs through all echelons of society.

The object of our concern in Zania was the Fleet Division of Safari International Zania (Manjaro Fleet). The Manjaro Fleet had under its control all safari vehicles based in the City of Manjaro and those based at the two safari lodges, in the Mungo and Prospect game reserves. The total number of vehicles in use through each season was between 90 and 120, some behing hired in during the peak season. The company employed 75 permanent and between 20 and 50 reserve drivers according to season. Company policy requires drivers to have detailed knowledge of the country, its history and people, game reserves, and animals and birds. In addition to the drivers, 50 staff are employed in the various operational, quality control and financial functions of Fleet. These functions are now considered in turn.

Operations was responsible for planning the utilization of all vehicles each day, allocating each booking to a vehicle and its driver, issuing instructions to the driver, completing paperwork for dispatch of the vehicle, liaison with staff from the touring company responsible for the booking, and the workshop staff with regard to servicing requirements and quality control of vehicle preparation. Within this function, work was done mainly on an *ad hoc* basis with no official individual responsibilities or authority among the staff. Those control mechanisms which were in force to ensure that vehicle use was effectively planned were little understood and used. Particular problems arose during the peak season when it was necessary to hire additional vehicles from other companies. Clients must have vehicles, yet outgoings need to be minimised. In the previous high season a substantial loss had to be borne as a result of excessive contracts with vehicle suppliers. In general, productivity, morale and loyalty were low in this vital group of employees and accusations of corruption were rife.

Quality control amounted to vehicle cleaning and servicing for which there were defined standards but no defined checking procedures. Delivery of quality rested mainly with the drivers. The permanent drivers were experienced and generally good, although no training had been given for 12 months and there were no plans for future staff development. Employment of reserve drivers was left to Operations staff, but with no supervision. As a result, temporary staff were of a poor standard, which led to an increase in dissatisfaction both from clients and from other company staff. Both categories of driver felt generally unhappy, neglected, even victimized. Management reacted with autocratic policies.

Accounts in Fleet Division comprised a comprehensive set of financial and administrative control systems which potentially enable detailed monitoring of every vehicle and driver used. Despite this, delays in transmitting information and limited use of the information, by staff and senior management alike, meant that these systems were of little day-to-day value. These difficulties had accentuated losses on hired vehicles in the previous year.

The difficulties highlighted above threatened organizational collapse. The recent high level of activity of the company had provoked a number of failures which were dealt with on a crisis management basis. Dealing with the next high season seemed to present insurmountable problems.

In discussion with participants the pressing and primary need was seen to be to install an organization that could provide necessary services and survive, and would be equitable. This organization would consist of many elements in close interrelationship ideally forming purposeful parts, exhibiting difficult to predict behaviour, and with significant environmental transactions. It would have to be capable of learning. The neurocybernetic metaphor obviously appealed to the analysts of this situation. This was confirmed by the unitary nature of the context. Both senior management and lower level employees seemed agreed on the basic need. Therefore, it seemed appropriate to draw upon a means of diagnosis and reorganisation which assumed that organizational reality is as the neurocybernetic metaphor suggests. Beer's viable system approach seemed ideal. The process of acceptance of this approach did not occur at an obvious temporal point, rather it became a part of the process of intervention—it followed a TSI logic.

5.6.2 Diagnosis and Redesign

We will start with what Beer calls the triple recursive-level in which our system-in-focus, Fleet Division, is embedded at recursion level 1. Recursion level 0 (the next higher level of recursion) is then Safari International Zania, which handles the majority of Safari Adventures Unlimited Zania's safari clients (Safari Adventures being at the next level of recursion up again). As Figure 5.3 shows there are five System 1 divisions at recursion level 0: Fleet Division, Workshops, Safaritrails, Incentives and Group Tours.

As we know the focus of this case study is Fleet Division. The purpose of this system-in-focus through which reorganisation becomes meaningful and which allows it to maintain an identity at recursion level 0 is:

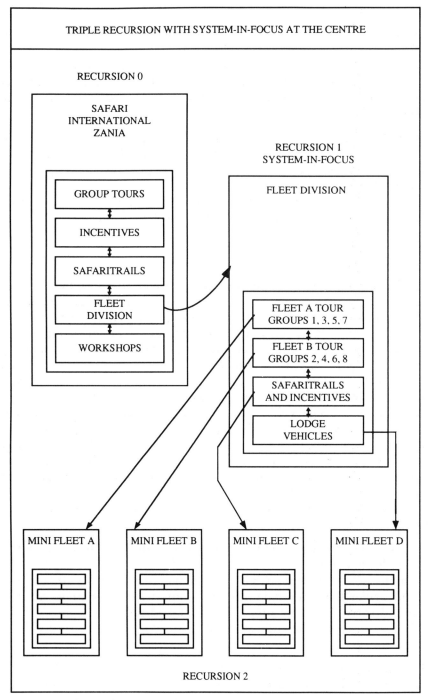

Figure 5.3 Triple recursion for the tourism example

- To develop and maintain an adequate fleet of company owned vehicles that will carry paying clients in Zania at the highest possible standard, with high calibre and presentable drivers to guide them throughout their trip. Also, to ensure that each vehicle is optimally utilized given constraints and uncertainty, thus realising preferable return on investment.

Fleet Division is thus a viable, autonomous, profit centre made up of fleet vehicles. Each System, 1–5, within Fleet will be discussed in turn below as we describe the application of viable system diagnosis to recursion level 1.

Recursion level 2 of the triple recursion is, of course, made up of the still-to-be-defined viable units that comprise Fleet Division.

System 1

The first major task that was undertaken involved dividing the fleet into a set of divisions of System 1, so as to create a number of viable units for the company. Four divisions were set up; the whole fleet becoming four mini-fleets. This System 1 reorganization is shown in Figures 5.3 and 5.4. Three of the mini-fleets were organised to deal with bookings from Group Tours, Incentives and Safaritrails, while the fourth comprised vehicles at two safari lodges. System 1(a) handled about half of Group Tours business, mostly consisting of small vehicle allocations, and had a complement of 30+ vehicles. System 1(b) handled the remainder of Group Tours business, Kuoni being a high volume client, and had 28+ vehicles at its disposal. System 1(c) dealt with business from Safaritrails and Incentives. System 1(d) dealt with business from the Prospect and Mungo Lodges. In all, 13 vehicles were stationed at these premier safari lodges.

The agreed purpose of each division of System 1 was defined as follows:

(1) To ensure that each vehicle booking is handled efficiently and all details confirmed.
(2) To ensure, as far as possible, that clients are provided with a vehicle and driver that they have selected—otherwise alternatives must be found through the set procedures (detailed below).
(3) To ensure optimum utilisation of vehicles within their "divisional control".

To help provide an incentive to drivers to care for the vehicles, a one-driver-one-vehicle approach was used. All vehicles, therefore, had a nominated driver, with a reserve driver chosen by the full-time driver

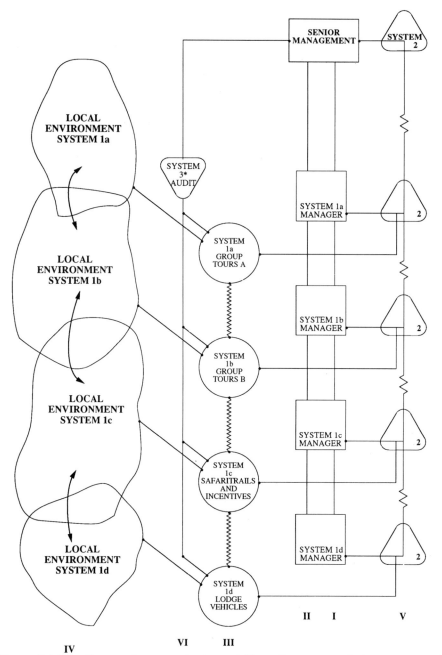

Figure 5.4 The System 1 reorganisation of Fleet Division and the six vertical channels (tourism example)

to ensure that someone is available to use the vehicle at all times. In this way each driver was attached to a division of System 1.

Each mini-fleet was allocated a member of staff from the fleet operations team, being responsible for planning and controlling the utilisation of their division of the fleet to an optimum level. This is a vital role because the vehicles and their use are the primary concern of the day-to-day operation of Fleet Division.

To ensure that all clients were treated equitably, but allowing for new and important business to be given special attention, it was necessary to establish clearly a set of operational procedures for charting vehicles. The following procedures were agreed and implemented. (The groupings referred to are of particular vehicle types for particular clients.)

(1) If a vehicle in a particular grouping within a division is available, it must be allocated to bookings for that group as they arise.
(2) If all the vehicles for that group are allocated according to Procedure 1, then another vehicle from within the division must be allocated, providing that a vehicle can be found that is not engaged in its own group's business.
(3) If all the vehicles in the mini-fleet are allocated, then a vehicle from one of the other mini-fleets can be re-allocated from its normal division, providing that a vehicle can be found that is not engaged in its own division's business.
(4) If all vehicles in all mini-fleets have been allocated, then a floating vehicle may be used. Floating vehicles are a group that are coming to the end of their productive life, are generally kept in Manjaro for peak-time city work, but may be used for last minute bookings or other emergencies (e.g. as replacements for breakdowns).
(5) If the entire fleet is allocated, or if a client will not accept an older vehicle, then a vehicle is hired from an outside supplier.
(6) Important and new contract bookings must be allocated relatively new vehicles and Procedures 1–5 will be bypassed.
(7) If a driver is requested by name then, if possible, that driver and vehicle are allocated to the requesting client.
(8) Some or all of the above procedures may be bypassed if there are last minute bookings (less than 48 hours), breakdowns or maintenance problems. This maintains flexibility in exceptional circumstances so that no client is without transportation.

These procedures cover the main activities of the system-in-focus as defined by its purpose. Simply by installing and promoting an understanding of these procedures, smoother running of operations and an image of better organisation was achieved. Not all these procedures are, of course, the task of System 1, according to the principles of viable system modelling. As each System, 2 to 5, is considered we will, at relevant points, refer back to these procedures and show how they act as "variety filters", helping to cope with the complexities associated with vehicle requirements.

Viable system diagnosis requires that we consider the System 1 environment (the operational environment) at this stage. The divisions of System 1 are affected by four main environmental factors—difficulties associated with spare parts availability; bad road conditions caused by heavy rainfall; corruption; and the poor educational and training standards of drivers. These environmental issues, when mixed with those dealt with by System 4, required careful yet innovative management and co-ordination from Systems 1 to 5.

System 2

While Procedures 1 and 2 govern the internal divisional use of vehicles, monitored and controlled by divisional managers, Procedures 3 and 4 require monitoring and control by a System 2 co-ordinator of the mini-fleets, which helps to ensure that an efficient and stable use of resources is realised. Together, these form the accountability function for operating company resources and they ensure that each day the normal bookings are co-ordinated within and between each mini-fleet, helping to optimise utilisation of the company's vehicles. System 2 also co-ordinates the flow of drivers, particularly when reserve drivers need to be called upon. Finally, since Fleet resources are limited, it is important that appropriate decisions are made concerning the number of vehicles which are allocated to each client group in each mini-fleet. System 2 monitors this, making "minor" changes where appropriate. Major changes are filtered up to a higher command level.

In summary, the formation of a floating vehicle pool, allocation procedures, the one-vehicle-one-driver policy and the use of nominated reserve drivers (all co-ordinated by System 2) provided the conditions for flexibility and the possibility for resource adaptation to counter local disturbances, but also provided a set of rules that reduced the number of possible situations (or states) to be managed. They also contributed to the minimisation of time lags before responses to disturbances.

System 3

While Systems 1 and 2 were (re)designed to deal with the normal day-to-day business of vehicle allocation in the Manjaro Fleet, there still remained a need for significant changes to System 3 where many essentially historic difficulties could be found.

Audit is the general label Beer attaches to audit and control functions designed to ensure that internal homeostasis is maintained. These "channels" are, however, often of a regular and routine nature and enter directly into System 1 (System 3* audit channels). They must be agreed upon, accepted and understood. If this is not done, then it can often lead to System 3 gaining a reputation for autocracy, as had been the case in Fleet Division. By involving System 1 in the design of these activities, senior management can promote shared knowledge and a democratic image. The main audit and control procedures identified and operationalised for Manjaro Fleet were: a Budget Review, Quality Control, Financial and Operational Audits, a Future Vehicle Requirements Forecast and Breakdown Records.

Some examples of these audits and the results obtained can be given. Quality control was necessary in order to ensure that vehicles remain usable throughout their productive life and to make certain that each vehicle with driver leaves the premises achieving the highest appropriate standards. An otherwise obsolete member of staff was used to carry out random checks each week, looking at drivers' uniforms and safari equipment, and for the required binoculars, reference books, cool-box and other items which enhance client enjoyment. The financial and operational audits included a summary of vehicle utilisation for each vehicle group on each mini-fleet, helping to ensure that vehicles and drivers were used evenly and equitably (respectively), particularly in less busy periods. In practice this process was viewed positively since it filtered out accusations of favouritism within Fleet operations. It also allowed periodic review of resource (vehicle) allocation by senior management. The Future Vehicle Requirements Forecast was particularly important bearing in mind that a large loss on hired in vehicles was experienced in the previous year. A comprehensive redesign helped establish effective feedforward control to ensure a reduction in future risks. When put together, the audit procedures provided a comprehensive variety absorption process that prevented senior management from getting an overload of information and thus being swamped with data irrelevant to their level of command. The staff at Fleet Division were educated in the importance and purpose of the auditing process to help reduce the degree of suspicion that might otherwise have been aroused.

Turning now to the functions of System 3 proper, it will be remembered that the operational procedures 1, 2, 3 and 4 (previously discussed) ensured normal vehicle utilisation within the framework of Systems 1 and 2. Procedures 5, 6, 7 and 8, however, are part of the management meta-system. Once decisions are made regarding these procedures it is System 3's responsibility to look after the consequences for internal stability. We will consider these issues in terms of what Beer calls the System 1–2–3 homeostat.

Beer employs six vertical channels to handle "variety" (a measure of complexity) in the model (see Figure 5.4). Channels (I) and (II) are at the centre of the vertical command axis and are tasked by Beer with the construction of the Resource Bargain and meeting Accountability and Corporate and Legal Requirements. They should also ensure the autonomy of the divisions of System 1. Channel (III) is governed by Procedure 3, with Channel (IV) representing the management of environmental disturbances. Channels (V) and (VI) are shown in more detail in their redesigned form in Figure 5.5. These are the high-level variety filters and are based on the use of co-ordination, review of performance, quality control and feedforward forecasting. They are also designed to assist the divisions of System 1 in carrying out day-to-day business (keeping the fleet on the road and in line with the purpose of the system-in-focus).

The two organisational characterisations shown in Figure 5.6 show that when the vertical channels are not properly put together, there is low variety filtering, information overload up to System 3 and hence a danger of Systems 3 to 5 "collapsing" into System 1 (Figure 5.6(a)). This was the situation in Fleet Division before our reorganisation, with Systems 3 and 5 wholly involved in day-to-day management. The situation after reorganisation resembles very much more Figure 5.6(b).

We have now built up a picture of the reorganised 1–2–3 homeostat necessary to establish internal homeostasis. It is from this base that we can construct our final viable system (re)organization by considering Systems 4 and 5.

System 4

This is an intelligence and development function that captures relevant information about the total environment of the system-in-focus (which is more than the operational environments of the parts of System 1). The total environment is represented in Figure 5.7. Issues of vehicle design, product plan, external training, societal constraints, market development and technological developments are highlighted. Interdependence between these areas is evident. Without an understanding of these links and intersects Fleet would soon lose touch with the market place and the future of its business. The two "total intersects" bring to the fore two central issues: development of driver guides and attention to vehicles and their development. Both must be planned for, so that the position of market leader is maintained.

System 4 is also important in relation to Procedure 5. If the System 3*

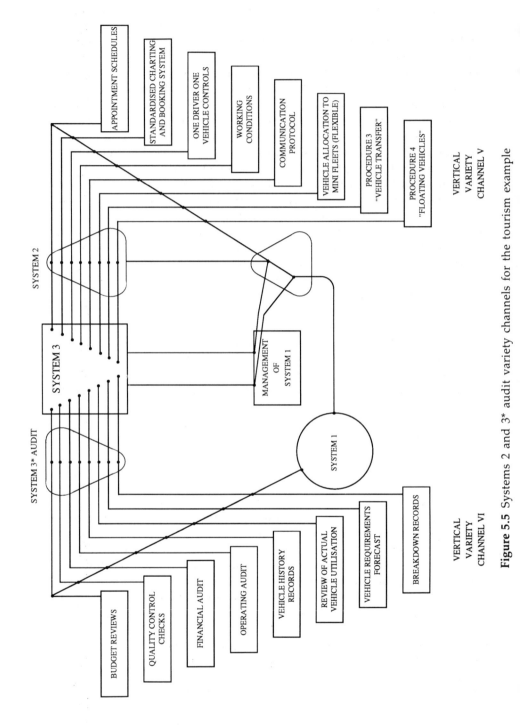

Figure 5.5 Systems 2 and 3* audit variety channels for the tourism example

SYSTEM 2

SYSTEM 3

SYSTEM 3* AUDIT

MANAGEMENT OF SYSTEM 1

SYSTEM 1

APPOINTMENT SCHEDULES

STANDARDISED CHARTING AND BOOKING SYSTEM

ONE DRIVER ONE VEHICLE CONTROLS

WORKING CONDITIONS

COMMUNICATION PROTOCOL

VEHICLE ALLOCATION TO MINI FLEETS (FLEXIBLE)

PROCEDURE 3 "VEHICLE TRANSFER"

PROCEDURE 4 "FLOATING VEHICLES"

VERTICAL VARIETY CHANNEL V

BUDGET REVIEWS

QUALITY CONTROL CHECKS

FINANCIAL AUDIT

OPERATING AUDIT

VEHICLE HISTORY RECORDS

REVIEW OF ACTUAL VEHICLE UTILISATION

VEHICLE REQUIREMENTS FORECAST

BREAKDOWN RECORDS

VERTICAL VARIETY CHANNEL VI

(a)

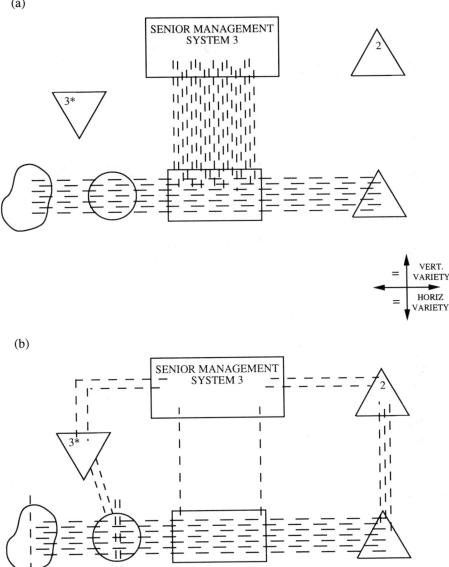

(b)

Figure 5.6 Two organisational characterisations: (a) without variety processes, (b) with variety processes

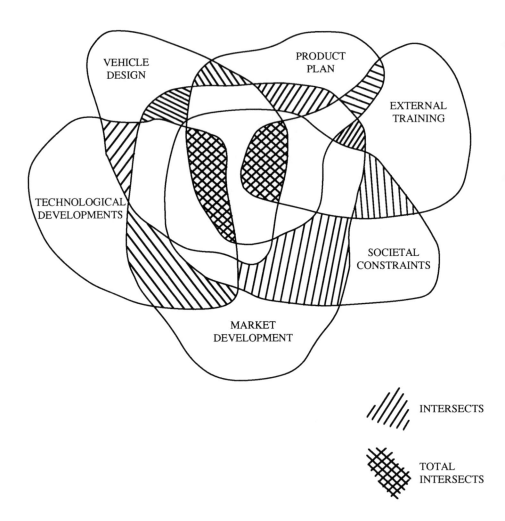

VEHICLE
DESIGN

PRODUCT
PLAN

EXTERNAL
TRAINING

TECHNOLOGICAL
DEVELOPMENTS

SOCIETAL
CONSTRAINTS

MARKET
DEVELOPMENT

INTERSECTS

TOTAL
INTERSECTS

Figure 5.7 The total environment of the system-in-focus (tourism example)

audit function forecasts overbooking, where the 1–2–3 homeostat would fail to meet the declared purpose, it would be vital that System 4 be aware of vehicles that were available externally and where they could be found. This might provide the edge over competition for easy access to Manjaro's superior vehicle contractors, and hence make an important contribution to preparations for the high season.

System 5

System 5 deals with strategic decisions and issues of management style. The procedures described earlier were discussed and agreed upon by all the staff at recursion level 1 and those affected at recursion level 0. They were not issued as unquestionable orders, but did create a foundation of the ethos (or culture) of Fleet Division. Once established, the procedures led to smoother relationships within all areas of the company and did resolve the difficulties that had previously led to accusations of corruption. In addition, an attitude of listening to what the staff had to say encouraged responsiveness (previously junior staff were paid little attention). This management style, complementary to a viable system reorganisation, generated positive responses throughout Fleet.

Only System 5 can initiate thought beyond the operational and other procedures (e.g. see Procedure 8 that typically would need System 5 decisions). We mentioned that shortage of spare parts affected the operations of System 1. System 2 could smooth out difficulties on a one-off basis, System 3 could inform of wider implications, System 4 could relate the problem to the total environment; but only System 5, with access to all relevant and necessary information, could consider this further and think about developing alternative strategies to sources of supply.

Attention was also given to the algedonic signal in System 5. Channels to alert this signal were identified and established. For example, vehicle breakdowns in high season, where a rapid decision was often required concerning complex allocation procedures, would trigger this signal.

5.6.3 Conclusion

We have completed the description of the diagnosis and reorganisation of Fleet Division. Previous to reorganisation the low morale, increasing number of breakdowns and the low vehicle utilisation seriously threatened the short-term survival of Fleet. It was, in essence, a non-viable organisation. The division would not have been able to cope with another high season. Senior staff were excessively involved in day-to-day affairs and were not, therefore, capable of directing time or energy to initiate changes. It was fortunate that the investigation began at the start of a two-month low season, allowing interventions to be carried out smoothly. The crying need was for some form of organisation "now, or bust".

A viable system (re)organisation proved to be ideal and generally acceptable to the staff, offering attractive advantages in the way its use helped remove corruption, increase equitability and democracy and, most important of all in this developing country, guarantee jobs in the short and medium term. Possibilities for learning and future viability were also offered in a competitive business, and uncertain and unstable political environments.

5.7 CRITIQUE OF VSD

A critique of Beer's viable system model is carried out below making use of the meta-paradigmatic net which we have developed for the purpose of critiquing methodologies.

Theory

(a) The cybernetic model is held by some to give an impoverished, or subset, picture of the organisation. It emphasises organisational structure and communication and control processes—the machine-like qualities of organisations—but neglects qualities brought by the human actors who make up organisations. Thus it has little to say about the social processes that go on in organisations, about organisational culture and about politics and power struggles in enterprises. There is something in this complaint although, as we have argued previously, the cybernetic approach offers a very rich exploration of the logic of the brain and organismic metaphors as well as of the machine metaphor. The VSM does neglect culture and power and in a TSI study it is usual to combine its use with attention to the culture and political metaphors. This is precisely what happened in the investigation of Fleet, when understanding was developed in terms of neurocybernetics, culture and politics (in the form of corruption). The dominant metaphor that emerged in the negotiation process was the first, but others were not ignored. Potential legitimacies and limitations of the use of the brain metaphor in practice were also made explicit.

(b) Connected to the first criticism it is often argued that the VSM neglects the purposeful role of individuals in organisations. Ulrich, for example, indites the model for being "tool" rather than "social systems design", for emphasising "purposiveness" instead of "pur-posefulness" and for encouraging "intrinsic control" but not "intrinsic motivation". This amounts to saying that the tendency of the model is to take some predetermined goal as given. It then seeks to pursue this goal as efficiently and effectively as possible by delegating control over means to the parts of the organisation. Those same parts, however, are not able to participate in goal determination. They are free only to the extent that they can develop alternative means of reaching the predetermined goal. It is true that the cybernetic model is one-sided in this respect, emphasising the pursuit of known goals rather that the way goals are arrived at. Descriptions of the VSM make no explicit mention of negotiation forums or participation to take account of individual viewpoints. But neither does the model reject participation. There is no reason why the VSM cannot be activated in a broader democratic context with channels for participation introduced according to management style. In the Fleet reorganisation, for example, all staffing levels were consulted and participated, and the management style adopted led to encouragement of a purposeful human contribution, making working-life meaningful for employees in their own terms while ensuring Fleet services were maintained. In this case the viable system model co-existed with intrinsic motivation. Of course, the criticism that the VSM says little about how participation in goal setting can be achieved remains.

(c) It is sometimes said that the cybernetic model emphasises stability at the expense of change. In fact the VSM provides for the possibility of stability or change. System 4 plays an important part in scanning the environment for possibilities which the organisation might take up. The System 3–4–5 homeostat seeks to balance the demands for stability against the demands for change. The model thus allows for continual adjustment and review. The charge of emphasising stability holds against early cybernetic models where interest lay solely in deviation counteracting; later models, however, can also incorporate deviation amplifying systems.

(d) It has been suggested that cybernetics encourages organisations to function on a set of *a priori* goals without regard to the field of relationships in which they find themselves, and that this can be dangerous in the long term as organisations might spoil their environments. This change fails to recognise, in respect of the viable system model, that the 3–4–5 homeostat is designed constantly to review corporate objectives. This is not a mechanical set-point approach, it is not a physiological process that regulates variables within a restricted range in order to maintain organismic integrity, neither is it passive evolution. Rather, it is active evolution involving conscious decisions in a feedforward mode. There may be goals, but they are not fixed and they can take account of the environment.

Methodology

(a) The cybernetic model is often accused of adherence to mechanical and biological analogies which are misplaced when applied to social contexts. Beer has consistently argued against this and shown that the VSM can, in fact, be generated from cybernetic first principles, constructing the model this way in *The Heart of Enterprise*. We would be the first to admit, however, that cybernetics itself is stronger in articulating the "complexity" metaphors of machine, organism and brain than the "participant" metaphors of culture and politics.

(b) One of the main cybernetic principles that underlies the work of Beer is the "law of requisite variety": that only variety can destroy variety. The VSM can be seen as a grand design for a variety engineering organisation. Yet variety has been criticised as a poor measure inappropriate for scientific work, and as unexceptional when applied to the management of social organisations. Poor measure it may be, but it is possibly the only type of measure appropriate to the science of organisation and it does seem to yield insight when reflected upon in practice—as the worked example of Fleet Division perhaps showed and the case study of the next section may convince the reader.

Ideology

Given the theoretical criticism that the VSM underplays the purposeful role of individuals, some have gone on to argue that its use is likely to lead to autocratic management within organisations. Beer claims that the model requires only that degree of control over individual freedom necessary in order to maintain cohesiveness in a viable system. A defence of the model can certainly be mounted along these lines, for unless systemic cohesion is maintained the parts will begin to get in each other's way and limit each other's freedom—the result will not be greater freedom but anarchy.

However, since the degree of systemic cohesion necessary is determined by the purposes of the organisation, we are driven on to ask who is responsible for determining purposes? Only if all participants have a say in the determination of purposes, and System 5 truly represents the whole system, can the parts be expected to accept as legitimate the limitations on their activity imposed in the name of systemic cohesion.

There is also the question of whether, whatever Beer's own intentions for the model, it cannot easily be corrupted into an autocratic management tool when applied in organisations with fixed power relationships and a hierarchical structure. Beer would like to claim that the decentralising nature of the model makes it completely inappropriate for such contexts, but there is little doubt that it could be misused to bolster existing power structures in many circumstances. The question might then be, would such organisations, which ignore such a fundamental principle of the VSM, still be viable?

Beer has done a good job in showing that control and freedom are not necessarily antithetical and in providing the basis for democratic management in a democratic context—if all have participated in a goal setting then they are likely to accept constraints imposed to facilitate goal achievement. It remains the case, however, that the model depends for its proper use and functioning on social conditions which it does not itself sufficiently seek to engineer—a democratic milieu.

Utility

Another criticism is that the VSM is difficult to apply in practice, particularly because of the resistance it is likely to provoke within an organisation. As long as the viable system model is perceived as simply a more efficient control device, resistance to implementation will obviously be strong. Let us accept, however, that it can offer the prospect of increasing personal freedom, as well as efficiency, in pursuit of more widely agreed goals. Then, with proper management, the situation could be different.

This is not to deny that introducing the VSM requires additional large-scale changes in organisational culture and that the model is largely silent about how these might be brought about. What is required is a more sophisticated methodology for using the VSM and work is being done on this. Our own sophisticated methodology is of course TSI, where the neurocybernetic concerns highlighted by the model are combined with cultural and political concerns in any analysis.

Summarising greatly, we find that the VSM survives most of the attacks made upon it. Perhaps there are two major unresolved difficulties. First, that the purposeful role of human beings within a VSM design has not been sufficiently well explored—but since the VSM does not dictate a management style, this is a task to be done rather than a task that cannot be done. Second is the criticism that a neurocybernetic perspective is only one way of conceiving any organisation. This is adequately dealt with in the logic of TSI when we offer a process of thinking about organisational situations in terms of many metaphors. TSI helps us to explore carefully the legitimacies of any perspective that we might propose to adopt.

5.8 CASE STUDY: XY ENTERTAINMENTS

There follows the case study which readers should use to try their hand at viable system diagnosis.

5.8.1 Introduction

XY Entertainments has grown up and is being run in a very *ad hoc* manner by its two directors, X and Y. At present the enterprise lacks even a rudimentary organisation chart. It is recognised by Y that, given the range and scale of current activities and the plans for expansion, there is now a need for more formal structures. Y is also aware of certain difficulties, including that of morale in the organisation. She wants a study to be done which will help her and X get an overview of the whole of XY's activities and enable them to begin to put right some of the perceived problems. At the same time, X and Y are keen to protect the informal atmosphere which they believe pervades the company.

5.8.2 Your Task

Using cybernetic modelling provide for Y an overview of XY and a diagnosis of where the "problems" lie. Also offer some tentative suggestions for redesign.

5.8.3 Further Information

Here is some further information about XY which you as the consultant have managed to gather from interviews with X, Y and other managers and staff.

XY Entertainments has expanded rapidly in size in recent years. Its activities include well developed and new operations in Bristol, partially developed operations in Weston-Super-Mare (an ongoing floating restaurant/discothèque and plans for a country club) and plans for operations in Bath (possible club, hotel, etc.) which are still at the blueprint stage. These activities are still run in a very informal and *ad hoc* manner by the two directors X and Y.

X is the owner of the group and is determined to make all the various operations profitable. He also possesses a sincere interest in conservation and this aspect of XY's "ethos" has determined the direction of many of its activities. The buildings which now house the XY Club, XY Hotel and Clifton Bar are renovated Grade II listed warehouses on the dockside in Bristol. These warehouses were built in 1831. They were to make way for modern office developments and roads. X, dismayed at the prospect of so much history being knocked down, has sought to preserve the character of these buildings so that they can be enjoyed by the people of Bristol. After lengthy negotiations with Bristol City Council, X was eventually granted a long lease on the premises. The converted warehouses have proved a great attraction to conservationists, to tourists and to the people of Bristol and have won five major awards.

The XY Club was opened first and proved to be an exceptionally profitable venture. It has recently suffered from severe competition from other clubs and possibly from some management neglect. Nevertheless, its early success financed the development of the XY Hotel and Clifton Bar. The XY Hotel is very successful with businessmen. It does well in the conference trade and houses a high class restaurant. The Clifton Bar was designed as a fashionable, dimly lit, basement pub, providing live music and discos for the younger set. Results have, however, been disappointing. Manager B feels that the Clifton Bar has lost out, in the fight for resources, with the more favoured Rose and Crown. The Rose and Crown is an old pub directly opposite the Club and Hotel. Control of this was recently negotiated by X and it has been totally renovated. As well as being an atmospheric pub, it offers good food and a "beer garden".

X is a dynamic entrepreneur who built up the business from scratch. He works on hunch rather than market research and some would say he is reckless in his approach. However, he saw the opportunities for development in the Old Town and Dock area of Bristol ten years before such ideas became popular. Most of his time and effort is spent in pursuit of new opportunities although he will, from time to time, involve himself in any parts of the existing business which happen to provoke his interest (apart from the affairs of the dance group, Silk Stockings, which he sees as Y's own adventure). This approach he regards as part of an informal management style. Although, of course, X consults Y about activities, it is clear that Y finds it difficult to keep up with the pace of the development going ahead in Weston-Super-Mare and Bath.

Given X's interests and management style, much of the running of the current enterprise is left to his co-director Y. Y also favours the informal style of management which proved such a success when the company was small. Her actual responsibilities remain vaguely defined and she manages mostly through observation and intuition, rather than on the basis of any measures of performance. She has to deal with problems when they arise in all parts of the business and to sort out an increasing number of petty disputes between other managers. For example, between Manager B and Manager G over resources for the Clifton Bar and Rose and Crown respectively. Her broad brief, which requires her to keep in touch with every aspect of XY's activities, imposes a great strain on Y who feels considerably overworked and under pressure. Recently she feels she has lost control over the business. This is especially the case because of the increasing time she now has to spend on the latest Bristol developments, the model agency and dance group. The model agency was an initiative of X's, but is now largely left to Y. Most of the 61 models are part-time, ranging from teenagers to the middle-aged. Business is fairly brisk. A deportment school is also run from the model agency.

The Silk Stockings dance group is Y's own recent speculative venture. The formation of the group created something of a stir among other managers, who saw it as a distraction and regarded it as a waste of money that could be better spent elsewhere. The group has experienced some success, but morale among its members is low because they remain unconvinced that they are taken as a serious venture in XY.

There are a number of other managers and staff responsible for various aspects of XY's business and their roles seem to be as follows.

A Responsible for publicity, promotions and some administration. Her greatest efforts seem to be on behalf of the Club, the Hotel and the Rose and Crown. She has considerable experience and her contacts and influence have helped give the company a reputable image with the public.

B Manages the XY Club and the Clifton Bar.

C Is assistant manager to B, helps G run the Rose and Crown and also assists A.

D Is responsible for general trouble-shooting, for overall control of bars, for the ongoing floating restaurant/disco at Weston-Super-Mare and for the conference facilities at the Hotel.

E Is restaurant manageress at the Hotel.

F Is responsible for room-bookings and housekeeping at the Hotel and for general stores for all the Bristol operations.

G Together with C runs the Rose and Crown and also helps with Club activities.

H Runs the model agency and the deportment school under the guidance of Y.

J Is the leading member of the dance group.

K Is a management trainee (the appointment of K is viewed with great suspicion by other managers and is another source of dispute in the company).

In general, morale among these managers and senior staff is not good. Although each is provided with a tight job description on joining XY, this soon breaks down under the informal, interventionist management style beloved of X and Y. The managers feel that under these circumstances it is impossible for them to do their jobs properly. They do not know where they are with X and Y, are not clear about what they are expected to achieve and have little idea of how well they are doing at any particular time. Whenever they want to take initiatives they have to go to X or Y for the money and this can prove extremely frustrating. It is remarkable how, in conversation with the managers, each comes across as primarily concerned with upward relations and communication. Each manager feels that relations with the directors are his/her real concern.

FURTHER READING

- Beer's trilogy on the VSM is, of course, fundamental:

Beer, S. (1979). *The Heart of Enterprise*, Wiley, Chichester.
Beer, S. (1981). *Brain of the Firm*, 2nd edition, Wiley, Chichester.
Beer, S. (1985). *Diagnosing the System for Organisations*, Wiley, Chichester.

- Beer's ideological position is spelt out in:

Beer, S. (1973). *Designing Freedom*, Canadian Broadcasting Company, Toronto.

- An acceptable secondary source on management cybernetics and a book of readings, including examples of the VSM in practice, are:

Clemson, B. (1984). *Cybernetics: A New Management Tool*, Abacus Press, Tunbridge Wells.
Espejo, R. and Harnden, R. (eds.) (1989). *The Viable System Model: Interpretations and Applications of Stafford Beer's VSM*, Wiley, Chichester.

- For a fuller account of the worked example in this chapter:

Flood, R. L. and Zambuni, S. (1990). Viable systems diagnosis I. Application with a major tourism services group, *Systems Practice*, **3**, 225–48.

- For the criticisms of the VSM and possible responses see:

Flood, R. L. and Jackson, M. C. (1988). Cybernetics and organization theory: A critical review, *Cybernetics and Systems*, **19**, 13–33.
Jackson, M. C. (1988). An appreciation of Stafford Beer's "viable system" viewpoint on managerial practice, *Journal of Management Studies*, **25**, 557–73.
Jackson, M. C. (1989). Evaluating the managerial significance of the VSM, in *The Viable System Model* (eds. R. Espejo and R. Harnden), pp. 407–39, Wiley, Chichester.

- You may also wish to consult the special issue of *Systems Practice*, Volume 3, Number 3, published in June 1990, which deals exclusively with the VSM.

Chapter 6

Strategic Assumption Surfacing and Testing (SAST)

We have had accounts of men as animals, men as machines, men as biochemical complexes with certain ways of their own, but there remains the greatest difficulty of achieving a human understanding of man in human terms.
R. D. Laing, *The Politics of Experience and the Bird of Paradise.*

6.1 INTRODUCTION

Having studied system dynamics and viable system diagnosis, both of which (although in very different ways) use models related to the situation of concern to assist decision makers, we arrive, with strategic assumption surfacing and testing (SAST), at a wholly different approach to the use of systems ideas. SAST looks different, and is different, from the previously considered methodologies because it focuses managers' attention on the relationship between the participants involved in a problem context, and not on the supposed characteristics of the "system" that constitutes the problem context. In terms of the "system of systems methodologies" matrix, it is the "participants" rather than the "systems" dimension that is now to receive the main attention. The human and political aspects of organisations are brought to the fore, while the issue of organisational structure slides into the background (but may re-emerge after issues of plurality are resolved). Not surprisingly, therefore, the "machine", "organism" and "brain" metaphors, are less in evidence, as the "culture" and "coalition" metaphors come into their own. SAST was designed as an approach suitable for ill-structured problem contexts where *differences of opinion* over which strategy to pursue prevent decisive action being taken.

An interesting feature of SAST, implicit in the work of its originators, is the assumption that once issues of pluralism have been overcome, the traditional methods of management science (those found corresponding to the simple–unitary area of the "system of systems methodologies") will be sufficient to finish the job. This is why we have placed SAST in the simple pluralist "cell" of the "system of system methodologies". SAST could in principle, however, be used in any pluralist situation to contribute to the development of mutual understanding, or learning about our and others' positions. It is just that to deal with complex–pluralist situations (we are speaking about ideal types) it would need much additional assistance, in ways not conceived of by the originators, from cybernetic thinking.

There are a number of versions of the SAST approach which differ in their precise details. The substance, however, is the same. The account here is drawn from the main sources with which either R. O. Mason or I. I. Mitroff, or both, have been associated. It is an attempt to present the substance in the clearest possible way and may not correspond to the detail of any one account. The methodology itself is approached through its underlying philosophy and the principles on which it is based.

6.2 PHILOSOPHY OF SAST

Those who have read Churchman on the systems approach will recognise in SAST a profound intellectual debt to his work and to the pragmatist tradition in American philosophy and culture. This is not the time to follow Churchman on an intellectual journey through the Western philosophical tradition. Nevertheless, it would be a pity not to take some advantage of Churchman's skill as a simplifier of that tradition for managers and systems analysts. Particularly as this will assist us greatly in understanding not only Mason and Mitroff's work, but also the whole of the "softer" systems tradition. "Interactive planning", the subject of the next chapter, "soft systems methodology", the subject of Chapter 8, and "critical systems heuristics", the subject of Chapter 9, have all been considerably influenced by Churchman. We preface our rendition of the philosophy specific to SAST, therefore, with some notes on Churchman's thinking.

6.2.1 Churchman's Philosophy as the Inspiration of SAST

Churchman's most pithy account of the thinking underlying his version of systems analysis comes in four statements at the end of his book *The Systems Approach*. There it is stated that:

"The systems approach begins when first you see the world through the eyes of another."

Here we have a lesson from the German philosopher Kant. We are reminded that we all tell a particular story of the world based on our own taken for granted, *a priori*, assumptions. However, it is as well to recognise that there are other equally legitimate stories based upon alternative sets of *a priori* assumptions. Once we recognise this we are *en route* for the systems approach because it becomes clear that "subjectivity" must be embraced in systems thinking; different evaluations of what we want to attain from systems, and of their current state of performance, are possible. The only way to come close to grasping the "whole system" is to sweep in as many different perspectives as possible.

"The systems approach goes on to discover that every world view is terribly restricted."

This opens the way, for Churchman, to a different understanding of "objectivity". Subjectivity is no longer to be rigorously excluded, but must be included in any definition of objectivity—so that the restricted nature of any one world view can be overcome. A further point is that, although every world view is terribly restricted, it is also likely to be highly resistant to change. Certainly world views cannot be seriously challenged by presenting them with new "facts", which they will simply interpret according to their fixed presuppositions. All this adds up to the need for an approach to objectivity based upon the work of the German philosopher Hegel. A prevailing world view (thesis) should be confronted by another world view based on entirely different assumptions (antithesis) in order to bring about a richer (more "objective") appreciation of the situation expressing elements of both positions while going beyond them as well (synthesis).

"There are no experts in the systems approach."

This is a statement that should be taken to heart particularly by systems designers themselves. When it comes to matters of aims and objectives (and of means), involving moral judgements, there are no experts. Systems designers must expose the restricted nature of their own world views by opening themselves up to the opinions of their enemies.

"The systems approach is not a bad idea."

Here Churchman is trying to capture the spirit of his mentor, the

American pragmatist philosopher, E. A. Singer. Increasing human purposefulness and participation in systems design in a never-ending process that needs pursuing in the "heroic mood". There is a need to bring about a consensus around a particular world view so that decisions can be taken. Before this world view can congeal into becoming the *status quo*, however, it should itself be subject to attack from forceful alternative perspectives.

Perhaps the most important aspect of all this to be clear about, is the shift proposed by Churchman in our understanding of "objectivity" in the systems approach. In the "hard" and "cybernetic" systems traditions, objectivity is perceived to rest on the efficacy of some model of the system of concern. Either the model represents the system of concern (as in system dynamics) or it can suggest, on the basis of the scientific laws it encapsulates, faults in the system of concern (as with viable system diagnosis). In both cases the objectivity of the model is demonstrated, and the results of the systems analysis guaranteed, if the implemented solutions derived from the model work in practice. For Churchman "systems", and whether they work or not, are as much in the mind of the observer as they are in the "real world". A model can only capture one possible perception of the nature of a social situation. Objectivity, therefore, can only rest upon open debate among many different perspectives. The results of systems analysis receive their guarantee from the maximum participation of different "stakeholders" in the design process. This is a fundamental shift indeed, and it is one which is necessarily adhered to (in theory at least) in all the "softer" systems methodologies that we shall from now on be considering. Once the claim to be modelling some "world-out-there" is abandoned, the only possible reason why anyone would want to follow the prescriptions of systems modellers and methodologists is that they can produce the means of better organising open and free debate about the value or otherwise of existing and proposed systems designs.

6.2.2 The Specific Philosophy of SAST

SAST is meant to be used with "messes", sets of highly interdependent "problems", where "problem" formulation and structuring assume greater importance than "problem solving" using conventional techniques. The specific philosophy of SAST is based upon four arguments about the nature of "problems" and their alleviation.

First, it is argued that most strategic problems in organisations are "wicked problems" of organised complexity, but that most management science methods are only suitable for simple, "well-structured problems". The usual management science approaches do not, therefore, help organisations to deal with their most important "problems".

Second, most organisations fail to deal properly with messes because they find it difficult to challenge, seriously, accepted ways of doing things. Policy options that diverge considerably from current practice are not given systematic consideration. SAST aims to ensure that alternative policies and procedures are considered.

Third, and stemming directly from Churchman, challenging currently preferred policies necessitates the generation of radically different policies or theories, since data alone, which can after all be interpreted in terms of existing theory, will not lead an organisation to change its preferred way of doing things. An organisation really begins to learn only when its most cherished assumptions are challenged by counter-assumptions. A variety of policy perspectives should, therefore, be produced, each supportable by the data available in the organisation. Different strategies based upon alternative world views must be developed in opposition to one another, each capable of interpreting the data differently.

Finally, it is recognised that tensions may well ensue from this process, since its success depends upon the different groups being strongly committed (initially at least) to particular policy options. However, to believe that ill-structured "problems" can be adequately tackled in the absence of such tensions is thought to be naive. Organisations are arenas of conflict between groups expressing alternative world views. This offers great potential for developing alternative strategies and policies, but it must also be managed. SAST attempts to surface conflicts and to manage them as the only way, eventually, of achieving a genuine synthesis.

6.3 PRINCIPLES OF SAST

From the philosophy of SAST are derived four clearly articulated principles which are incorporated into the methodology. SAST is:

- *Adversarial*—based on the belief that judgements about ill-structured problems are best made after consideration of opposing perspectives.
- *Participative*—it seeks to involve different groupings and levels in an organisation, because the knowledge and resources needed to solve complex problems and implement solutions will be distributed around a number of individuals and groups in the organisation.
- *Integrative*—on the assumption that the differences thrown up by the adversarial and participative processes must eventually be brought together again in a higher order synthesis, so that an action plan can be produced.
- *Managerial mind supporting*—believing that managers exposed to

different assumptions will possess a deeper understanding of an organisation, its policies and "problems".

The idea that an approach can be both adversarial and integrative may appear perverse to some. That it is not, was strongly brought home by one particular intervention in a firm that was in the process of introducing a quality management programme. In that firm there was an apparent consensus around the need for the kind of quality management programme underway. In fact, this apparent consensus was founded upon very varied interpretations of the key concepts in the programme. Only through a process of adversarial debate could these very significant differences be highlighted and the ground prepared for a more soundly based consensus built upon common understanding.

The four principles of SAST are employed in all the phases of the methodology itself.

6.4 SAST METHODOLOGY

6.4.1 Introduction

The methodology can be regarded as having four major stages:

- group formation;
- assumption surfacing;
- dialectical debate;
- synthesis.

We shall consider these in turn.

6.4.2 Group Formation

The aim of this stage is to structure groups so that the productive operation of the later stages of the methodology is facilitated. As many individuals as possible who have a potential bearing on the definition of the "problem", and its proposed solution, should be brought together. It is important that as many possible perceptions of the "problem" as can be found are included. These individuals are then divided into small groups on the basis of one or more of the following criteria:

- advocates of particular strategies;
- vested interest;
- personality type;
- managers from different functional areas;
- managers from different organisational levels;

- time orientation (short-/long-term perspective);
- etc.

In choosing the criteria to be used, the aim should be to maximise similarity of perspective *within* groups (to get coherent group activity) and to maximise different perspectives *between* groups. Each group's perspective should be clearly challenged by at least one other group.

6.4.3 Assumption Surfacing

Each group should develop a preferred strategy/solution. The aim of the assumption surfacing stage is then to help each group uncover and analyse the key assumptions upon which its preferred strategy/solution rests. Three techniques assume particular importance in assisting this process.

The first, *stakeholder analysis*, asks each group to identify the key individuals, parties or groups on which the success or failure of their preferred strategy would depend were it adopted. These are the people who have a "stake" in the strategy. The process can be helped by asking questions like:

- "Who is affected by the strategy?"
- "Who has an interest in it?"
- "Who can affect its adoption, execution or implementation?"
- "Who cares about it?"

Thus the list of relevant stakeholders drawn up when this technique was being used in an evaluation exercise with a Council for Voluntary Service included:

- funding agencies;
- local authorities;
- local politicians;
- existing voluntary organisations;
- people in need;
- other local people;
- trade unions;
- various statutory agencies;
- Council for Voluntary Service staff;
- volunteers;
- The Executive Committee of the Council for Voluntary Service.

The main criterion used for constructing this list was which groups would be affected by the success or failure of the Council for Voluntary Service. Using the list to ask questions about how each of these groups would see success for the Council, it was possible to build up an extremely rich picture of the potential expectations held of it.

The second technique is *assumption specification*. For the stakeholders identified, each group then lists what assumptions it is making about each of them in believing that its preferred strategy will succeed. Each group should list all the assumptions derived from asking this question of all the stakeholders. These are the assumptions upon which the success of the groups preferred strategy/solution depends.

The third technique is *assumption rating*. This involves each group in ranking each of the assumptions it is making with respect to two criteria. For each of the listed assumptions each group asks of itself the following:

- "How important is this assumption in terms of its influence on the success or failure of the strategy?"
- "How certain are we that the assumption is justified?"

The results are recorded on a chart such as that shown in Figure 6.1. Because of their lack of importance, those assumptions falling on the extreme left of Figure 6.1 are of little significance for effective planning or "problem solving". Those falling in the top right (certain planning region) are important, but it is those in the lower right-hand quadrant (problematic planning region) which are most critical. Because of their uncertainty they deserve close attention.

Dialectical debate proceeds best if only the most significant assumptions are considered. Each group should now, therefore, list the most significant assumptions on which its preferred strategy depends.

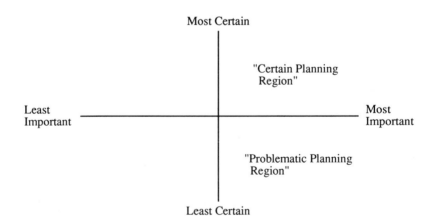

Figure 6.1 Assumption rating chart

6.4.4 Dialectical Debate

The groups are brought back together and each group makes the best possible case for its favoured strategy, while clearly identifying the most significant assumptions that it is making. Questions of information only are allowed from other groups while these presentations are being made. It is important that each group comes to understand the key assumptions upon which the strategies of all other groups rest at this stage.

Open, dialectical debate is then permitted between the groups. Each group should have its list of key assumptions on display. The debate may be guided by asking questions such as:

- "How are the assumptions of the groups different?"
- "Which stakeholders feature most strongly in giving rise to the significant assumptions made by each group?"
- "Are different assumptions rated differently as to 'least important'/'most important', 'least certain'/'most certain' by the groups?"

And especially:

- "What assumptions of the other groups does each group find the most troubling?"

After the debate has proceeded for so long, each group should consider adjusting its assumptions. This process of "assumption modification" should continue for as long as progress is being made.

6.4.5 Synthesis

The aim of the synthesis stage is to achieve a compromise on assumptions from which a new higher level of strategy/solution can be derived. Assumptions continue to be negotiated and modifications to key assumptions made. A list of agreed assumptions should be drawn up. If this list is sufficiently long, then the implied strategy can be worked out. This new strategy should hopefully bridge the gap between the old strategies and go beyond them as well. The assumptions on which it is based can be evaluated as it is put into effect. If no synthesis can be achieved, points of disagreement are noted and the question of what research might be done to resolve those differences is discussed. Meanwhile, any strategy put into effect can be more fully evaluated.

Mason has detailed what he sees as the advantages of the "dialectical approach", captured in the SAST methodology, over the alternative "expert" and "devil's advocate" methods of planning. In the expert approach some planner or planning department simply produces an "objective" plan, based upon the "best" evidence, for managerial consumption. The planners' assumptions remain hidden and the opportunity is lost to produce plans premised upon other points of view. In the devil's advocate approach, managers and planners produce a planning document which is then subject to criticism by top management. The criticism may uncover some assumptions. However, this approach often encourages top management to be hypercritical, with the added problem that, if they are too opposed, the suggested plan disintegrates with no alternative to replace it. In these circumstances planners may be tempted to produce "safe" plans to protect themselves from severe criticism. Again, with the devil's advocate approach, the chance is lost to develop alternative plans constructed on different world views. A dialectical approach, such as SAST, is seen as overcoming all the weaknesses of the other two methods.

6.5 SAST IN ACTION: THE EXAMPLE OF WINTERTON CO-OPERATIVE DEVELOPMENT AGENCY

The worked example now provided to illustrate the use of SAST, within the TSI framework, concerns a project that was undertaken for a Co-operative Development Agency (CDA). We call the CDA, here, Winterton CDA. CDAs serve particular regions and aim to foster, encourage, develop and promote industrial and commercial activity through the formation of co-operative enterprises—enterprises owned by the people who work in them and which are also, usually, managed collectively. The project was to look at the general operation of the CDA to see how it could more efficiently serve the county in which it operated, and how it might market its services in order to achieve its objectives. In thinking about the overall situation of Winterton CDA, a range of metaphors was appropriate and helpful. The "organism", "brain" and "cultural" metaphors all brought some insight. It seemed apparent that the project needed to explore possible ways forward for the CDA at the same time as suggesting what institutional changes would be necessary to realise those ways forward. It needed to concern itself with both the norms and values in the CDA as well as with issues of organisational structure. For this reason a methodology based upon complex–pluralist assumptions was chosen as "dominant" to guide the study. This was Checkland's "soft systems methodology", and its use did indeed lead to useful suggestions for attitudinal, procedural and structural changes, some of which were implemented (see the worked example of this soft systems intervention in Chapter 8).

SAST appears in this case as a "dependent" methodology, which became dominant for a short period of time, to tackle what became an exceptionally important area of disagreement in the CDA about the desirability and feasibility of one possible future strategy which emerged in the course of employing Checkland's approach. It was suggested (and captured in one "root definition"—see Chapter 8) that a useful way to consider Winterton CDA was as

> "a system seeking to recruit individuals to form workers' co-operatives in particular fields where business opportunities exist."

The possible strategy floated here was flagrantly a "top-down" way of carrying out co-operative development work, as opposed to the more usual "bottom-up" approach. The top-down approach involves identifying business opportunities and then recruiting individuals into co-operatives to exploit those opportunities. It is usually viewed with great distrust in co-operative circles. The preferred approach is bottom-up, essentially encouraging and assisting groups already thinking about starting co-operatives in particular fields. Within Winterton CDA the idea of trying a top-down strategy had some support, although there was also vehement opposition from other development workers.

The dominant metaphors of use for understanding this situation seemed to be those of "culture" and "coalition"; in the latter case because the CDA could be seen as consisting of two groups pulling in different directions. It was important to address this issue as quickly as possible because it was clearly of such significance for future planning in the CDA. A quick run through of the SAST methodology was suggested. This approach is clearly designed to address "pluralism", while its lack of concern about complexity (see Chapter 2 and elsewhere in this chapter) was a positive advantage in the circumstances. The need was for a rapid resolution of the disagreement, not a study on the detailed structural arrangements whereby the top-down approach could be institutionalised. SAST, therefore, assumed for a time the role of dominant methodology. The description of its use which follows is in terms of the four stages of the methodology.

Group formation was easily accomplished. The development workers naturally fell into two groups, one consisting of those with some sympathy for the top-down approach and the other consisting of those opposed. The opposed group was asked to make the best case it could against top-down. It was felt that this, rather than asking them directly to make the case for bottom-up, would lead to the most fruitful debate.

The separated groups were then asked to go through the assumption surfacing phase, by using the stakeholder analysis, assumption specification and assumption rating techniques. The groups came up with different lists of stakeholders, obviously influenced by initial perceptions about which individuals or groups might/might not support a case for the top-down strategy.

Stakeholders listed are shown in Table 6.1.

The combined, long list of stakeholders facilitated the emergence of numerous assumptions supporting/against the top-down strategy as each group, during assumption specification, asked of itself what it was assuming about each stakeholder in believing its arguments to be correct. These were rated as to their importance and certainty by the groups on the assumption rating chart. Tables 6.2 and 6.3 contain lists of those assumptions rated most significant by the two groups, (i.e. those appearing in the right-hand quadrants of Figure 6.1). The particular stakeholder generating each assumption is noted in brackets.

The groups were then brought back together to engage in dialectical debate. During the presentations it became clear that the groups were emphasising assumptions derived from consideration of different stakeholders as the main props for their arguments. Group 1 (for top-down) drew heavily on the stakeholders' "funding bodies" (increase in credibility, ensures continuous support, carries out expectations) and "unemployed" (provides employment, gives unemployed a solution in a package). Group 2 (against top-down) concentrated on assumptions generated by the stakeholders "the development workers themselves" (mixed feelings, lack of knowledge about business opportunities, lack of experience in the area), "potential clients" (lack of group cohesion, lack of willingness to co-operate, lack of commitment to business idea), and

Table 6.1 Stakeholders listed in a study for a Co-operative Development Agency

Group 1 (for top-down)	Group 2 (against top-down)
the development workers	the development workers
the unemployed	potential clients
local authorities	the ideologically motivated
business improvement schemes	local authorities
established co-operatives	Department of Trade and Industry
funding bodies	existing co-operatives
other CDAs	people already in work
marketing agencies	
trade unions	
general public	
other businesses	

Table 6.2 The top five assumptions concerning the stakeholders recorded in Table 6.1

Group 1 (for top-down)	Group 2 (against top-down)
another way to set up workers' co-operatives (potential clients)	mixed feelings of the development workers towards the strategy (development workers)
increases the CDA's credibility in job creation (funding bodies)	lack of group cohesion among the co-operators (potential clients)
ensures continuous support to the CDA (funding bodies)	lack of willingness to co-operate among the co-operators (potential clients)
carries out the expectations of the funding bodies (funding bodies)	getting people who are not motivated (the unemployed)
strengthens the co-operative sector (established co-operatives)	less development workers' time on helping existing co-operatives (established co-operatives)

"established co-operatives" (less development worker time for them, suspicion). This analysis helped clarify for the participants the nature and the basis of the arguments for and against top-down, and contributed to a highly effective and productive debate.

When argument was centred around particular issues, other interesting results emerged. The two groups interpreted the reaction of the stakeholders "funding bodies" from entirely different perspectives. Group 1 insisted that top-down would assist the CDA's credibility in job creation, fulfil the expectations of the funders, and so ensure continued support. Group 2 believed that top-down might be seen as a waste of development workers' time on a risky venture, and this dangerous experiment could lose the CDA credibility with the funders if it failed. On the issue of whether top-down promoted industrial democracy, Group 1 argued that more people in workers' co-operatives would inevitably bring this effect; Group 2 argued that the very idea of top-down took choice away from the individuals concerned; and Group 1, back again, argued that many of these were unemployed and had few choices anyway, so work in a co-operative could only increase these.

The most troubling assumptions of the other side for Group 1 (for top-down) were the divisions among the development workers themselves and the possible lack of commitment from those brought together in a top-down scheme. Group 2 (against top-down) worried that if no top-down work took place, a genuine opportunity to set up more co-operatives might be foregone and chances to improve the lot of the

Table 6.3 Other significant assumptions concerning each stakeholder recorded in Table 6.1

Group 1 (for top-down)	Group 2 (against top-down)
provides employment (unemployed)	lack of knowledge of business opportunities hinders "top-down" (development workers)
provides the unemployed with a solution in a package (unemployed)	
a more effective way of starting workers' co-operatives (development workers)	lack of experience of the development workers in this area of activity (development workers)
establishes a successful precedent (others CDAs)	lack of commitment to business idea among the new co-operators (potential clients)
increases numbers working in co-operatives (established co-operatives)	against principle of self-determination (ideologically motivated)
increase in industrial democracy (trade unions)	could be criticised as a waste of development workers' time (funding bodies)
	very dangerous if failed (funding bodies)
	suspicions of other co-operatives, fear of hierarchy and getting co-operatives a bad name (established co-operatives)
	too risky a venture for them (funding bodies)
	no previous association of co-operative members (potential clients)
	may have nothing in common with other co-operators (potential clients)

unemployed, and to gain credibility with funders, would be missed.

Despite attempts at assumption negotiation and modification, it proved impossible to arrive at any overall synthesis during the final stage of the methodological process. Consensus was, however, reached on particular matters such as the need to seek out sources of information about business opportunities, to research other top-down experiences, and on the desirability of some experiments with a modified top-down approach (which were, indeed, carried out).

The intervention in Winterton CDA was, therefore, most useful in assisting creativity, in generating a very rich and full discussion, and in helping to clarify where differences of opinion lay. Although overall synthesis proved impossible to achieve, the chances of genuine consensus around specific issues was improved and this brought benefits. The inclusion of the items mentioned above in an action plan would not have been possible without the changes in perception brought about through the use of SAST.

6.6 CRITIQUE OF SAST

Having gained an appreciation of SAST and the way in which it is employed, we are now in a position to appraise its usefulness to systems practitioners. We carry out the analysis in the usual way, drawing upon the meta-paradigmatic net previously developed. This should ensure that a rounded assessment is achieved.

Theory

(a) As the Winterton CDA example showed, SAST is largely true to the four tenets on which it is built. It is adversarial, integrative and profoundly managerial mind supporting. In the right circumstances it can encourage and orientate a participative style of problem management. The involvement of different groups, advocating alternative positions, brings a large spread of opinion to bear on any problem situation and should ease implementation of proposed courses of action. In Winterton, the situation made genuine participation possible and these advantages were gained. There will be many circumstances, however, where barriers to the extension of the participative principle exist, and in such instances many of the benefits of SAST will be lost. SAST depends for its full and successful operation on genuine participation being possible. It should be remembered that the participative principle derives directly from the philosophy of SAST, and if that philosophy is distorted in use, no justification remains for the methodology.

(b) Mason and Mitroff make clear that they regard SAST as coming into its own in the face of complex, ill-structured problem situations. Certainly it is suitable for simple–pluralist problem contexts. Its appropriateness in complex–pluralist contexts is, however, doubtful, for although it would help in tackling the pluralist aspects of such contexts, it has little relevance to the "complex". There seems to be an unwarranted assumption with SAST that once pluralism has been dissolved, then the difficulties stemming from the complex nature of the context will disappear as well. The analysis of Chapter 2 points to the need to see the complex character of some problem contexts as presenting peculiar difficulties of their own. Since SAST tends to ignore these, assuming that all the difficulties stem from pluralism, it offers only a partial solution to those set in complex–pluralist contexts, and requires some further thinking if it is going to make a genuine contribution in that domain.

Methodology

(a) As was mentioned, SAST for the most part honours the principles on which it is based and these principles can be seen to be of importance. Perhaps it is a little too ambitious in seeking overall synthesis, but this may be no bad thing.
(b) Of considerable concern, however, is the fact that circumstances in many organisations may frustrate honouring of the participative principle. If so, SAST's usefulness as a methodology is inevitably curtailed, and its legitimacy must, in terms of its own philosophy, be open to question. It becomes little more than a kind of expanded multigroup brainstorming without any justification for its results.

Ideology

In coercive contexts it will be impossible to achieve the adversarial and participative debate necessary for the proper application of SAST. Integration is achieved in such contexts by power and domination rather than through consensual agreement. Any employment of SAST is likely to get distorted and to provide benefit only to those possessing power in the organisation. Mason and Mitroff identify the main weakness of SAST as being its dependence upon the participants being willing to lay bare their assumptions. In coercive contexts, the powerful are unlikely to want their assumptions revealed. Very little attention is given to the possibility of the misuse of SAST by powerful groups.

Utility

(a) Cosier and his associates argue that the empirical evidence for the effectiveness of what they call the "dialectical inquiry systems" (DIS) methodology is not as convincing as its theoretical and philosophical support. The limited field studies reported by its proponents have not, in Cosier's view, demonstrated that the DIS technique leads to improvements in objective performance or to more effective plans. Cosier, therefore, carried out some controlled laboratory and field tests to compare the results of using DIS to the results of using alternative planning approaches, such as the devil's advocate. DIS failed to show itself unequivocally as a superior aid. Indeed, Cosier argues that, although the conflict component of DIS is functional, this can be better delivered by the devil's advocate approach, and without the formality, complexity, and need for training in dialectical method implied by DIS.

Cosier's contribution is useful, but more because it helps clarify some of the important features of SAST than because the criticisms are well directed. As Mitroff and Mason argue, the problem with Cosier's critique is that it assesses DIS as an approach to "well-structured problems" rather than, what it is intended to be, an approach to "ill-structured problems". In extracting problems from the "real world" for the purposes of his experiments, Cosier has inevitably imposed more structure on them than would normally be present with ill-structured examples. If he had not done so he would hardly be able to judge whether the DIS or devil's advocate or expert methodology provided the "best" solution. DIS comes into its own only in dealing with "messy problems", when basic "problem formulation" is at issue.

(b) The evident power of this Mitroff and Mason response is, however, to some extent double edged, since it clearly carries the implication that SAST can never be subject to the kind of empirical verification which Cosier attempted. There is no way we can ever be sure, on the basis of empirical evidence, that some other planning technique might not have produced "better" results. We are drawn back, therefore, to the philosophy of SAST, and the way that philosophy is operationalised in the methodology, as the only possible guarantee for the approach. Mason and Mitroff recognise this well enough and search for a guarantor in aspects such as participation, the controlled conflict encouraged, and the provision for challenging assumptions. All the more reason, of course, for honouring the philosophy in practice. Cosier himself admits, as we saw, that the philosophy and theory behind SAST are convincing, so perhaps we should leave this argument here. As a final point against Cosier, the Winterton example demonstrates that the employment of SAST need not be formal or complex or require training in dialectics.

SAST is most appropriately used, therefore, when "problems" to be dealt with are highlighted by the culture and coalition metaphors, and when it seems sensible to apply a methodology which assumes that problem contexts are simple–pluralist. In such contexts it can assist in structuring the exploration of different world views and help to bring about a synthesis, or at least accommodation, among participants so that action can be taken.

6.7 CASE STUDY: THORNTON PRINTING COMPANY

6.7.1 Your Task

You are an outside consultant brought in to consider the appropriateness of the managing director's strategy for dealing with the problems of Thornton Printing Company. You are impressed by the proposed quality management programme, but worried about whether enough thought has gone into preparing for its introduction. Your training in TSI tells you that unless more work is done, the programme may flounder on existing fundamental weaknesses in the company which the programme does not address. You want to use TSI to tackle these problems in due course, but first you need to convince the managing director of the validity of your immediate concerns. To achieve this you initially choose SAST as your dominant methodology, hoping to reveal the assumptions upon which the quality management programme is based. Your task, therefore, is to use SAST to reveal the assumptions underlying the quality management programme and then to assess whether this strategy is appropriate or whether any other strategy should be adopted. In particular you should:

- identify all the relevant stakeholders (i.e. all those with a vested interest in the quality management programme);
- specify what assumptions are being made of each of these stakeholders in assuming that the quality management programme can cure the main problems facing Thornton;
- rate the key assumptions being made as to their importance and certainty;
- on the basis of your feelings about the actual nature of the stakeholders involved, set out the strengths and weaknesses of the quality management programme.

If you are doing this exercise in groups you can progress to dialectical debate, one group having been given the brief of defending the managing director's strategy, another having been told to attack it.

Readers are further invited to return to this case when they have finished the book to consider, in terms of TSI, which other systems methodologies should be employed to address the many problems facing Thornton Printing Company as set out below and as revealed by SAST.

6.7.2 Description of the Situation

Thornton Printing Company engages in the printing of labels for other companies' products, and the printing of tickets. It also manufactures label application machines for other companies.

Thornton was set up in the early nineteenth century and, although none of the Thornton family is still connected with the firm, its ethos is still that of a family business. The present managing director is concerned that every employee should feel that he or she is a full member of the company, have pride in his or her work and in a quality product, and should be willing to work hard in the company. This is far from the current reality of the situation, however, as indeed the managing director realises.

In recent years Thornton's business environment has changed very rapidly and has forced inevitable changes in the business which have made the family firm ethos difficult to sustain. Thornton's inability to adapt satisfactorily to changing circumstances, exacerbated by turbulent industrial relations, has moreover led to disappointing financial returns over the last three years, projected to get worse into the future.

Printing technology has been changing very rapidly over the past ten years, with new products frequently coming onto the market. Many small and efficient firms have managed to take advantage of this situation to establish themselves and to gain a reputation for producing and delivering labels quickly and cheaply to exact customer specifications. The number of direct competitors to Thornton has risen from around 30 to, perhaps, 400 in that ten-year period. It is apparent, to use the organisation theory jargon, that Thornton's environment has changed from being simple, homogeneous, stable and friendly, to being complex, diverse, turbulent and hostile.

Thornton's response to these market changes has been largely unco-ordinated. The managing director has attempted to formulate overall company strategy, advised by an executive team set up for the purpose, but on a "muddle-through" basis. Only very general statements have been issued and these have had little resonance or effect on a fundamentally conservative higher and middle management team. New departments have been set up and a number of "outsiders" recruited but this has simply led to the proliferation of different perspectives in the business, and all sense of a shared vision and purpose have been lost.

Thornton's organisational structure remains very centralised and highly bureaucratic. It is an organisation run according to the "machine" model. With the traditional emphasis having been on the production function, Thornton appears weak in certain other essential areas of business activity. It does little research and development and, in fact, has no separate department for R and D. This has, inevitably, led to it falling behind its competitors in product innovation. The firm has poor communications with its market and plays no role in trying to nurture its environment. It lacks a public relations department and its budget for this activity is extremely low compared to its main competitors. Thornton's marketing has been far too passive in the face of aggressive tactics from competitors. Its salesforce lacks proper training and professionalism and does not seem motivated to establish and develop customer relations. Sales personnel are unable to service customers properly because of a simple lack of knowledge about what the company can offer. Internally, communication between sales/marketing and production planning is weak, and this causes difficulties in scheduling and in maintaining proper utilisation of the diverse high technology machines.

The situation within the production function itself has reached a crisis point. Traditionally, managers and supervisors have felt that employees do not work hard enough and have imposed close supervision and control of subordinates. This has now degenerated into "management by threat" as market pressure has led to very high targets for output being set and detailed work routines and procedures being enforced. There are many errors and mistakes leading to high levels of waste and spoilt work, and low quality products. This in turn leads to excessive overtime being worked to correct these failings, and this increases costs. Morale is extremely low, the workers refuse to collaborate with their supervisors and industrial relations "blow ups" between management and unions or shop stewards are frequent.

From the managers' point of view, they are simply trying to pull the organisation together in the face of intense competition in the market. The supervisors feel that the situation is now largely out of control and they do not know which way to turn. There is an incentive scheme for workers in place, but this is easily manipulated and so is ineffective. The supervisors feel they are getting no clear direction set for them by management. The unions feel that they are not consulted about company policy and that communication between managers and supervisors, and supervisors and workers, is very poor. The workers, mostly, have boring and monotonous jobs. They work a two shift system and are organised according to work study methods, with tasks broken down into simple, repetitive, easily learned operations. They are suspicious of management and resentful, especially since management recently cut the subsidy to the workers' canteen. They feel they are blamed for poor quality work which, in fact, often results from the poor quality materials with which they are supplied. The specialised materials needed for the new high technology machines are difficult to check for quality when they arrive, and the workers feel that some suppliers deliberately try to get away with providing poor preparatory products (e.g. printing plates). In the circumstances the workers fail to see why they should show the "flexibility" needed to ensure the best utilisation of the new high technology machines.

In the face of these external threats and internal problems, Thornton could obviously do with a well trained and highly aware management team. In fact, this is lacking. Management jobs are specialised and there is little team spirit. Amazingly, a number of the senior managers fail to see the scale of the difficulties facing Thornton and are reluctant to change. There is no management training either for senior or middle managers. There is no standardized personnel policy, with each manager carrying out, in his/her own way, coaching and performance appraisal. Most frequently these activities are not done at all, so there is no proper management of subordinates and human relations problems proliferate.

6.7.3 Proposed Response

The managing director of Thornton Printing Company, alarmed by falling profits, a weakening market position and the many difficulties of the firm, is determined to put things right by introducing a comprehensive quality management programme into the company. To this end, the managing director and his executive team have formulated their own quality proposals, the broad outlines of which are set out below.

The proposals are based first and foremost on the notion of "conformance to requirements". A strong corporate culture is to be propagated, and introduced from the top, emphasising the importance of quality and conformance to requirements. There is to be a "quality co-ordinator" to act as a champion for the programme, as an information channel and facilitator, and as a trouble-shooter. The programme is to be introduced with quality management sessions for top managers. Once top managers have learned the key concepts they will be responsible for passing these on to their subordinates. Gradually the programme is to be cascaded down to the shop floor where the workers will demonstrate they have absorbed the principles by applying them in their day-to-day work. When specific problems of quality arise, quality teams will be set up to deal with them. It is recognised that, for this implementation process to work, there must be much more effective communication down the line, supported by feedback and follow-up, and that managers and supervisors will have to change their conception of their roles and become "leaders", creating excellence and quality by motivating and educating their subordinates rather than by tightly controlling and threatening them.

"Conformance to requirements" is to apply both to relationships with customers and suppliers, and to all work related activities in the organisation.

With regard to customers the aim will be to learn customers' needs much more accurately and to provide them with the best possible service. The managing director has become convinced that "excellent" companies are also highly innovative, and the aim is to innovate in co-operation with customers, developing an "enhancing" relationship with them. Suppliers are expected to contribute to quality by supplying "zero defect" products and materials.

In terms of internal activity, it is essential that quality requirements be made clear and specific and that they be communicated effectively. Agreed quality output requirements from each process are to be used to establish a "prevention" approach to quality. The aim is to "get things right first time" in order that there are "zero defects" and so no avoidable deviations from output requirements. If there is a deviation this must be regulated immediately. Non-conformance to requirements is to be eliminated.

In order to ensure employees get it right first time, it is important that they develop the right attitude to quality. Their awareness of the importance of quality must be raised. The emphasis put on quality will obviously help with this, as will the setting of agreed output standards which will allow measurement of the "price of non-conformance". Additionally, in the programme, upward communication from below is to be encouraged and recognition given to employees who achieve high quality standards. Hopefully, employees will be motivated to "own" quality themselves, and will take over the quality control function. Inevitably there will have to be changes in work organisation to make jobs more interesting and meaningful.

The managing director is convinced that if "conformance to requirements" can be achieved the organisation will become much more adaptive to its environment, morale will improve, fewer mistakes will be made, difficulties will decrease, productivity will increase, and there will be a resulting improvement in profits.

6.8 FURTHER READING

- The main text to consult for strategic assumption surfacing and testing is:

Mason, R. O. and Mitroff, I. I. (1981). *Challenging Strategic Planning Assumptions*, Wiley, New York.

- For the advantages of SAST over other planning approaches:

Mason, R. O. (1969). A dialectical approach to strategic planning, *Management Science*, **15**, B403–14.

- For the critique of SAST see:

Cosier, R. A. (1981). Dialectical inquiry in strategic planning: A case of premature acceptance? *Academy of Management Review*, **6**, 643–8.
Cosier, R. A., Ruble, T. L. and Aplin, J. C. (1978). An evaluation of the effectiveness of dialectical inquiring systems, *Management Science*, **24**, 1483–90.
Mitroff, I. I. and Mason, R. O. (1981). The metaphysics of policy and planning: A reply to Cosier, *Academy of Management Review*, **6**, 649–51.
Jackson, M. C. (1989). Assumptional analysis: An elucidation and appraisal for systems practitioners, *Systems Practice*, **2**, 11–28.

- We noted the importance of C. West Churchman's work as an inspiration to Mason and Mitroff and also to Ackoff, Checkland and Ulrich. Churchman's main volumes are:

Churchman, C. W. (1968). *Challenge to Reason*, McGraw-Hill, New York.
Churchman, C. W. (1968). *The Systems Approach*, Dell Publishing, New York.
Churchman, C. W. (1971). *The Design of Inquiring Systems, Basic Concepts of Systems and Organisation*, Basic Books, New York.
Churchman, C. W. (1979). *The Systems Approach and its Enemies*, Basic Books, New York.
Churchman, C. W. (1981). *Thought and Wisdom*, Intersystems Publications, Seaside, California.

- A special *Festschrift* issue of the learned journal *Systems Practice*, Volume 1, Number 4, devoted to C. West Churchman, provides further insight into his life's work.

Chapter 7

Interactive Planning (IP)

If you read the newspapers and are still satisfied with the state of the world, put this book down; it is not for you. My objective is not to convert those who are satisfied—even though I believe they need conversion—but to give those who are dissatisfied cause for hope and something to do about it.

R. L. Ackoff, in Preface to *Redesigning the Future*

7.1 INTRODUCTION

Russell Ackoff's work has had a major impact upon all of the various branches of the management sciences about which he has had his say: operational research, corporate planning, applied social science, social systems science, management information systems—to mention only the most obvious. One explanation for the depth and breadth of Ackoff's influence lies primarily in the power of his vision of the management sciences. The job of the management scientist is not to build mathematical models which purport to predict the future and, therefore, help key decision makers prepare their enterprises for the inevitable. Rather, it is to assist all of the participants of an organisation to design a desirable future for themselves and to invent ways of bringing it about.

While carrying out development work with leaders of the Mantua ghetto in Philadelphia, Ackoff was pleased to find many of the lessons he was trying to impart to management scientists captured in the motto of the Mantua Community Planners: "Plan or be planned for." The sentiments of this motto, in turn, bring to mind the words of the English poet William Blake: "I must Create a System, or be enslav'd by another Man's." It is indeed the case that the spirit of Blake's maxim is well captured by Russell Ackoff's work. He has shown why it is apposite to the management sciences, and why it is just as relevant, probably more relevant, to the modern era (the "systems age") as to the time when Blake wrote it. Ackoff's achievement goes beyond this, however. For in his book *Creating the Corporate Future*, subtitled "plan or be planned for", Ackoff sets out a detailed methodology through which desirable futures can be planned and pursued. This "interactive planning" has as its operating principles that planning should be continuous, holistic and participative, and has, as its most original element, the idea that the phases of the planning process should be centred around the design of an "idealised future". It is a methodology which effectively realises the insight of "plan or be planned for" (and Blake's vision) by endorsing it in its philosophy and providing a set of practical procedures through which the philosophical message is empowered. Thus, Ackoff would not only be sympathetic to Blake's maxim, but could point to interactive planning as the means of doing something about it.

More prosaically, and in terms of the logic of this book, the power of Ackoff's work can also be seen to lie in the manner in which it addresses a wide variety of organisational concerns as revealed by a number of important metaphors. It responds to the idea that organisations depend upon a "coalition" of stakeholders and that they are "cultures", as well as recognising that they should be designed to promote learning, like "brains". The "system of systems methodologies", set out in Chapter 2, would record Ackoff's interactive planning as assuming problem contexts are complex–pluralist, since it pays attention to both the complexity of the organisations that managers face and the pluralism inherent in those organisations conceived as purposeful systems.

Detailed discussion of interactive planning follows, adopting the normal style of this book and considering in turn philosophy, principles and methodology.

7.2 PHILOSOPHY OF IP

Like his friend and colleague C. West Churchman, Ackoff was much influenced by the pragmatist philosphy of E. A. Singer. We charted in the previous chapter how Churchman's reworking of that philosophy produced a new understanding of "objectivity" in the systems approach. Ackoff, as well, has contributed to and endorsed that new understanding. For him, the conventional view that objectivity results from constructing value-free models, which are then verified or falsified against some "real world", out there, is a myth. Objectivity in the field of social systems science has to be rethought. Purposeful behaviour cannot be value-free. Objectivity, therefore, should be seen as resulting from the open interaction of multifarious individual subjectivities. It is "value-full", not value-free.

From this, stem a number of significant Ackovian conclusions. The need for wide participation and involvement in planning and design follows. So does the notion that "rationality" should be seen interactively. The attribution of irrationality by an analyst to a client, for example, is simply a statement that their models of reality differ. If the analyst would serve that client, he/she would be better off attributing rationality to the client and irrationality to himself/herself, so that improvement is sought in terms of the client's own criteria. Also linked, is the idea that one of the major banes of the professional planner's life, how to quantify quality of life so that it is possible to plan well for others, can be sidestepped once it is recognised that people should plan for themselves. All that is needed is a planning methodology that people can use with the aid of professional planners, and which makes their own ideals and values paramount.

Ackoff's general philosophical orientation, which we have been discussing so far, takes on a precise form once we relate it to the changes he sees as taking place in the world in which planners and systems scientists have to operate. In order properly to appreciate these changes, Ackoff believes that we need a changed conception of the world and a changed conception of the nature of corporations. Then perhaps we will be able to recognise what kind of planning approach is required by the new circumstances.

A new conception of the world is wanted if we are to understand the profound changes advanced industrialised societies are undergoing. About the time of the Second World War, Ackoff reasons, the "Machine Age"—associated with the industrial revolution—began to give way to the "Systems Age". The systems age is characterised by increasingly rapid change, by interdependence and by complex purposeful systems. It demands that much greater emphasis be put upon learning and adaptation if any kind of stability is to be achieved. This, in turn, requires a radical reorientation of world view. Machine-age thinking, based upon analysis, reductionism, a search for cause–effect relations and determinism, must be complemented by systems-age thinking which proceeds by synthesis (or putting things together) and expansionism (understanding starts from the whole), tries to grasp less direct producer–product relations, and admits the existence of free will and choice.

Those who would manage corporations in the new systems age also need to alter the way they think about these enterprises. In the past, it has been usual to regard corporations either as "machines" serving the purposes of their creators or owners, or as "organisms" serving their own purposes. Today a much richer conception is needed. Organisations should be considered as serving three sets of purposes. They are themselves purposeful systems and have their own goals, objectives and ideals which must be taken into account. But they also contain, as parts, other purposeful systems: individuals, whose aspirations must be met. And they exist, themselves, as parts of wider purposeful systems whose interests also should be respected. Hence corporations have responsibilities to themselves (control problem), to their parts (humanisation problem) and to the wider systems of which they are parts (environmentalisation problem). Managers should seek to serve the purposes of all three "layers", developing all the organisation's "stakeholders" and removing any apparent conflict between them. If this is done, all the "stakeholders" of the organisation, whether internal or external, will continue to pursue their own interests through it, and the organisation will remain viable and effective.

These changing conceptions of the world and of the corporation demand a different kind of planning which properly reflects the new thinking—interactive planning. As we have already suggested, for Ackoff planning should be participative and should be about enabling others to plan effectively for themselves. That said, Ackoff sets up the case for interactive planning by comparing it to three other ideal types of planning: reactivist, inactivist and preactivist.

Reactivist planners are always looking to the past and want to return things to the state of affairs they believe existed in some "golden age" in the past. They deal with problems in a piecemeal fashion rather than systematically and, of course, are out of touch with present realities. *Inactivist* planners are wedded to the present. They want to keep things as they are. They too treat problems separately as they attempt to "muddle-through" and "satisfice", avoiding any real change. Organisations governed by inactivist thinking only survive as long as circumstances are favourable to them. *Preactivist* planners are future orientated. They welcome change for its own sake and believe that quantitative forecasting techniques will enable them to predict the future, so that organisations can be designed to perform "optimally" when it arrives. This "predict and prepare" thinking is what Ackoff so criticises in operational research. To Ackoff it is illogical, since if the future was so determined that we could accurately predict it, there would also be nothing we could do about changing or preparing for it. Fortunately, we are able to affect the future by what we do now, and that means we need a different kind of planning.

Interactivist planners do not want to return to the past, to keep things as they are, or to accept some inevitable future. They take into account the past, the present and predictions about the future, but use these only as inputs into a process of planning aimed at designing a desirable future and inventing ways of bringing it about. They believe that the future can be affected by what organisations and their stakeholders do now. What they all should do, therefore, is reach out for ideals. If inactivists satisfice and preactivists optimise, then interactivists "idealise".

Sometimes Ackoff presents the difference between interactivists and other types of planners in an alternative formulation. According to this representation, while other planners seek to "resolve" or "solve" problems, interactivists want to dissolve them. *Resolving* problems is the approach favoured by most managers. It is a "satisficing", trial and error approach, based upon a mixture of experience and common sense. Managers using this approach seek a course of action which is "good enough". The resolving method eschews any scientific assistance. *Solving* problems is the optimising approach practised by most operational researchers and management scientists. It employs scientific methods and techniques and mathematical models. Unfortunately, in its enthusiasm to make reality fit the tools at its disposal, it often ignores or distorts the essential properties of "messes". *Dissolving* problems, the interactivist's solution, involves changing the system and/or the environment in which the "mess", the "set of interrelated problems", is embedded so that "problems" simply disappear. The minority of managers and management scientists who favour dissolving problems idealise rather than satisfice or optimise, and pursue the "development" of organisations rather than simply growth or survival.

Ackoff provides us with a good example of the dissolving (or "design") approach at work in a large machine tool manufacturing company. This company was faced with abrupt changes in demand for its products and tended to respond by alternatively hiring and firing personnel, many of whom were skilled workers. This policy led to low morale, poor productivity and bad labour relations. Management sought to "resolve the problem", tackling symptoms as they arose on the basis of experience and common sense. Because the "problem" did not go away, however, and indeed seemed to be getting worse, it was decided to use the skills of some operational researchers to "solve" it once and for all. The problem was defined by the operational researchers as one of production smoothing. Data were collected and the relevant system identified and modelled. Optimum solutions were suggested on the basis of the performance of the model. Unfortunately, the results obtained were only slightly better than those yielded by the managers' feel for the situation. Obviously the success of the simulation depended crucially on accurate forecasts of demand being incorporated into the model, but the dynamics which gave rise to demand were in reality just too complex to model.

Finally, a design or "problem dissolving" approach was tried. The "problem" was formulated as one which required a reduction in the fluctuations in (rather than simply a response to) existing demand and the organisation was redesigned to achieve this. It was found that demand for road-building equipment was counter-cyclical to that for machine tools and, furthermore, production of road-building equipment required much of the same technology and marketing and distribution skills, and some of the same parts and sub-assemblies. Adding road-building equipment as a product line reduced combined fluctuations in demand to a small fraction of the fluctuations from machine tools alone. Stable employment was achieved with a consequent improvement in productivity, cash flow difficulties and the industrial relations climate.

Interactive planning, therefore, is the specific methodology recommended by Ackoff to translate his general philosophy into practice. We shall now consider the "principles" of interactive planning.

7.3 PRINCIPLES OF IP

There are three operating principles of interactive planning which we need to discuss before setting out the methodology itself. These are the "participative" principle, the principle of "continuity" and the "holistic" principle.

The principle that planning should be *participative* rests upon two connected ideas in Ackoff's thought. The first is that the process of planning is more important than the actual plan produced. It is by being involved in the planning process that members of the organisation come to understand the organisation and the role they can play in it. It follows, of course, that no one can plan for anyone else—because this would take away the main benefit of planning. The second idea is that all those who are affected by planning should be involved in it. This is a moral necessity for Ackoff, but it also stems directly from the philosophical argument that objectivity in social systems is "value-full".

The participative principle states, therefore, that all stakeholders should ideally participate in the various stages of the planning process. To help in the institutionalising of this, Ackoff has produced an organisational design for participative planning. In this design the different levels of the enterprise are organised into planning boards, with heads of units at each level being members of boards at three levels: their own and the ones immediately above and below. At the highest level, representatives of external stakeholders are represented on Board 1 and, at the lowest, all workers are members of their unit's Board. Although this arrangement may seem unwieldy and time consuming at first, with some managers being on as many as perhaps ten boards, Ackoff's experience is that the benefits in terms of co-ordinated activity, organisational integration and motivation (which are what a manager should be spending his or her time on anyway) are very considerable.

Of all the questions asked of the participative principle, the most frequent must surely be: "What is the role of professional planners in this process?" and "How does higher management react to having to involve other stakeholders, especially low-level employees, in planning?" Ackoff replies that professional planners are by no means excluded from the process; it is simply that their role has changed. They now use their expertise not to plan for others, but to help others plan for themselves. Thus the benefits of the "solving" approach (and the "resolving" as well) can be included in an essentially "dissolving" orientation. On the stakeholder involvement issue, Ackoff admits that there can be a reluctance to permit full participation. However, in these circumstances, if other groups can first be gained admittance as "consultants", it is usually then possible to increase their involvement over time.

The second principle is that of *continuity*. The values of the organisation's stakeholders will change over time and this will necessitate corresponding changes in plans. Also, unexpected events will occur. The plan may not work as expected, or changes in the organisation's environment may change the situation in which it finds itself. No plan can predict everything in advance, so plans, under the principle of continuity, should be constantly revised.

The final principle is the *holistic* principle. We should plan simultaneously and interdependently for as many parts and levels of the "system" as is possible. This can be split into: (a) a "principle of co-ordination", which states that units at the same level should plan together and at the same time—because it is the interactions between units rather than their independent actions which give rise to most difficulties; and (b) a "principle of integration", which insists that units at different levels plan simultaneously and together, because decisions taken at one level will usually have effects at other levels as well.

With these principles in mind we can now pass on to consideration of the interactive planning methodology itself.

7.4 IP METHODOLOGY

7.4.1 Introduction

There are five phases of interactive planning. These, however, must be regarded as constituting a systemic process, so the phases may be started in any order and none of the phases, let alone the whole process, should ever be regarded as completed. The five phases are:

- formulating the mess;
- ends planning;
- means planning;
- resource planning;
- design of implementation and control.

7.4.2 Formulating the Mess

During this stage "problems" and prospects, and threats and opportunities facing the organisation are highlighted. A recommended way of doing this is to work out the future the system *is currently in*. This is a projection of the future that the organisation would be faced with if it did nothing about things, and if developments in its environment continued in an entirely predictable way. Such a projection requires, according to Ackoff, three types of study:

- systems analysis—giving a detailed picture of the organisation and how it works, who it affects and how, and its relationship with its environment;
- an obstruction analysis—setting out any obstacles to corporate development;
- preparation of reference projections—which extrapolate on the organisation's present performance in order to predict future performance if nothing is done and trends in the environment continue as now.

Synthesising the results of these three types of study yields a reference scenario which is a formulation of the mess the organisation is currently in.

7.4.3 Ends Planning

Ends planning concerns specifying the ends to be pursued in terms of ideals, objectives and goals. The process begins with "idealised design", which is both the most unique and most essential feature of Ackoff's approach. An idealised design is a design for the organisation which the relevant stakeholders would replace the existing system with today if they were free to do so. An idealised design is prepared by going through three steps:

- selecting a mission—which is a general-purpose statement incorporating the organisation's responsibilities to its environment and stakeholders, and propounding a vision of what the organisation could be like which generates commitment;
- specifying desired properties of the design—a comprehensive list of the desired properties stakeholders agree should be built into the system;
- designing the system—setting out how all the specified properties of the idealised design can be obtained.

It is desirable to go through these steps twice to prepare two idealised designs—one constrained, assuming no changes in the wider containing "system", the other unconstrained (i.e. with changes in the containing system allowed). If the differences between the two versions are great, then the organisation will clearly have to concentrate much effort in bringing about changes in the so-called "wider system" during the rest of the planning process.

Idealised design is meant to generate maximum creativity among all the stakeholders involved. To ensure this, only two types of constraint upon the design are admissible. First, it must be technologically feasible, not a work of science fiction. It must be possible with known technology or likely technological developments; but it should not, for example, assume telepathy. Second, it must be operationally viable. It should be capable of working and surviving if it were implemented. Constraints of a financial, political or similar kind are not allowed to restrict the creativity of the design.

Ackoff is equally clear that the aim of idealised design is not to produce a Utopia which specifies what the "system" should be like for all time. This would not be sensible since the values of stakeholders, and what they hold to be ideal, are bound to change. Hence they should be able constantly to modify the "system". Nor would Utopia be possible, because the designers will not have at their disposal all the information and knowledge necessary to resolve some important design issues or to predict the state of the organisation's environment far into the future. For all these reasons, it is essential that the designed system be capable of rapid learning and adaptation. It must be highly flexible and be constantly seeking to improve its own performance. In short, what is intended is the design of the best "ideal-seeking system" that the stakeholders can imagine. This will certainly not be static, like a Utopia, but will be in constant flux as it responds to changing values, new knowledge and information, and buffeting from external forces.

An "ideal-seeking system" obviously requires a very particular kind of organisational design, capable of rapid and effective learning and adaptation. Ackoff, in fact,, supplies an outline for such a "responsive, decision system". This contains five essential functions:

- identification and formulation of problems (threats and opportunities);
- decision making—determining what to do about the threats and opportunities;
- implementation—doing it;
- control—monitoring performance and modifying actions to prevent repetition of any mistakes;
- acquisition or generation, and distribution of the information necessary to carry out the other functions.

There are further recommendations in Ackoff's work about the design of appropriate management information systems, about issues of organisational structure (e.g. centralisation versus decentralisation) and, as we have seen, on how to achieve a participative organisation.

Those organisations willing to undertake idealised design should, according to Ackoff, reap considerable benefits. In particular, the process is said to:

- facilitate the participation of all stakeholders in the planning process;
- allow incorporation of the aesthetic values of the stakeholders into planning;
- generate a consensus among those who participate;
- release large amounts of suppressed creativity and harness it to individual and organisational development;
- expand participants' concept of feasibility, revealing that the biggest obstruction to the future we most desire is ourselves;
- ease implementation, since people are more inclined to implement plans in which they have a say.

The remaining three stages of the planning process are directed at approximating the idealised design as closely as possible. We shall spend less time on them, and interested readers should consider Ackoff's own work, especially *Creating the Corporate Future*.

7.4.4 Means Planning

The output of Stage 1 of interactive planning was a reference scenario, setting out the future the organisation is currently locked into if it does nothing and if the environment does not change its behaviour drastically. The output from Stage 2 was an "idealised design" setting out in detail the future the organisation would like to have. During Stage 3, means planning, policies and proposals are generated and examined with a view to deciding whether they are capable of helping to fill the gap between the desired future and the way the future looks like being at the moment. Creativity is needed to discover ways of bringing the organisation towards the desirable future invented by its stakeholders. Alternative means to reach the specified ends must be carefully evaluated and a selection made.

7.4.5 Resource Planning

During this stage of planning, Ackoff recommends that four types of resource should be taken into account:

- inputs—materials, supplies, energy and services;
- facilities and equipment—capital investments;
- personnel;
- money.

For each type of resource, questions have to be asked in relation to the chosen means. For example, it must be determined how much of each resource is required, when it will be required, and how it can be obtained if it is not already held.

7.4.6 Design of Implementation and Control

This "final" phase of interactive planning concerns itself with seeing that all the decisions made hitherto are carried out. "Who is to do what, when, where and how?" is decided. Implementation is achieved and continually monitored to ensure that plans are being realised and that desired results are being achieved. The outcome is fed back into the planning process so that learning is possible and improvements can be devised.

So much for the philosophy and principles behind interactive planning and the details of the methodology, we now need to see it at work.

7.5 IP IN ACTION: THE EXAMPLE OF SUPER FRESH

7.5.1 Introduction

In this section we are going to consider an interactive planning consultancy worked on by members of INTERACT, the Institute for

Interactive Management. We are indebted to A. Barstow for allowing us to include his account of this project in the book.

7.5.2 Super Fresh

In 1982, the Great Atlantic & Pacific Tea Company (A & P) supermarket chain closed over 40 stores in the Philadelphia area, resulting in the loss of more than 2000 jobs. Volume-driven profits based on very narrow margins, the historical pattern in food retailing, were under pressure from a changing environment.

A & P had been in trouble nationwide from the early 1970s. Mounting losses had resulted in several changes in management and ownership, and the number of stores had been cut from around 3500 in 1970 to near 1000 in 1982. In 1979, A & P was acquired by Tengelmann, a large German food merchandiser. The new corporate strategy was to scale down A & P and to increase the rate of return on the chain's remaining assets. A higher proportionate return on equity became the new bottom line.

In the Philadelphia area, A & P considered its major problem to be the high labour costs of its unionised workforce. Despite high sales per employee, as compared to the rest of the industry, labour costs were higher than average: 15% of operating revenues as opposed to 10% for the industry. A & P began layoffs, which, due to seniority clauses in the labour contracts, affected mostly part-time, younger, and lower-salaried workers.

Early in February 1982, Wendall Young, President of Local 1357 of the United Food and Commercial Workers (UFCW), contacted several consultants to discuss the then-pending closure of the Philadelphia stores and to consider possible ways forward. Local 1357, which represented most of the employees of A & P, had already lost 40% of its members because of numerous supermarket and department store closings within the previous few years. Young knew the situation was critical, but he had a plan: to accumulate a large fund of employee contributions, and to borrow whatever was necessary beyond that to buy 21 of the soon-to-be closed stores.

With the facilitation of outside consultants, the Union began to use mess formulation techniques to outline the issues facing the proposed plan. The participants in the process emphasised the need to reform management policy and practice, regardless of who was managing. After all, the primary interest of Young and the UFCW locals was to protect the jobs of A & P employees and to avoid the impact that mass closing would have on the Union's pension fund.

The key role for the external consultants was to assist Union leadership in educating its members about the need for the Union to change its traditional roles, in the face of a changing environment. There was considerable scepticism and questioning about whether such education would be a proper role for the Union, and whether sufficient knowledge and expertise were available to make the plan work. The main question for A & P management was whether the union could succeed where the company had failed.

Despite reservations among some of its top officers, Local 1357 made its bid to buy 21 of the stores on 2 March 1982. Two weeks later it was announced that 600 members had pledged $5000 each as seed money to build a purchase fund. This was a radical departure from traditional union roles such as organising, bargaining, and pension administration.

In time it became clear that the union plan to buy 21 stores was not feasible. The union and its outside consultant designed a new idealised plan, which became known as the "Quality of Work Life Plan". Its prominent feature was worker participation in management of the stores. The new position taken by Union Local 1357 caused A & P to rethink its position and consider alternatives to mass closings.

A & P recognised that the workers had invaluable knowledge, hitherto untapped, about the operations of the stores. A & P executives became more receptive to the concept of worker participation in management, and in sharing earnings that might be realised by revising provisions in the existing labour contract concerning wages, hours and benefits. A & P agreed to consider the plan.

The ends planning phase of interactive planning and management was used to design the Super Fresh Quality of Work Life programme. Both union and management participated in the design of a structure that could realise the intent of their agreement: that the Company shall share power with the employees.

The development of the programme can be described in two stages: design and implementation. In the first stage, idealised design, approximately 30 people were involved. Included were corporate employees from A & P and Super Fresh employees, from the president and store managers to full-time and part-time hourly employees, and staff from the Union locals. All meetings included representatives from both labour and management.

Three groups were formed, each of which generated an idealised design of a supermarket chain. These groups were then reshuffled into two groups, each of which produced a synthesis of the designs. These two designs were synthesised by a smaller working group. This design was then presented to the original 30, who after a few modifications, approved it. The final design was printed in a pamphlet entitled, "Quality of Work Life for United Food & Commercial Workers Local 56 and Local 1357 with Super Fresh Food Markets".

A system of "Planning Boards" was proposed. This provides the opportunity for all employees to participate in the planning of the corporation by means of a structured management system throughout the organisation. Planning Boards are formed at every level of management, with every manager heading a Board whose membership includes his or her manager. Each Board is responsible for the horizontal coordination of the activities within its unit. Vertical integration ensured the presence of three management levels on each Board. There is direct contact and interaction with as many as five levels of management, since most managers will serve on Boards in each of three capacities: manager, manager's manager, and member.

A & P and UFCW Locals 1357 and 56 reached an agreement incorporating this plan in May 1982. *The New York Times* (22 May 1982) called it an agreement for a "new life" for the A & P chain. The agreement had three innovative features.

- A & P agreed to reopen 21 stores as units in a newly created subsidiary. The new chain was named Super Fresh Food Markets, Inc.
- Profit sharing was accomplished through the Employee Incentive and Investment Fund. Every store that succeeded in keeping its yearly labour costs below 10% of operating revenues would receive 1% of the store's gross sales apportioned among eligible employees according to the number of hours each worked in the course of the year. An employee became eligible after a period of one year. The 1% share would be reduced if labour costs exceeded 10% of revenues and would be increased if labour costs fell below 9%.
- Management and the unions agreed to utilise a Quality of Work Life (QWL) structure to provide a mutual basis for "problem solving", which was to be implemented concurrently with the opening of the stores. It was further decided to utilise mutually agreed upon outside sources to provide guidance and advice to increase the effectiveness of this programme.

To attain these innovative features the union conceded three main things.

- Total compensation was to be reduced through several methods, including a 20% wage cut, the elimination of various overtime provisions, and reductions in vacation time.
- A permanent two-tiered wage system was introduced, whereby new hires received lower wages and fewer benefits for work equivalent to that performed by higher-paid existing employees.

- Chainwide seniority and transfer rights for all employees were conceded.

The results in this case were remarkable. In the face of store closings, conflict was dissolved and a new venture based on management–union co-operation was created and realised. Super Fresh opened its 29th store by December 1982 and hired 2015 workers during a period characterised by the highest unemployment rate since the Second World War. The original goals were 24 store openings and 2000 hired workers by the end of 1982. The very same stores that had been closed down only six months earlier began to establish record sales and profits almost every week. In June 1983, A & P announced its first profitable quarter in two years. In November 1986 A & P renamed its 47 Washington and Baltimore stores Super Fresh. As *Businessweek* said, and Tom Peters repeated in his book, *Thriving on Chaos*, "A & P's rivals said [it was] crazy to offer one percent bonuses in a business where profit margins aren't much larger. But the dividends from the Philadelphia experience have silenced them."

7.6 CRITIQUE OF IP

Theory

(a) We begin with some very positive points. It will be obvious from what has been said about Ackoff's writings, and the work done in Chapter 1 of this book on metaphors, that much of the power of interactive planning stems from its ability to address a wide range of possible organisational "problems" as revealed by a number of systems metaphors. Ackoff uses some very insightful metaphors in considering how to respond to organisational problems in the "systems age". He is not happy that looking at corporations as machines or organisms is very productive in the present situation. He wants to replace this thinking with the idea that organisations are "purposeful systems", containing other "purposeful systems" and being part of "wider purposeful systems". This new vision, as it is expressed in the detail of the interactive planning approach, seems to combine much of the best that can be gleaned from the brain metaphor with considerable inputs from the culture and coalition metaphors as well.

   The idea of the organisation as a brain leads to, and supports, the emphasis upon learning and adaptation. The stakeholder view of the organisation, evinced by Ackoff, simply restates the perspective of the pluralist version of the political situation—the coalition metaphor as we named it. Idealised design is all about developing a strong organisational culture shared by all the participants and which encourages maximum creativity.

The same broad (and deep) response to organisational problems is revealed when we relate Ackoff's work to our "system of systems methodologies" set out in Chapter 2. Interactive planning is an ambitious attempt to handle simultaneously both the complexity of the problem situations facing modern organisations and the pluralism which inevitably follows from their serving diverse stakeholders.

(b) We must now consider if there are any problem situations for which the theory of interactive planning does not equip it adequately. If we begin by asking what systems metaphors interactive planning does not employ, and what assumptions it does not make about problem contexts, we shall quite quickly be able to grasp the essentials of a persistent line of critical assault that has been launched at Ackoff's work. It seems as though interactive planning fails to take account of the possible existence of coercive situations in organisations (simple–coercive and complex–coercive problem contexts). If participants are in a coercive relationship to each other, they do not share common interests, their values and beliefs are likely to conflict, they cannot agree upon ends and means and "genuine" compromise under present systemic arrangements is not possible. The only reason the "system" holds together is because of the existence of coercive forces binding the less powerful into it. A couple of more detailed critical points follow from this.

(c) It is argued that Ackoff's work is set squarely in a consensus world view. He believes that there is a basic community of interest among stakeholders which makes them willing to enter into interactive planning and to participate freely and openly in idealised design. There are no fundamental conflicts of interest between "system", "super-system" and "sub-systems" which cannot be dissolved by appealing to this basic community of interests. Ackoff, then, denies the existence of fundamental conflict and, according to critics, has to deny its existence. If irreconcilable conflict between stakeholders were frequent (as some assert it is) then his methodology would be impotent because no agreement could be reached in such cases concerning the idealised future. For Ackoff, conflict is only "apparent" ; it can be resolved at a higher level of desirability when people contemplate the desirable future they share in common. The critics argue that conflict is endemic in many social and organisational systems, and that incompatibility of ends is not rare. It is easy to see that some social systems operate in ways which make it impossible for different groups all to achieve their ends.

Ackoff does not think very much of the critics' argument. He observes that he has not in his work come across the "irresolvable conflicts" that the critics talk about. All the conflicts he has met, he has been able to address with the interactive planning approach. He suspects that the critics merely assert that such conflicts exist. If they went out and tried to use interactive planning on conflicts they see as irresolvable, they might find out differently. But they are unlikely to do so because this might shatter a dogma they value more than the truth.

(d) Ackoff's work is further criticised because of its alleged failure to come to terms with "structural" features of social reality such as conflict and power. No reference is made to structural inequalities in organisations determining conflict. For Ackoff, conflict seems always to be at the ideological level and is essentially dealt with by ideological manipulation. Perhaps it is possible temporarily to alleviate conflict at the ideological level by getting people to believe they have interests in common. But the "subjective" belief of groups about their interests does not necessarily coincide with their objective interests. Permanent reconciliation of conflicts between stakeholders would need to be in terms of objective and not merely subjective interests. This point links to Ackoff's lack of attention to power relationships in organisations. Power can operate in very subtle and covert ways. It can mean that some issues never reach the agenda for debate. It can mean that some groups suffer from "false consciousness" and fail to recognise and represent their own interests properly. Wherever structurally based conflict and power relationships exist in organisations, they can severely affect the way interactive planning is used and the results it brings. It seems, to the critics, that Ackoff takes no account of these matters; that his approach is not, therefore, useful in coercive contexts.

Ackoff simply does not accept the existence of the "structural" aspects of social reality that the critics discuss. The chief obstruction between people and the future they most desire is, for him, the people themselves, and their limited ability to think creatively and imaginatively. Provide people with a mission, with a mobilising idea, and the structural constraints on their development can largely be overcome.

Methodology

It is argued by the critics that it is only because Ackoff believes in a basically consensual social world that he is able to believe in the efficacy of participation as the remedy for so many difficult organisational issues.

Participation is essential to interactive planning: philosophically because it provides the justification for believing in the "objectivity" of the results, and practically because it generates creativity and commitment and ensures implementation. Perhaps because of its significance, Ackoff plays down the obstacles to full and effective participation. To get started, interactive planning depends on all the stakeholders being prepared to enter into participative planning concerning the future. But will the powerful be willing to forego their dominant position and submit their privileges to the vagaries of idealised design?

Ackoff replies that full participation may certainly meet with some resistance from powerful stakeholders. But there are ways around this, such as by introducing other stakeholders as consultants first, then gradually increasing their role. In any case, the criticism that full and equal participation cannot be immediately realised is a poor reason for not making whatever progress can be made.

Ideology

(a) Even if interactive planning can be got underway, the critics suggest, another difficulty will be encountered. Interactive planning depends for the objectivity of its results on free and open discussion between stakeholders. But planning is complex and time consuming. We cannot realistically expect that less privileged stakeholders will be able to participate equally in the planning process. Any discussion or debate among stakeholders can only be exceptionally constrained. The less privileged will feel threatened by the massive resources that can be mobilised by the powerful. In intellectual terms, they may find themselves under the sway of a "dominant ideology" through which they fail altogether to recognise their own true interests. Whatever help the analyst can give to less fortunate groups, the various stakeholders will enter the process of interactive planning with widely divergent intellectual, political and economic resources. In coercive contexts, therefore, the results of interactive planning will favour the powerful; it is impossible for Ackoff's methodology to bring about the "objectivity" for which he hopes.

(b) It is further argued that Ackoff's belief in a consensual social world, and in the efficacy of participation, is sustained because he artificially limits the scope of his projects so as not to challenge his clients' or sponsors' fundamental interests. If the position of powerful stakeholders is not threatened by idealised design, because significant issues are kept off the agenda for debate, then the powerful might well be willing to let other groups participate. And it might seem that all stakeholders share common interests.

If, however, Ackoff were to broaden his studies to challenge the hierarchical nature of organisations, the ultimate decision-making rights of powerful stakeholders, or the unequal distribution of organisational resources to different stakeholders, then he would soon provoke conflicts which revealed deep status and economic inequalities in organisations which could not be spirited away by idealised design.

Ackoff responds that he makes what changes are possible in the circumstances prevailing. Better this than wait for some judgement day when all wrongs can be corrected. If he works with managers, then that is because they are often the most enlightened group and can see that benefiting other stakeholders will also benefit themselves.

Utility

(a) Ackoff has demonstrated the usefulness of interactive planning as a practical systems approach in hundreds of projects with organisations of all types in the United States and elsewhere. It has been one of our jobs, in the critique, to try to understand from the theoretical point of view why interactive planning is so successful. We have demonstrated that the theory underpinning Ackoff's work is itself powerful and that this is the primary reason for the success of interactive planning. This prevents cynics claiming that it is not interactive planning but something about Ackoff himself, his personality perhaps, which leads to the success of his projects.

(b) Our critique sections are also designed to help us specify in what circumstances methodologies might not work. The debate between Ackoff and his critics cannot be finally decided here. Ackoff asserts that the social world is basically consensual, his critics assert that it is characterised by power imbalances, structural conflict and the existence of "false consciousness". From the TSI perspective, however, interactive planning does seem to ignore important aspects of some organisations that are revealed by the political metaphor in its coercive (prison) setting (and by considering coercive problem contexts). The reader must decide whether his or her view of organisations (as guided by the metaphors) leads him/her to feel the need for a systems methodology more in tune with the coercive perspective; or whether Ackoff's interactive planning seems adequate.

7.7 CASE STUDY: A COFFEE SELLING ORGANISATION

7.7.1 Introduction

The following recounts the main features of post-computerisation in the Sales department of a coffee selling organisation. As you will see, the situation is far from *ideal* for any of the parties concerned. The Managing Director has decided to call in consultants. Other main actors, as you will discover, are the Sales Manager, Sales Coordinator, MIS/finance Manageress, and a variety of customers. The task that you are asked to tackle follows.

7.7.2 Your Task

This task is best approached by a group. If possible, therefore, read the information below and then organise yourselves so that you represent about five relevant actors. Think very hard about the perception and needs of the actor you are playing, of course injecting your own knowledge and understanding. Then, with one person acting as an interactive planning oriented consultant and facilitator, pass through the methodology. Formulate the mess (look for problems and prospects, and threats and opportunities), carry out ends planning (look for ends to be pursued in terms of ideals, objectives and goals), carry out means planning (generate policies and proposals and examine them considering how well they help to meet the desired future), and then focus on resource planning (how much is required, when, and how can it be obtained).

After you have completed these tasks, reflect upon how well the group operated, and whether any hidden agendas were at work.

7.7.3 A Coffee Selling Organisation

Hull Far East's main business in Hong Kong comes from the selling of coffee that they package in a factory. There are three main divisions in Hull Far East. They are Production, Far East Sales and Hong Kong Sales. The Far East Sales division is responsible for market development in the Far East: namely, places like Singapore, Taiwan and Korea.

Our main concern is the local distribution department of the Hong Kong Sales division. Operations in this department is broken up into Hotels, Agents, Fast Food Restaurants and Supermarkets. So far the local agents' orders constitute the biggest share of the sales of coffee and food products. Of late, however, there is an increasing demand from hotels and fast food restaurants.

The orders from the local agents and supermarkets have always been in large quantities and they would place orders well in advance of the need date. The orders that are coming from hotels and fast food restaurants are usually placed the day before or on the same morning as the goods are required. Although the actual orders from these sectors are small, the frequency of orders is high.

There is a changing profile in the market demand. This is evident in the hotels and fast food restaurants business. The contribution to the sales of Hull Hong Kong from these sectors rose from 10% a year ago to approximately 25% today. But to remain competitive in these business sectors, Hull Hong Kong must be able to cope effectively and efficiently with orders from customers. It is important that orders from these sectors are properly serviced as the increasing contribution from the sales to these two sectors indicates the growing importance of these markets to the company.

All orders throughout Hong Kong are made by phone via the Sales Coordinator. Prior to computerisation, sales orders were taken down manually by the Sales Coordinator and were then issued out to the storekeeper before delivery to the customers next day. Normally, orders that arrived before noon were delivered by the next morning.

After computerisation, there was an apparent increase in the work to be carried out by the Sales Coordinator. The sales orders that arrived before noon were not now being delivered until two days later. This caused considerable inconvenience to customers, some of whom (e.g. hotels) do not keep stocks of coffee.

Although Hull Far East is the leading supplier of coffee in the region, the Sales Manager is worried that the competition is gaining market share at a rapid pace. This is especially true because of their ability to offer cheaper coffee and a better delivery service. He is also firm in his belief that the backlog of sales orders has arisen because of cumbersome procedures introduced in computerisation. These, he argues, are the main cause of his mediocre sales performance.

The Sales Coordinator pointed out that the computerisation had introduced a lot of manual work. For example:

- the manual sorting of invoices printed by the computer to go along with the delivery orders which were sorted according to the different vans;
- having continuously to refer to customer files to obtain customer account numbers before being able to process the orders;
- time spent in altering and changing form sizes on the printer for invoices;
- manual checking of the finished goods stock quantity by the Sales

Coordinator before order confirmation. This was done because the finished goods stock figures on the computer were of questionable accuracy.

The Sales Coordinator also noted that the MIS/finance Manageress felt the need to do computer back-up and batch update around noon time. This caused the computer to be inaccessible to the users for two hours. The processing of sales orders, as a result, could not be completed during the morning.

The MIS/finance Manageress, for her part, has shown great pride in the computerisation project undertaken by her MIS department. She feels that the users are at fault for not communicating their requirements clearly to her earlier. She strongly maintains that the chosen package, which was supported by Headquarters in the United Kingdom, is the best package for Hull Far East. There is a very strong sense of ownership by the MIS/finance department over the use of the new computer system, but the same feeling is missing in the other departments, namely Production and Sales.

The Managing Director wants the issues arising from the computerisation to be addressed quickly by outside consultants.

One of the departments identified by the Managing Director as "difficult" was the Sales department, especially the order processing area. The Order Processing section had as its responsibility the following duties:

- ensuring order entry for each sales order;
- preparing delivery orders for the store people;
- invoicing customers;
- scheduling daily delivery;
- ensuring that customers have not exceeded their credit limits—if they had, clearance would be needed from the Sales Manager before proceeding with the delivery; and
- planning the delivery schedule/route for the three delivery vans.

The key problems identified were:

- a reduction in efficiency of the order processing operation resulting in delays in dispatch;
- additional workloads especially at month-end; and
- apparent lack of benefits to the users as a result of computerisation.

The Sales department comprises the Sales Manager, six sales executives, one assistant manager in charge of products, one secretary for the Sales Manager and the Sales Coordinator.

Usually the Sales Coordinator is responsible for the main coordination of the whole order processing operations. She is also responsible for mailing credit notes to customers and liaising with the Accounts section for payment notification. On many occasions in the past, she received help from the secretary with some of her order processing functions due to work overload. Recently the old secretary resigned and a new appointment was made. The Sales Manager felt that the new secretary should not help to do the order entry job, but should concentrate on secretarial duties which had increased due to the introduction of new products. The Sales Manager felt that he should be allowed to employ a sales clerk to help the Sales Coordinator in her duties. The Managing Director disagreed.

7.8 FURTHER READING

- Ackoff's main works relevant to this text are:

Ackoff, R. L. (1974). *Redesigning the Future*, Wiley, New York.
Ackoff, R. L. (1978). *The Art of Problem Solving*, Wiley, New York.
Ackoff, R. L. (1981). *Creating the Corporate Future*, Wiley, New York.

- Also of considerable interest on interactive planning are:

Ackoff, R. L. (1981). The art and science of mess management, *Interfaces*, **11**, 20–26.
Ackoff, R. L. (1983). Beyond prediction and preparation, *Journal of Management Studies*, **20**, 59–69.
Barstow, A. (1990). On creating opportunity out of conflict: Two case studies, *Systems Practice*, **3**, 339–55.

- For the critique of Ackoff see:

Jackson, M. C. (1982). The nature of soft systems thinking: The work of Churchman, Ackoff and Checkland, *Journal of Applied Systems Analysis*, **9**, 17–28.
Ackoff, R. L. (1982). On the hard headedness and soft heartedness of M. C. Jackson, *Journal of Applied Systems Analysis*, **9**, 31–3.
Jackson, M. C. (1983). The nature of soft systems thinking: Comments on the three replies, *Journal of Applied Systems Analysis*, **10**, 109–13.

- Further insights into Ackoff's life and works can be found in the special *Festschrift* issue of *Systems Practice*, Volume 3, Number 2, published in April 1990.

Chapter 8

Soft Systems Methodology (SSM)

A trap is a trap only for creatures which cannot solve the problem that it sets. Man-traps are dangerous only in relation to the limitations on what men can see and value and do. The nature of the trap is a function of the nature of the trapped. To describe either is to imply the other.
Sir G. Vickers, *Freedom in a Rocking Boat* (Part I, The Trap)

8.1 INTRODUCTION

C. West Churchman and Russell L. Ackoff in the 1950s and 1960s were pioneers in the social systems sciences. Churchman developed a powerful philosophical base which, as we have seen, provided the grounding on which the methodological principles of strategic assumption surfacing and testing (SAST, explored in Chapter 6) were constructed and, as we will find out, provided much of the inspiration behind critical systems heuristics (unravelled in Chapter 9). Ackoff pursued a more practically directed career, culminating in his work with INTERACT (Institute for Interactive Management) in Philadelphia. Neither of these huge contributors to soft systems thinking has lost sight of his original intent, to work with complex issues while acknowledging the subjective appreciations of human participants. Churchman's and Ackoff's contributions have been covered in the previous two chapters..Soft systems is not complete and does not finish with these remarkable contributions, however.

Emerging in the 1970s and developing in the 1980s was a new brand of soft systems thinking. Also inspired by Churchman's work, Peter Checkland began to explore systems engineering methodology, applying it to messy managerial situations rather than to so-called structured problems, with the intent of finding out whether this approach could be appropriately evolved and employed in "soft" systems situations. As the investigations proceeded a number of key "discoveries" began to crystallise. These were to lead to a wholly different approach to soft "problem solving", soft systems methodology (SSM), as we shall discover in this chapter.

Essentially, SSM has been developed for use in ill-structured or messy problem contexts where there is no clear view on what "constitutes the problem", or what action should be taken to overcome the difficulties being experienced. In fact, SSM in action should prevent decision makers from rushing into poorly thought-out solutions based on preconceived ideas about an assumed problem.

In terms of the logic of this book, SSM would be considered redundant in unitary contexts where there is genuine agreement about what should be done, although not necessarily how to do it. Time spent on drawing out possible other ways forward that may offer potential benefit, which is a main strength of SSM, would largely be wasted. In the case study in Chapter 5, using viable system diagnosis, the issue was organisation "now, or bust", a priority that was grasped through the "creativity" phase of TSI. The company concerned would have benefited little at that time from a soft systems study. In coercive contexts, it is impossible to generate mutual understanding, another key feature and strength of SSM, because of the effects of power which can completely undermine any interpretative process of enquiry. SSM is, therefore, best employed in pluralist contexts, where there is a basic compatibility of interests, where values and beliefs of participants diverge and yet where genuine accommodation and compromise is possible. Further, since systems (in fact organismic) models are always used in the methodological scheme, SSM clearly assumes that pluralistic issues are tied in with complex issues of organisational structure and process. SSM finds its legitimacies and avoids its limitations in complex–pluralist problem contexts.

The new insights of SSM and the effects that these had on soft "problem solving" will now be considered in the details of the philosophy, principles and methodology of SSM.

8.2 PHILOSOPHY OF SSM

Churchman's understanding of subjectivity leads to the conclusion that the results of systems interventions receive their guarantee from the maximum participation of those involved; the "sweep in" principle as it has been called. Adopting a systems approach involves discovering this and also going on to realise that every world view is terribly restricted. Churchman's development of these ideas has clearly taken an ethical route, dealing with issues arising for future generations and opposition to the ideas from religion, aesthetics and politics. This left the way open for someone sagacious enough to explore the notion of subjectivity in a more pragmatic way, by asking questions about the different ways people perceive problem situations, how these can be represented and how learning can be generated from this. Focusing on this line of development, however, ran the risk of sidestepping potent ethical and political issues. As we shall see in the critique of SSM later in this chapter, this is precisely the reason why SSM helps in pluralist but not in coercive contexts. Werner Ulrich, however, took a greater interest in Churchman's ethical line of thought and hence developed an approach that would be more appropriate in problem contexts where, for example, political and coercive forces are at work. Ulrich's contribution, critical systems heuristics, is deferred for further discussion until Chapter 9. Now let us consider Checkland's "discoveries".

The revelations that have wooed a large number of contemporary systems thinkers are threefold and, not surprisingly, are related. They can be summarised in the following way.

- Hard systems approaches are fundamentally based on a means–end approach.
- "System" as a concept or notion is best employed as a means of organising our thoughts about problem situations, rather than as a way of describing in a real sense portions of reality.
- There are two paradigms, hard and soft, based on contrasting assumptions that lead to very different methodological principles.

We will now explore each of these important observations.

The philosophy of SSM breaks away from the traditional, hard view of the nature of problems. The hard view regards problems as real and solvable, assuming that ends are easily and objectively definable. The primary concern of hard methodologies, therefore, is how we should reach predefined ends, what are the best means available, or "*How* should we do it?" SSM, by contrast, believes that problem situations arise when people have contrasting views on the "same situation". The notion of a plurality of possible viewpoints, and consequently acceptance of many "relevant problems" emerges. SSM, therefore, rejects the means–end approach. The much more interesting questions concern the ends themselves: "*What* should be done?" becomes the main focus of SSM. To answer this question SSM attempts to draw in and explore a diversity of viewpoints as part of the decision-making and intervention process.

Another key observation that Checkland puts firmly on the agenda is that "system" as a concept is better reserved for ordered, abstract thinking about the world rather than as a way of stating how the world is. The argument is that as soon as we assume a world comprising systems then we will start investigating that world by looking for systems. Our methodologies will be system-seeking ones, even when we wish to study social situations. So we will inevitably identify functional social systems, be they organisations, groups of friends or, presumably, ethnic groups and nations. This is abhorrent to interpretive thinkers, such as Checkland, who understand social situations through action concepts (words that describe actions) which are meaningful in terms of social rules and practices (the described actions are understood through agreed interpretations of intentions or conventions) and constitutive meaning (fundamentally the reasoning why something should or should not be done in a particular way). Social dynamics, according to this formulation, are explained as the interrelationship between interpretations of humans, which significantly overlap, forming cultures. Cultures are exemplified by shared social rules, practices and constitutive meanings. Of course, in such social dynamics, there will be some areas where overlap is not as strong as others, nevertheless the conflict that then arises is containable within the cohesiveness of culture. No matter how deep the conflict may seem, the different interpretations are assumed not to be frozen, but very much open to change. Generation of mutual understanding will, therefore, be possible for the soft systems analyst and of course, as an issue, that has influenced the principles that underpin SSM. The idea of "system", therefore, is misconceived when employed as a functional goal-seeking means of stating what is, because it misses the essence of social dynamics, and is far better reserved as a means of organising our thoughts and transferring our ideas in a meaningful way to others.

It is probably the "means–end" and "system" discoveries that more than anything led Checkland to conclude that there are two paradigms in systems thinking, the second of which is the paradigm inhabited by SSM. With Paradigm 1, the hard paradigm, the real world is assumed to be systemic and the methodologies that we use to investigate that reality are systematic. The switch to Paradigm 2, the soft paradigm, turns things around stating that the real world is problematical but the process of enquiring into it, the methodologies, may be systemic. This transfers the notion of systemicity from the world to the process of enquiry into the world. For this profound observation the management and systems sciences are indebted to Checkland.

In essence it is the hard, machine, organismic and neurocybernetic assumptions about the nature of social reality which are rejected in favour of a soft culture-based view (although, as we shall see, organismic assumptions remain of secondary importance).

8.3 PRINCIPLES OF SSM

There are four main principles that a user should be aware of and remain aware of when employing SSM. These concern learning, culture, participation and the "two modes of thought".

SSM articulates a process of enquiry, it is a *learning* system that leads to purposeful action in a continuous cycle. This differs from hard systems approaches which adopt means–end directives, seeking to achieve preset goals. Checkland talks of SSM in terms of "management", seeking to achieve organised action, coping with an ever-changing flux of interacting events and ideas. Learning is about perceiving and evaluating parts of the flux before deciding and taking action, which then becomes a part of the flux with new perceptions, evaluations and actions emerging. These need to be learnt about as well. Learning, then, is like a never-ending cycle which has no beginning or end. There is, as Churchman pointed out, the need for Singerian enquiry where there are no clear starting or finishing points. With SSM, ways forward are decided upon in terms of relevance (to those involved), cultural feasibility (constraints that must be met) and systemic desirability (essential systems thinking that must not be violated).

Of these three "ways forward", *cultural* feasibility can be picked out as the peculiar and key feature of SSM, dominating or absorbing the notions of relevance and systemic desirability. The idea of culture powerfully guides the SSM user, stating categorically that there are organisational and/or social constraints in the "real world" which potential changes, recommended by intervention, must meet. This clearly reflects the philosophical base of SSM, particularly the idea of the cohesiveness of social rules and practices.

The interpretive grounding of SSM leads very strongly to the principle of *participation*. This is so important that we might go so far as to say that, without guaranteed participation of those involved, any application of SSM must be invalid in its own terms. What this means is that, given the validity of a wide variety of perceptions about a situation, it is not only desirable to encourage participation but in fact is necessary to do so if we are to stand any chance of bringing about successful results which can be justified and successfully implemented.

The process of SSM can be distinguished into *two modes of thought*: abstract and ideal systems thinking, and specific context-related "real world" thinking. One is a stream of logic-based enquiry, the other a stream of cultural enquiry. It is argued that these must remain distinct so that pure systems thinking can be carried out with the aim of developing ideal models for discussion. These must not be muddled in their development by reflecting upon and mixing in the messiness of the "real world" situation. The experienced user of SSM will move easily between the real world and the world of abstract systems thinking, but will remain conscious of making the shift.

Making sure that we keep these principles in mind, we will now move on to consider soft systems methodology as an approach to "problem solving".

8.4 SOFT SYSTEMS METHODOLOGY

8.4.1 Introduction

We shall now develop an appreciation of SSM. The methodology might be thought of as a seven stage process of enquiry. There is no predefined beginning or end in practice, although we will go through the process from Stage 1. The seven stages have been drawn up in diagrammatic form in Figure 8.1, but it must be noted that this is only one means of forming a structure through which the methodological process can be understood. It should not be conceived of as a linear progression. Checkland says that as long as the logical connections are kept in mind, the actual "problem solving" activity can move flexibly among the stages. An SSM user who has fully internalised the methodology may not use the stages to guide his/her activity at all, but simply employs the methodology as a point of reference to make sense of what is being done in the real world. This is what has recently been called a Mode II usage of SSM as opposed to the more formal Mode I procedure. In order to introduce the reader to the methodology we must present it Mode I style, in terms of seven stages. Let us, therefore, turn to those stages.

8.4.2 Stages 1 and 2: Finding Out

There are a number of methods that Checkland recommends for "finding out". First is to gather information about structure and processes by observation (e.g. informal analyst observation or more formal sampling procedures), collecting secondary data (e.g. minutes of committee meetings), and importantly through informal interviews. These findings can be summarised in a "rich picture". A rich picture is a cartoon-like expression which, in the spirit of such representations, allows for certain

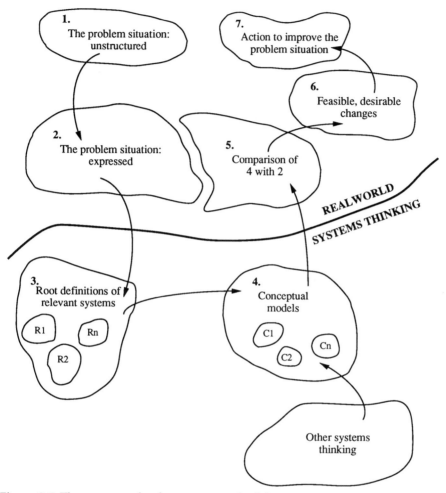

Figure 8.1 The process of soft systems methodology

issues, conflicts and other problematic and interesting features to be accentuated. The rich picture expression represents the climate of the situation. An example is given in Figure 8.2.

An alternative approach is to move on to Stages 3 and 4 of the methodology as a way of promoting Stages 1 and 2. This is done by developing "primary task" root definitions and conceptual models, which must be relevant to the situation, and then comparing these to the "real world", using the comparison to guide the finding out. Checkland notes, however, that this can direct subsequent thinking to a concern only for improving the efficiency of current operations.

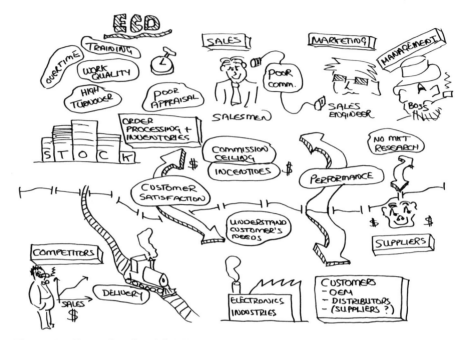

Figure 8.2 Example of a rich picture

A third approach currently being explored uses three types of analysis. The first takes the intervention in the situation as its subject matter, considering "clients" (who cause the intervention to take place) and "would-be problem solvers" (who conduct the study). The latter develop a list of possible people who could be considered "problem owners". Analyses 2 and 3 draw upon two different metaphors, a culture metaphor and a narrowly defined power metaphor. Analysis 2 is "social system" analysis of roles, norms, etc. Analysis 3 is "political system" analysis based on the idea that power can be understood as the exchange of commodities of power in organisations. Analyses 1, 2 and 3 make up the stream of cultural enquiry—a review of the context within which the methodology is being used. This enquiry continues, of course, throughout the study.

From the rich picture, or one of the other ways of finding out, a number of themes surface which can then be captured as a set of relevant viewpoints, or "relevant systems". This part of the process is effectively interfacing the two modes of thought, systems thinking and "real world" thinking, where themes of context-related "real world" thinking become relevant systems of idealised abstract systems thinking. A number of diverse relevant systems are generated. These will mostly be developed into ideal "root definitions" and "conceptual models", before being brought back into the "real world" for context-related examination.

8.4.3 Stage 3: Formulating Root Definitions

While Stages 1 and 2 help in the creation of diverse relevant systems, which are pure views of purposeful activity that may promote action for improvement in the problem situation, Stage 3 is concerned with expanding each of these into concise well formulated verbal statements. Each statement will be quickly tried out by moving around Stages 2–5, as the systemic learning principle underlying SSM recommends. A root definition is an idealised view of what a relevant system should be. The aim is to draw out the essence of what is to be done, why it is to be done, who is to do it, who is to benefit or suffer from it and what environmental constraints limit the actions and activities. This is achieved by formulating the statement around six elements:

- Customers—the victims/beneficiaries of the purposeful activity.
- Actors—those who do the activities.
- Transformation process—the purposeful activity which transforms an input into an output.
- Weltanschauung—the view of the world that makes the definition meaningful (i.e. the constitutive meaning as discussed under the philosophy of SSM).
- Owners—who can stop the activity.
- Environmental constraints—those constraints in its environment that this system takes as given.

These are easy to recall using the CATWOE mnemonic.

Two tips are worth noting. First, that the formulation of root definitions most easily falls into place if Ts (transformations) and Ws (Weltanschauungen) are considered first. In other words, "What is the core process at work in the idealised system and what is it doing?" and "Why is this being done?" Second, when deciding upon T, be very careful to ensure that the output is clearly something which can be transformed from the input. For example, it is simply nonsense to think of people being transformed into money—what kind of physical process could achieve that?

Root definitions taken forward should include "primary task" examples, built around officially declared tasks and more controversial "issue based" examples (leading to systems not likely to be institutionalised in the "real world"). These can then be translated into conceptual models.

8.4.4 Stage 4: Building Conceptual Models

Whereas the root definition from Stage 3 is an account of what the idealised system is, the "conceptual model" built directly from the root definition, in Stage 4, is an account of the activities which the ideal system must do in order to fulfil the requirements of the root definition. A hint here: if there is one rule in SSM, then that rule states conceptual models *must* be developed from their relevant root definitions and from nothing else.

A conceptual model is constructed by drawing out the minimum number of verbs that are necessary to describe the activities that would have to be present to carry out the task named in the root definition. These are then logically ordered according to how they depend on each other and how they would work together in the "real system". These "human activity system" models will at the first stage of their development contain around seven verbs. A usual feature is to have a number of verbs, in one sub-system, concerned with the operations of the system, and a couple of other verbs, in another sub-system, concerned with monitoring and controlling and thus the long-term viability of the system. The basic model of around seven verbs can, if necessary, be expanded to higher levels of resolution by taking each activity within it as the source for a new root definition and conceptual model. Having formulated conceptual models it is often useful to think ahead to what comparisons with the "real world" they are likely to yield. This saves unnecessary time being spent on conceptual models unlikely to provide interesting comparisons at Stage 5 and provoke useful debate at later stages. If none of the models seems particularly interesting, or provoking, the user of the methodology has to back-track to Stages 2 and 3 to formulate new relevant systems and root definitions.

8.4.5 Stage 5: Comparing Models and "Reality"

The aim behind the comparison stage is essentially to generate debate about possible changes that could be made to bring about improvements in the problem situation. It is argued that differences between the idealised models and "reality" highlight likely changes that would have to be made in order that reality better reflects the pure systems thinking contained in the models. This may challenge some basic assumptions held by participants and lead to alternatives that may not have been considered outside of the SSM process. Checkland has outlined various ways of making full use of the potential of comparison.

First, we may take a number of models and look for the main differences that stand out against current perceptions. Second, and more thoroughly, a formal listing of differences can be made for each conceptual model and annotated with questions for which answers are sought in the situation itself. For example, "Does this activity exist in the real world?" "How well is it done?", etc. Third is the idea of scenario writing, a dry run on paper describing how the system captured in the conceptual model is expected to behave into the future (a sort of immensely "weak" qualitative system dynamics simulation). The output which is the scenario, it is suggested, can be compared to any knowledge of such events in the past by those in the problem situation. Fourth, a model of the part of reality similar to the model can be constructed, with a view to mapping between the two which might highlight significant differences worthy of discussion. These four means of comparison naturally lead on to, or integrate with, the process of defining changes.

8.4.6 Stage 6: Defining Changes

The carrying out of "model-reality" comparisons inevitably involves consideration of possible changes. The kinds of change considered, however, are not necessarily black and white choices such as, "Is this desirable feature of the model in the 'real world'?" No, then it must be introduced. That could happen, but the models are not constructed as blue-prints for design. The real point, Checkland would stress, is that the models are meant for generating meaningful debate where participants discuss potential improvements that are worthy of consideration. By this time, we have ensured that the models conform to systemic desirability (since they have emerged from the logic-based stream of enquiry) and we have some idea of whether they are culturally feasible (we have been carrying out cultural enquiry). The debate stages finally confirm which changes are indeed culturally feasible in this organisation at this time. We may then be in a position to take action.

8.4.7 Stage 7: Taking Action

Taking action means implementing changes that are both desirable and feasible. Often such changes can be classified as attitudinal, structural and procedural. It is proposed that we may want to use SSM to develop a system by which the defined changes may be implemented.

8.4.8 Conclusion

SSM is essentially a means of introducing some ordered, structured systems thinking into the flux of events and actions that is everyday life. It is doubly systemic since it promotes a systemic learning process, orchestrating different appreciations of the situation, which is never-ending, and it also introduces systems models as part of that learning process. The systemic learning process aims to create a temporarily shared culture in which conflicts are accommodated so that action can be taken. It is governed by the culture metaphor. The supporting systems models of possible human activity systems are primarily organismic in nature, although alternatives have been explored. The aim of introducing systems thinking in this way into everyday decision making is to promote rigour. It allows continous checking of new avenues of exploration and back-tracking when blind alleys are discovered. The whole process of exploring alternative ways forward can be done consciously and rigorously.

Although we have described SSM as a seven stage, somewhat rigid, process we must emphasise again that it is very rarely used that way. Each use of the methodology must be adapted to the context in which it is employed—it is this which makes SSM more than a technique. Different users will also bring their own flavour to the methodology. During any study employing SSM, it is as important to reflect upon the context of use (cultural enquiry) and the way the methodology is being used, as it is to go through the stages themselves. Every use of SSM tackles problem situations but should also involve reflection on the methodology and the way it can be employed. So there is learning in the world about the problem situation and also about the methodology itself.

As a final point it should be mentioned that SSM does not have to be the tool of experts doing a study from outside the problem situation. It can be employed by managers as part of their everyday work. In all circumstances it is much better if as many people as possible in the problem situation become involved with the study so that they own the results and are willing to implement the findings.

8.5 SSM IN ACTION: THE EXAMPLE OF WINTERTON CO-OPERATIVE DEVELOPMENT AGENCY

8.5.1 Introduction

This study for Winterton Co-operative Development Agency (CDA) was the broader study from which the specific SAST study described in Chapter 6 developed. For the background to CDAs and the study the reader is referred back to Chapter 6. The two studies together can be regarded, of course, as an example of a TSI investigation into the affairs of Winterton CDA. It might be useful just to remind the reader that this broader project was to look at the general operation of the CDA to see how it could more efficiently serve the county in which it operated, and how it might market its services in order to achieve its objectives. SSM was chosen as the dominant methodology because the study required consideration of both norms and values (cultural issues) and organisational structure and processes (systemic matters for which organismic models would be useful).

The study undertaken was a very conventional Mode I use of SSM in which the methodology guided the project to the extent that the Figure 8.1 representation of SSM was pinned to the wall of Winterton CDA with deadlines noted on it.

8.5.2 Description of the situation

Winterton CDA grew out of research on job creation and the economic problems of the county carried out by the Industrial Studies Unit of the University of Winterton. A Steering Committee was formed to set up a local CDA and the Agency started its operations in 1985. The running costs of the Agency are financed by grants from the county's local authorities and from the European Regional Development Fund.

Winterton CDA is based at two offices, in different towns in the county, provided by local councils. It is managed by a General Council, made up of representatives of various interest groups, which meets quarterly to discuss the activities of the Agency and decide policy issues. Besides the quarterly General Council Meetings, there is a Support Committee Meeting each month to discuss various activities of the Agency. The Support Committee contains elected representatives of the General Council and the Agency's development workers. The workers themselves also meet every Wednesday morning to review work done in the previous week and decide on the work for the coming week.

At the time of the project Winterton CDA employed five development workers. Since Winterton CDA is itself run as a co-operative, no hierarchical structure was imposed. The duties of the development workers overlapped considerably, with only a rudimentary division of labour. The main duties undertaken by the Agency were those of promotion (introductory days, seminars, exhibitions, advertising, public relations); training (especially for unemployed people); advice to potential co-operatives (feasibility studies, market research, the business plan, accounts and book-keeping); and advice to established co-operatives.

The development workers' sense of unease with their situation constituted a complicated "mess". They were not happy with the division of offices which meant duplicating documents and filing systems. Moreover one office had minimal activities and was difficult for the public to reach. All were dissatisfied with aspects like job allocation, job rotation and skills sharing. They had different points of view on, for example, the balance between the need for specialisation and collective decision making. The insecurity of funding from the sponsoring bodies also had a psychological effect on the development workers. Finally, they were disappointed by the number of workers' co-operatives being set up by the Agency, the number of enquiries from the public, and the number of people who came to the Agency to ask for help. They sensed there must be something wrong with their marketing strategy.

8.5.3 Application of SSM

Stages 1 and 2

Stages 1 and 2 were concerned with constructing the verbal rich picture just displayed. From this rich picture it was decided that various mismatches between structure and process could be detected. The absence of a division of labour to a certain extent was causing confusion in responsibilities. The weekly allocation of work could not effectively respond to the fast changing process in the Agency. Furthermore, for a newly established CDA, marketing activities should perhaps be the most important aspect of process, but they were not adequately catered for in the structural arrangements. There was no special element in the structure in charge of the marketing system and a lack of careful planning of marketing activities.

Having examined the "climate" of the problem situation in this way the marketing system was selected as an important system for further study and five relevant systems named:

(1) The Marketing System
(2) The Support Generation System
(3) The Segmented Market System
(4) The "Top-Down" System.
(5) The Image Building System

It was felt that addressing the problems of the marketing system would inevitably "sweep in" many of the other difficulties faced by the Agency. For the rationale behind relevant System 4 the reader is referred back to the worked example in Chapter 6.

Stage 3

Five root definitions (RDs) were constructed for the five relevant systems and checked against the CATWOE mnemonic. These five are listed below, with a sample CATWOE analysis of RD1.

RD1. A Winterton CDA owned system aiming to transform potential worker co-operators into actual worker co-operators through a series of analysed, planned, organised and controlled marketing activities so that both parties (Winterton CDA and potential worker co-operators) will benefit.

C = Winterton CDA and potential worker co-operators.
A = Those carrying out the analysed, etc., marketing activities.
T = Potential worker co-operators into actual worker co-operators.
W = Marketing can convert potential into actual worker co-operators.
O = Winterton CDA.
E = Resources, knowledge available to development workers, etc. (assumed too obvious to state in the RD).

RD2. A development worker managed system seeking to transform potential sources of support for Winterton CDA's marketing activities into actual useful support provided on a continuous basis.

RD3. A Winterton CDA owned system aiming to improve marketing effectiveness by employing appropriate marketing techniques to reach particular identifiable groups of potential worker co-operators.

RD4. A Winterton CDA owned system seeking to recruit individuals to form workers' co-operatives in particular fields where business opportunities exist.

RD5. A Winterton CDA managed system aiming to improve the attractiveness of the CDA and its services to potential customers, in order to encourage more groups of people to form workers' co-operatives.

Stage 4

At this stage a conceptual model (CM) was built on the basis of each RD setting out what the system must do to accomplish the task defined in the RD. Two examples, CM3, The Segmented Market Model, and CM4, The "Top-Down" Model, are provided in Figures 8.3 and 8.4.

Stage 5

After building the conceptual models at Stage 4, they were compared with the "real" situation in the Agency as painted in the "rich picture". For each activity in each of the conceptual models, the following questions were asked:

• "Is this activity done at present?"

From potential market

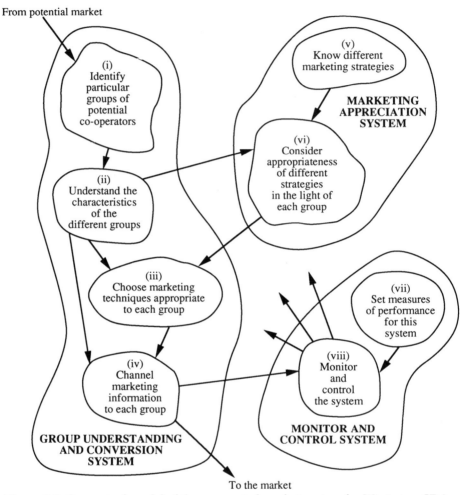

Figure 8.3 Conceptual model of the segmented market system for Winterton CDA

● "If so, how?"

The answers were recorded in tabular form (not shown here).
  The main points from all the comparisons are now summarized.

(1) The planning and organizing of marketing activities is mainly carried
    out on an *ad hoc* basis. The lack of overall planning and organising
    of marketing activities causes inefficiency in allocating and utilising
    the resources of the Agency. Poor planning also results in not
    prioritising the Agency's target groups of potential co-operators.

(2) Understanding of the potential market of worker co-operators, the

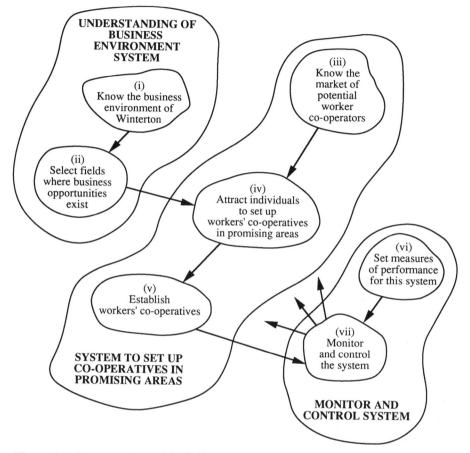

Figure 8.4 Conceptual model of the "top-down" system for Winterton CDA

characteristics of potential co-operators and the general business environment in the county, etc., is mainly obtained by guesswork and common sense. This carries a high risk of misunderstanding the actual situation.

(3) In general, marketing activities have tended to get ignored; and the importance of applying different strategies to different situations has not been recognised. The main reason for this may be the time available and "invisible pressure" from funding and other influential bodies. Keeping funders happy involves considerable time and effort.

(4) Little work has been done on knowing people's perceptions of workers' co-operatives, nor has the Agency worked out an "image" for itself.

(5) Present advertising policies mainly involve using leaflets, press releases and posters, etc. It seems they are inadequate; other possibilities must be considered.

(6) Monitoring and control activities are carried out instinctively at worker meetings, or at internal reviews. But present control devices seem inadequate and there is no standard against which to measure actual performance. In other words, the control system is not working properly.

Stage 6

After asking the questions "Is this activity done at present?" "If so, how?", to identify weak or non-existent "hows" at the comparison stage, another question was asked to suggest possible "hows". The question was:

● "How might the activity be done?"

The desirability and feasibility of each "how" was then debated with the development workers. The results were again displayed in tabular form. Since many of these results found their way into recommendations for change at Stage 7 we shall not detail them here.

Stage 7

Stage 7 is action to improve the problem situation. The recommendations made to the Agency and some responses are organised below under the categories of attitudinal change (people's perceptions of the situation), structural change (task and role responsibilities) and procedural change (process and work activities).

Attitudinal Change

Soft systems studies are often most successful in bringing about attitudinal change. Working closely with clients over a prolonged period with a methodology like SSM almost inevitably affects the culture of an organisation. This was particularly the case with Winterton CDA—a small organisation still finding its feet. During the course of the study the Agency came to accept that marketing activities should be regarded as important and receive continuous and systematic attention. Viewing the Agency as a marketing system became natural for the development workers. It is such attitudinal change that paves the way for necessary structural and procedural alterations.

Structural Change

(a) It was recommended that the Agency might consider assigning to an individual or individuals special responsibility for its marketing activities. These responsibilities could be formalised with each development worker's role and tasks outlined. In fact, the next vacancy that arose in the Agency was filled by a person with marketing expertise.

(b) It was accepted that a greater division of labour was necessary. The development workers, to a much greater extent, had special responsibilities assigned.

Procedural Change

The following changes designed to improve the planning and organising of marketing activities were recommended and, to some extent, acted upon.

(a) There should be regular examination of secondary sources of data and relevant marketing articles in order to achieve a better understanding of the environment which affects the Agency and of the marketing strategy of other CDAs.

(b) A marketing audit should be carried out at least once a year. The aim would be to reveal opportunities for development and the main problem areas facing the Agency. The results should be subject to full discussion, so that relevant corrective action can be taken.

(c) The Agency should keep under review its target market segments and be careful to devise particular marketing strategies for different segments.

(d) The Agency should attempt to make use of existing supporters and find new supporters to help it with its marketing activities. It should attempt to enlist the assistance of these groups in particular marketing activities. Involving established co-operatives in marketing is a possible idea.

(e) People's attitudes to co-operatives and Winterton CDA should be monitored perhaps using a questionnaire. Such surveys can always reveal areas for improvement.

(f) Improvements in presentation, advertising and publicity must be considered in the light of attitudes and as part of a long-term image building strategy.

(g) Arrangements should be made to show interested individuals a successful co-operative in operation.

(h) It seemed inevitable that a degree of "top-down" work must begin.

This should take the form of "experiments" which are monitored so that continual improvements can be made in this activity. Other CDAs' experiences with "top-down" should be considered. Information should be sought about business opportunities in the county.

8.5.4 Conclusion

In this instance SSM proved to be a highly effective tool for action research. It not only facilitated learning about the Agency, but also learning about the use of the methodology itself. For example, because the methodology is so focused on bringing about attitudinal and cultural change the involvement of the problem-owners throughout the intervention is crucial to success. This study also helped convince the authors of the sense of using different systems methodologies together in a complementarist fashion—in this case SSM and SAST; although the VSM was also employed at one stage in discussion over the division of labour in the Agency.

8.6 CRITIQUE OF SSM

The worked example above shows the main features of a "traditional" application of SSM. Our critique, however, relates to both the traditional and the more contemporary ideas, the latter having been explained earlier.

One point worthy of note, before we begin, is that almost all of the criticisms levelled at Ackoff's "interactive planning" approach can also be raised against Checkland's SSM. In order to avoid too much duplication we have deliberately dealt with these matters in summary form in what follows. The reader, however, might like now to reconsider the critique of Ackoff's work as it would apply to Checkland's.

Theory

(a) The first criticism concerns the restrictive nature of the interpretive theory upon which SSM is explicitly based. Interpretive thinkers see social reality as the self-conscious creation of human actors. "Problems" arise when individual actors' perceptions of reality do not overlap. It is then the job of the interpretively minded systems thinker to seek to establish or re-establish mutual understanding—to bring perceptions back into congruence so agreement can be reached on what action to take. This is really a very limited view of why problem situations occur. It ignores, for example, the cybernetic insight that organisations can fail to function properly because communication and control systems are poorly designed. The idea of cybernetic "laws", which must be obeyed when all complex systems are being organised, is simply not taken seriously by the soft systems thinking of Checkland. Further, the possibility that difficulties arise in organisations because different individuals and groups have differences of real interest cannot be conceptualised within the logic of SSM. It is a common-sense notion that organisations are arenas of political infighting and conflict over status and resources, but there is little in SSM (except the impoverished study of power relations which is Analysis 3) which seems to acknowledge the existence of such tensions.

In essence, and to use Habermas' threefold categorisation of human interests, SSM serves only the "practical" interest in bringing about mutual understanding. The technical interest in the prediction and control of natural and social affairs cannot be encompassed within the rationality of SSM. Similarly, the emancipatory interest in communication free from distortion and in realising participative decision making free from the effects of power relationships is not granted attention. In holding to one limited rationality, SSM is "isolationist" in character. In seeking to absorb hard systems approaches as a special case of the soft (suitable when a means–end logic applies) and to deal with issues of power within the interpretive rationality, Checkland makes unjustifiable "imperialist" claims for SSM.

(b) A related criticism turns on the idealist rather than materialist basis of Checkland's methodology. SSM is fundamentally idealist; ascribing to ideas the prime motive force in the construction and change of social reality. A materialist position, by contrast, sees ideas not as autonomous but as reflecting material and economic interests. The upshot of Checkland's idealism is the conclusion that the only way to change social systems is by changing people's world views or *Weltanschauungen*. This, of course, is what SSM sets out to do. If the materialist position is correct, however, it is extremely difficult to change people's world views without first doing something about the political and economic structures which condition those world views. It must be a matter of debate whether world views are relatively fluid and are capable of radical change in response to the pressure of alternative perspectives, or whether they can become "stuck" because the balance of social and economic forces they represent is unchanging. To fail to make any attempt to link ideas to social and economic circumstances, to make no attempt to address this serious issue, is a definite weakness of SSM.

(c) Adopting an idealist position and working from within interpretive social theory, it is argued that Checkland cannot properly address issues of conflict and coercion. All conflict must apparently be of an ideological nature so that it can be removed by promoting mutual understanding. Coercion, brought about by power relationships, cannot be recognised at all either in its naked form or in its more subtle types when it acts to keep important issues off the agenda for debate or succeeds in inculcating "false consciousness" into the minds of oppressed groups.

Methodology

(a) Changes emerging for implementation are supposed to be both systemically desirable and culturally feasible. However, in practice, the criterion of cultural feasibility dominates that of systemic desirability. Agreed changes can stem from a variety of conceptual models, each of which is built according to systems logic, but the changes that then come through are not themselves tested for coherence as a package against any systems logic. It is difficult to see, therefore, how the set of agreed changes meets any criterion of systemic desirability—cultural feasibility is, in fact, the sole arbiter. This represents the triumph of the culture metaphor over the organismic metaphor in Checkland's thinking. It is the complete abandonment of the idea that organisations can be made more effective and efficient if they are designed according to a set of systems principles. It is further confirmation of the isolationism inherent in SSM.

(b) Cultural feasibility, therefore, plays an extremely important role in SSM. But is it coherent? In almost all multi-institutional settings and even in most single organisations it will be impossible to identify a unique culture against which to judge feasibility. SSM simply seems to neglect the existence of different sub-cultures in organisations and in social settings. Presumably, then the *real* test of feasibility is whether a change is acceptable to the "dominant" culture in the problem situation. This dominant culture may, of course, be a coerced culture—an issue which cannot be considered within the bounds of SSM.

(c) The previous point of criticism seems to highlight a contradiction that goes to the very heart of SSM. Interpretive thinking embraces a form of relativism where every viewpoint must be accepted as equally valid. Generating mutual understanding by exploring world views is a process that theoretically can and should go on for ever. This poses a major difficulty in practical situations since there is no means of changing from abstract debate of alternative *Weltanschauungen* to pragmatic problem solving. SSM resolves this difficulty in an extremely unfortunate way. It simply leaves closure of the debate to the prevailing power structures as reflected in the dominant culture of the organisation.

(d) As in Ackoff's interactive planning, participation also plays a significant role in SSM as the guarantee that the results obtained are legitimate and that they will secure sufficient support to be implemented. However, Checkland does not specify how far this participation should run or who should be involved. Participation is obviously of crucial importance at Stages 5 and 6 of the methodology when comparisons between CMs and the "real world" are being made, and feasible and desirable changes are being agreed. However, no ground rules are established for what is to count as "genuine" participation. In the absence of such rules it is all too easy for those with power to dominate the debate and have their own priorities reflected in the outcome. Checkland should insist that the debate stages are conducted as far as possible according to the rules for establishing "communicative competence" laid down by Habermas. Instead he seems quite happy to accept for implementation changes that emerge from debates in which the different resources available to participants ensure only "distorted communication".

Ideology

(a) It can be argued given the points made above, and as was argued in the case of Ackoff, that the failure to establish the grounds for genuine participation means that the methodology will always serve those with power in a social situation.

(b) Despite Checkland's claim that the methodology is neutral in practice, it has been claimed that the theory on which it is based inevitably conditions it to be managerialist and reformist. It is managerialist because it seems inevitably to serve powerful groups like managers. It enables such groups to establish or regain their ideological hegemony. It is reformist because it works only at the ideological level and leaves untouched existing distributions of influence, power and wealth. Ideas can lead to changes in structures and procedures but they are also often frozen, mirroring existing social inequalities.

SSM does not reflect on the changes it provokes or seek to ensure that they lead to any emancipatory end result, so it is likely to assist with only reformist changes, reorientating the *status quo* in a manner beneficial to those with power.

Utility

SSM is best suited to situations where there is a coalition of organisational stakeholders and the need is to create, temporarily at least, a shared appreciation among these stakeholders of what is the best way forward from a given problem situation. It is extremely adept at providing creative solutions that enable organisational actors to escape the "traps" into which their current thinking has led them. If the problem situation is one in which organisational design of complex systems is required, however, SSM has to be used in conjunction with other approaches which have developed further the machine, organismic and neurophysiological metaphors: with cybernetic approaches, for example. In coercive contexts SSM is to be avoided because of the ease with which it lends its support to already powerful decision makers.

8.7 CASE STUDY: ELECTRONIC COMPONENTS DISTRIBUTORS

8.7.1 Introduction

Electronic Components Distributors (ECD) has traditionally been a market leader in its field. Recently, however, there has been a rapid increase in competition and company results have begun to look very worrying. In some quarters there is even a sense of panic. The Managing Director has decided to seek the advice of management consultants.

8.7.2 Your Task

In the role of management consultants, your task is to investigate the situation and carry out "strategic options analysis", looking at potential ways forward for the company. After an initial TSI appraisal, soft systems methodology has been chosen as an appropriate methodology for the study. Use the methodology to learn about the situation detailed below, and to come up with several contrasting strategic possibilities for ECD.

8.7.3 Background Information

Electronic Components Distributors (ECD) is a manufacturer's representative and distributor for electronic components. It is one of the largest companies of its type in New Zealand and had a sales turnover of about US$40 million in 1988. Profits recently have tended to increase by about 20–25% every year. The company markets 15 different product lines from the United States and Europe. The company's product lines are shown in Figure 8.5. These products are sold to the local electronics industry, which has been booming recently.

ECD has a very large customer base. Big multinational corporations contribute about 70% of the total sales. The remaining 30% are generated from both local and overseas electronics contract manufacturers, and other small local business organisations. There are two broad categories of customer: OEM (original equipment manufacturers) and distribution customers. For OEM customers, ECD acts as a representative and is paid a commission on business transacted on behalf of its overseas principals.

Product Category A

Product Line A1: ⌐
Product Line A2:
Product Line A3:   Semiconductor components
Product Line A4:
Product Line A5:
Product Line A6: ⌐

Product Category B

Product Line B1: ⌐
Product Line B2:
Product Line B3:   Passive components
Product Line B4:
Product Line B5: ⌐

Product Category B

Product Line B6: ⌐
Product Line B7:   Electromechanical components
Product Line B8:
Product Line B9: ⌐

Figure 8.5 ECD's product line card

The products are shipped directly from factories to customers. For distribution customers, ECD acts as a broker: buying, keeping stocks and reselling them to end customers. Sub-distributors are also appointed by ECD to sell to low volume users, such as universities, other institutions and the general public.

By 1989, the business environment had changed considerably. Many competitors had entered the market, competing head-on with ECD. The number of competitors had increased from about 5 to 50 in the span of six years. The competitors were very aggressive and were very successful in penetrating many of ECD's key accounts, and nowadays are enjoying substantial shares of this business arena. The market environment is getting increasingly complex, hostile and turbulent.

The sales revenue for 1989 increased by 20% over the previous year but the increase in profit dropped to about 7.5%. The cost of sales also increased tremendously. This dramatic turnaround worried shareholders and the Managing Director.

For many years, ECD has had no proper corporate objectives or strategies to guide the company for the immediate and long term. The only real objective is quantitative and that is the sales quota set each year for the sales and marketing department. Other loosely defined objectives are not well understood by most departments. Departments tend to take their own initiatives and set their own goals and objectives.

ECD is organised as shown in Figure 8.6. The Product Marketing, Sales, and Customer Services Managers all report to the Director of Sales and Marketing. This Director, together with the Financial Controller and Personnel Manager, work for the Managing Director.

ECD appears weak in many key areas of its business activities. It does very little market research. When "the need arises", the marketing department is responsible for carrying out this task. A quick "opinions of salespeople" review is conducted on an irregular basis. Most of the data thus collected are inaccurate. The advertising and promotional activities are also very minimal. They are solely done by the Marketing Manager who carries the added responsibility for new business development. Internal communication between sales, customer service and marketing is very poor.

The managers spend a lot of their time and effort on "fire fighting", concerned more with solving immediate daily operational problems than on making policy decisions and monitoring and controlling staff performance. The middle management team still adopt "old machine thinking and working habits". However, they do this inefficiently. Subordinates have regularly been told to carry out certain tasks without proper guidance. No standards are set. There are no proper job definitions and there is overlapping of job responsibilities. A poorly planned

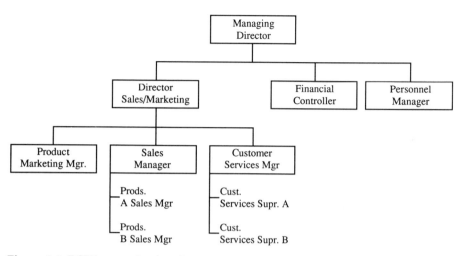

Figure 8.6 ECD's organisational structure

employee appraisal system is being used. It is a closed appraisal (employees are not involved) and is done at the end of each year. The annual pay increments of employees depend on how well they fare in this appraisal.

ECD has maintained a team of very young salespeople. Their average age is about 28 years. Unfortunately, they lack proper training and professionalism, and do not seem motivated to establish and develop good customer relations. Lack of knowledge about what the company can offer leads to an inability to service customers properly.

The pricing method is based on the traditional way of "cost plus mark-up" for all brokerage business. The mark-up can range from 25% to 40% and the sales staff are not allowed to sell below 25% mark-up unless authorised by the Sales Manager. As for the OEM sales, the pricing is set solely by the respective principals. The salesforce will negotiate on their behalf. If special pricing is required, authorisation will be sought from these principals. On occasions profit margins derived from commissions on these sales can be as low as 5%.

The marketing department is also responsible for conducting product training for the sales staff. The Sales Manager and Customer Services Supervisors are responsible for the initial training of new sales staff and customer services representatives respectively. There is no continuous training programme. After salespeople have been on-board for a few months or after probation, they simply slot into their jobs and are scarcely trained again. An annual budget of about 0.1% of sales is set aside for "settling-in" training. Staff development programmes are also lacking and the company provides limited subsidies, on a case by case basis, to employees who want to attend outside courses.

In a good year, a salesperson can earn commission as high as eight to nine months of basic salary equivalent. Salespeople are still unhappy with the commission scheme as it has a ceiling imposed on it. To meet a sales quota, most salespeople only sell high margin and easy to sell products. Low margin and difficult to sell products, which require a lot of sales follow-up, have been ignored. There are no additional incentives to motivate extra effort. The Sales Manager is responsible for setting an annual sales quota after consulting with individual salespeople. Each salesperson is required to submit a six month rolling sales forecast at the beginning of each month. The majority of salespeople submit their reports and forecasts late. There is no proper routeing and call plan. Most salespeople make only one to two calls per day. The morale of the salesforce is low.

The customer services department is overloaded with work. Many errors are committed in order processing and this causes delays with order confirmation. Shipments have been irregular, which detrimentally affects customers' production plans. Many customers are annoyed and frustrated. Many of the customer service staff work overtime, including weekends, to get their job done. They are not given overtime pay, but enjoy variable bonuses of about one-half to one month's pay for every three months' salary. The morale of these people is also low. Many have resigned over the year, being replaced by new people.

At the last physical inventory check, the warehouse contained about US$1 million worth of stock. About US$200 000 is dead stock and the rest mostly excess stock. There is, however, insufficient buffer stock for popular products, and products with long lead time, to support the market upturn. As a result many customers have placed their orders with ECD's competitors. Many orders have been lost to competitors who seem to have geared themselves better for the changing market environment.

The company's shareholders are obviously disappointed with the company's performance, and have been putting pressure on the Managing Director to get the situation under control. The Managing Director is overwhelmed with difficulties and does not know how to begin "problem solving". He has decided to consult a management consulting group.

8.8 FURTHER READING

• The main texts for the ideas of soft systems methodology are:

Checkland, P. B. (1981). *Systems Thinking, Systems Practice*, Wiley, Chichester.

Wilson, B. (1984). *Systems: Concepts, Methodologies and Applications*, Wiley, Chichester.

Checkland, P. B., and Scholes, J. (1990). *Soft Systems Methodology in Action*, Wiley, Chichester.

- Checkland's two chapters in an edited book by Rosenhead are also of value:

Rosenhead, J. (ed.)(1989). *Rational Analysis for a Problematic World*, Wiley, Chichester.

- For the critique of SSM see:

Jackson, M. C. (1982). The nature of soft systems thinking: The work of Churchman, Ackoff and Checkland, *Journal of Applied Systems Analysis*, **9**, 17–28.

Checkland, P. B. (1982). Soft systems methodology as process: A reply to M. C. Jackson, *Journal of Applied Systems Analysis*, **9**, 37–9.

Jackson, M. C. (1983). The nature of soft systems thinking: Comments on the three replies, *Journal of Applied Systems Analysis*, **10**, 109–13.

Chapter 9

Critical Systems Heuristics (CSH)

This much is certain, that whoever has once tasted critique will be ever after disgusted with all dogmatic twaddle. . .

Immanuel Kant, *Prolegomena*

9.1 INTRODUCTION

The systems tradition has long been strong in methodologies for the efficient design of systems to achieve known goals. In this volume system dynamics and viable system diagnosis attest, in their different ways, to this strength. More recently Churchman, Mason and Mitroff, Ackoff and Checkland have provided soft systems methodologies capable of operating in situations where there is a lack of agreement over goals among the different participants, and capable in pluralistic situations of achieving sufficient consensus for some agreed course of action to follow. Until very recently, however, there has been a gap in the systems tradition, in that there has been no systems approach which has provided a means for critically reflecting either upon the goals attained and means used by hard systems thinking, or upon the nature of the consensus achieved and the changes brought about through soft systems thinking. In this respect Ulrich's book *Critical Heuristics of Social Planning*, published in 1983, fills a major gap in the literature. The aim in this book is nothing less than to set out an appropriate philosophy for an emancipatory systems approach, and to develop a method which can be used by planners and concerned citizens alike to reveal the "normative content" of actual and proposed systems designs. By "normative content" Ulrich means both the underlying value assumptions that inevitably flow into planning and also the consequences and side-effects for those affected by the planning.

In arguing for a critical systems approach, Ulrich distances himself from the currently dominant use of the systems idea in what he calls "systems science" (operations research, systems analysis, systems engineering, system dynamics, cybernetics). In systems science, he argues, which is dominated by limiting mechanistic and organismic analogies, the systems idea is used in the context of "instrumental reason" to help us decide *how to do things*. It refers to a set of variables to be controlled. Ulrich's aim involves using the systems idea as part of "practical reason", to help us to decide what we *ought to do*. Within practical reason, the systems approach can assist us to use our freedom of choice to design better human (social) systems. A "purposeful" systems paradigm can be constructed that can be used by planners to reflect critically upon existing social system designs and to explore potential alternative designs. And procedures can be developed which should allow those who have to live with the results of plans to challenge the "systems rationality" of the planners.

From the TSI point of view, Ulrich's primary contribution must be in having provided a practical method, with a sound philosophical base, for proceeding in more "coercive" situations. In coercive contexts, where the powerful seek to impose their proposals upon other participants (planners planning for others), critical systems heuristics enables us to reveal the "true" interests and motivations underlying these proposals, assists with challenging the proposals and constructing counter-proposals, and insists that no plans are rational which have not been approved by the "affected but not involved".

In terms of our reasoning in Chapter 2, Ulrich has produced a methodology that helps in coercive contexts, but rather like Mason and Mitroff and their SAST approach, he leaves us with the view that having properly dealt with coercion there remains only the simple task of employing traditional management science methods to complete problem resolution. Mason, Mitroff and Ulrich all follow Churchman in sharing the opinion that it is the human problems which make management science difficult. Problems inherent in designing complex systems are not recognised. That is why we consider Ulrich's work as simple–coercive.

We approach the methodology of critical systems heuristics (CSH) through our usual route of philosophy and principles.

9.2 PHILOSOPHY OF CSH

For Ulrich, the purpose of systems thinking is scientifically to inform planning and design so as to secure an improvement in the human condition. The systems approach is, therefore, an exercise in practical reason, not theoretical reason. Its aim is to help us decide what *ought* to be done, not to produce knowledge of what *is*. The main issue is, for Ulrich, that he finds the two classical epistemological positions relating to practical reason to be untenable.

On the one hand the "scientistic" approach (followed by systems science) believes that no scientific guidance can be provided in formulating what ends to pursue, only on what is possible and on what means will secure predefined ends. Ulrich is unwilling to leave the matter of what we ought to do to "decision" or, indeed, to accept the means–end distinction which gives scientism sole discretion with regard to means: "Do not means involve value judgements and consequences too?"

On the other hand, there is the "dialectical" approach to the problem of practical reason, as suggested by Habermas for example. This approach sees practical rationality as emerging from a discursive process of will-formulation conducted according to the norms of "communicative competence". Ulrich accepts this as a theoretical ideal, but believes it fails to provide usable advice on how to proceed before the Utopia required for "undistorted communication" is achieved.

Ulrich, therefore, advocates a "third way" between these two classical epistemological positions. This seeks to extend science and rationality to the matter of "ends", but to do so in a way which is eminently practicable in the "here and now" of everyday circumstances. No theoretical grounding may be possible but practical heuristic guidelines, Ulrich believes, can be provided. We shall now consider further how these ideas work out by looking at what Ulrich means by "critical systems heuristics".

Ulrich uses all three terms—"critical", "systems" and "heuristic"—in the sense given to them by Kant. To be critical one must reflect upon the presuppositions that enter into both the search for knowledge and rational action. A *critical* approach to systems design means planners making transparent to themselves and others the normative content of designs. All designs and proposed designs must be submitted to critical inspection and not presented scientistically as the only "objective" possibility. Ulrich takes the *systems* idea in Kant to refer to the totality of relevant conditions upon which theoretical or practical judgements depend. These include metaphysical ethical, political and ideological aspects. In attempting to grasp the "whole system" we are inevitably highly selective in the presuppositions we make. Ulrich follows Churchman ("every world view is terribly restricted") in seeing Kant's systems idea as an admonition to reflect critically on the inevitable lack of comprehensiveness and partiality of all systems designs. It is by reference to the whole systems concepts entering into these partial presuppositions that critique becomes possible. Finally, *heuristics* refers to a process of uncovering "objectivist" deceptions and of helping planners and concerned participants to "unfold" messy issues through critical reflection. It also signals that Ulrich is not going to attempt to ground critical reflection theoretically but to provide a method by which presuppositions and their inevitable partiality can be kept constantly under review. These arguments are further developed in a debate with the ideas on social systems design present in or inferred from the writings of Popper, Habermas and Kant.

Popper's primary concern is with the logic underpinning "theoretical reason", with how we find out what is. The only rational application of theoretical reason is, for Popper, in instrumental reason which helps us to decide how to do things. As far as social systems design is concerned, therefore, reason can only help us with technical questions such as the most efficient means to achieve predetermined ends. Rational discussion about ends, and even about the value content of means, is apparently not possible. The central question of practical reason, "What ought we to do?", is placed by Popper beyond the scope of critical reflection. Practical reason is reduced to instrumental reason. This same attitude still pervades systems science. The goals served by systems science go unexamined as all the effort is put into finding the most efficient means for achieving predetermined ends. Ulrich wishes to make the question of what we ought to do subject to critical reflection.

Habermas' work is much more useful to Ulrich's enterprise because he recognises that instrumental reason is not the only legitimate application of reason. Practical reason and emancipatory reason (aiming at freedom from oppression) are equally important, with their own proper object domains. All three forms of reason are capable of being critically reflected upon. In order that questions such as "What ought to be done?" can be properly decided, according to Habermas, a process of rational argumentation must be established. All citizens, or at least all those affected by a planning decision, must be allowed to participate in the argument surrounding that decision. And the debate must be so arranged that all ideological and institutional constraints on discussion are eliminated, so that the force of the better argument persists. Through an analysis of the structure of actual speech situations, Habermas determines what this ideal-speech situation, free from all constraints, must be like— a theory of undistorted communication. Ulrich regards Habermas' work as providing a useful theoretical boundary experiment but as having little practical application. In order to enter into Habermas' debate, speakers must be willing and able to exhibit communicative competence. This tends to presuppose the very rationality the debate was designed to ensure. Habermas, in attempting to ground his critical reflection theoretically, cuts himself off from "realities" of the practical world in which personal and group interests inevitably contaminate any such debate. Far better, Ulrich argues, to ground critical reflection on practice heuristically, provide a method by which practical judgements can be constantly reflected upon and their partiality revealed by ordinary everyday accounts of the nature of social experience.

It is on a reconstruction of Kant's philosophy that Ulrich attempts to build his critical heuristics on a systems basis. Kant hoped to justify the kind of knowledge we have about the world. He was particularly concerned about what he called synthetic *a priori* concepts. These concepts were deeply implicated in the production of knowledge but were little understood and difficult to justify. Kant proceeded critically to reflect upon the necessary conditions for thought. He attempted to show the theoretical necessity of three sets of synthetic *a priori* concepts. First are two "pure forms of intuition"—space and time—present in the very possibility of things as appearances. Second are the 12 "categories", pure concepts of understanding necessary to connect perceptions together. Finally, there are three "transcendental ideas"—the World, Man and God. These transcendental ideas reveal to us the necessary conditional character of our understanding of the totality. Kant then tried to show that these synthetic *a priori* concepts contributed valid knowledge about the world.

Ulrich builds on Kant's work but subtly transforms it in order to make it applicable to planning and systems design. Certain presuppositions in the form of boundary judgements inevitably enter into any social systems design. Ulrich proceeds to reflect on which of these synthetic, relatively *a priori* concepts have *heuristic* necessity. Concepts are heuristically necessary if, only by making them explicit, it becomes possible critically to reflect upon the presuppositions entering into planning and social systems design. The concepts meeting this criterion are arranged according to the pattern set out by Kant. To Kant's space and time, the concept of purposefulness is added as an extra dimension necessary to map social reality. Twelve critically heuristic categories are established around a fundamental distinction between those "involved" in any planning decision (client, decision maker, planner) and those "affected" but not involved (witnesses). Three quasi-transcendental ideas are developed— the systems idea, the moral idea and the guarantor idea—as critical standards against which the limitations of particular social system designs can be compared. These concepts should enable any existing social system to be examined with a view to discovering the norms, values, etc., that went into its design. They should enable any potential systems design to be interrogated as to its presuppositions.

Ulrich has shown the heuristic necessity of certain concepts for understanding social system designs. He now has to demonstrate how, making use of these concepts, particular social system designs can be validated and accepted for implementation. Here Ulrich follows Habermas rather than Kant and requires some sort of participative debate to provide the final justification for practical knowledge. Habermas' forum of speakers exhibiting communicative competence has, however, already been found impracticable. Ulrich suggests instead a "dialectical" solution to the problem. It is not enough that the involved, making use of the heuristically necessary concepts, be self-reflective about the partiality of their social system designs. They must be subject also to a dialogue with the witnesses—in practice, representatives of those affected but not involved. The witnesses need only state their concerns in everday language since the "polemical employment of reason" (from Kant) in itself will be enough to reveal that the social system designs of the involved are based upon challengeable assumptions. It will become clear that only agreement among all affected citizens can finally lead to conclusions about what ought to be done. Ulrich's dialectical solution, therefore, is to bring the systems rationality of the planners directly into contact with the "social rationality" of those who have to live in and experience the social system designs. The reader will recall, at this point, Churchman's maxim that "there are no experts in the systems approach", and his argument that systems designers should expose the restricted nature of their own world views by opening themselves up to the opinions of their "enemies".

We shall take up various aspects of Ulrich's overall philosophy in discussing the principles and methodology of CSH.

9.3 PRINCIPLES OF CSH

The principles which guide the practice of critical systems heuristics might reasonably be taken to be four in number. There is the concept of "purposefulness": the additional dimension necessary to map social reality. And there are the three "quasi-transcendental" ideas designed to be used as critical standards—the systems idea, the moral idea and the guarantor idea.

Kant concluded that space and time were necessary mapping dimensions for the object domain of Newtonian natural science. Ulrich reasons that, in considering social reality and seeking its improvement, planners inevitably come up against human "intentionality" (self-consciousness, self-reflectiveness and self-determination), as well as the dimensions of space and time. Plans have a "meaning" to concerned actors and "matter" to them. A "pragmatic" mapping dimension which respects human intentionality and human purposefulness is, therefore, necessary in dealing with social reality. This somewhat abstruse idea lies behind Ulrich's advocacy of a "purposeful systems paradigm" and his insistence that social systems be adequately designed to become purposeful systems—otherwise they are likely to serve people and purposes other than those intended. By specifying what is meant by purposeful systems, Ulrich is also able to reveal shortcomings in mechanistic and organismic designs. Very briefly, in a purposeful system, the ability to determine the purpose must be spread throughout the system; the system should produce knowledge relevant to purposes and encourage debate about purposes; and all plans or proposals for design should be critically assessed in terms of their normative content. Critical systems heuristics is about the design and assessment of purposeful systems.

We turn now to the three "quasi-transcendental" ideas. In Kant the notions of the "World", "Man" and "God" are employed to reveal to us the necessary conditional character of our understanding of the totality. These notions are adjusted by Ulrich using three questions formulated by Kant, to produce the "systems", the "moral" and the "guarantor" ideas; notions applicable to social reality and capable of acting as critical standards against which the limitations of social system designs can be compared.

In considering the "World" (its existence and limits), Kant was pointing to the question, "What can I know?" The systems idea, as we have already met it, captures Kant's intent with respect to social reality. We must reflect upon the inevitable lack of comprehensiveness in our attempts to map social reality and to produce social system designs. The systems idea acts as a critical standard which forces us to consider this matter.

In considering "Man" (his immortal soul and freedom of the will), Kant was pointing to the question, "What might I do?" Transferring the intent to social reality gives birth to the moral idea. The planner aims to design better social systems for all, but should constantly ask what values are built into the designs, and consider the moral imperfection of the designs. The moral idea asks the social systems designer to seek continually to improve the human condition through his/her designs, but to be always aware, as well, of the moral implications of those designs. Moral limitations and shortcomings are best revealed by having regard to the "affected but not involved".

In considering "God", Kant was pointing to the question, "What may I hope?" In the social realm this translates into the guarantor idea. There can be no absolute guarantee that planning will lead to improvement, but the planner should seek to incorporate as many sources of imperfect guarantee as possible. A social systems designer should seek opinions from many experts and from different stakeholder groups. Proper procedures should be put in place for consultation, and agreement should be sought between those involved in the plan and those affected. After all this, however, the planner should still continue to reflect on the lack of guaranteee for his/her designs.

The systems, the moral and the guarantor ideas should be used by planners as critical standards against which they can evaluate the limitations and partiality of their own designs. They can also be used by those affected by plans to show the plans' lack of comprehensiveness (systems idea), their ethical inadequacy (moral idea) and their undemocratic nature (guarantor idea). As we shall now see, when we look at the methodology of CSH, Ulrich believes both usages to be essential.

9.4 CSH METHODOLOGY

9.4.1 Introduction

The methodology of critical systems heuristics falls into two parts. The first part is concerned to help planners to make transparent to themselves and others the presuppositions that inevitably enter into social system designs. To assist with this, 12 "critically heuristic categories" are established which can be used to interrogate system designs and potential designs. The second part offers a practical tool which ordinary citizens can use to engage planners in rational discourse about the partiality of their plans. This tool, or method of arguing, is called the "polemical employment of boundary judgements". It is necessary, as we know, because the planners (the involved) must not only be self-reflective about their designs, but also subject their designs to debate with the "witnesses"—in practice, representatives of those affected but not involved. Only if agreement is then reached between involved and affected can the plans be passed as "rational".

9.4.2 The 12 Critically Heuristic Categories

In order to reveal the "whole system" judgements, or presuppositions, entering into social system designs, Ulrich suggests using the concept of "boundary judgements". When planners apply systems design methods to the "real world" they inevitably make assumptions about what is inside the system of concern and what belongs to its environment. These boundary judgements reflect the designer's "whole systems judgements" about what is relevant to the design task. They also represent "justification break-offs", since they reveal the scope of responsibility accepted by the designers in justifying their designs to the affected. Thus boundary judgements provide an access point to the normative implications of systems designs. The task is to find a means of interrogating systems designs to reveal the boundary judgements being made, and a means of postulating alternative boundary judgements, that is, of asking what the boundaries *should be*.

In order to facilitate this task, Ulrich has produced a checklist of 12 "boundary questions". These flow from 12 critically heuristic "categories" (cf. Kant) established around the distinction between those "involved" in any planning decision (client, decision taker, designer) and those "affected" but not involved (witnesses).

The questions relating to the client concern the "sources of motivation" flowing into the design. They are about its "value basis". The questions relating to the decision taker examine "sources of control". They are about the design's "basis of power". The questions relating to the designer concern "sources of expertise". They ask for the "basis of guarantee". And the questions relating to the witnesses, reflect on the "sources of legitimation" considered in the design. So they ask for its "basis of legitimation". The client, decision taker, designer and witnesses distinction yields, therefore, four groups of questions.

There are three questions asked of each of these four groups—giving the complete set of 12 boundary questions. The first question is about the "social roles" of the involved or the affected; the second refers to "role-specific concerns"; and the third to "key problems" surrounding the determination of boundary judgements with respect to that group.

The power of the 12 questions to reveal the normative content of systems designs is best seen if they are put both in an "is" mode and an "ought" mode, and the answers contrasted. For example, we would compare the answer to the question, "Who *is* the actual *client* of the system's (S's) design?", with answers to the question "Who ought to be the *client* (beneficiary) of the system S to be designed or improved?" We set out the 12 questions, side by side, in the "is" and "ought" modes in Tables 9.1 and 9.2.

Using the 12 boundary questions should allow both planners and concerned citizens to get at the normative premises that inevitably flow into any actual systems design. For Ulrich, no systems design can be regarded as "rational" unless it does make explicit its own normative content. This, however, is not the only criterion of rationality. It is also necessary that those affected by the design, those who have to live in the world created by the design, validate its consequences. There can be

Table 9.1 The 12 critically heuristic boundary questions in the "is" mode

(1)	Who *is* the actual *client* of S's design, i.e. who belongs to the group of those whose purposes (interests and values) are served, in distinction to those who do not benefit but may have to bear the costs or other disadvantages?
(2)	What is the actual *purpose* of S's design, as being measured not in terms of declared intentions of the involved but in terms of the actual consequences?
(3)	What, judged by the design's consequences, is its built in *measure of success*?
(4)	Who is actually the *decison taker*, i.e. who can actually change the measure of success?
(5)	What *conditions* of successful planning and implementation of S are really controlled by the decision taker?
(6)	What conditions are *not* controlled by the decision taker, i.e. what represents *"environment"* to him?
(7)	Who is actually involved as planner?
(8)	Who is involved as *"expert"*, of what kind is his expertise, what role does he actually play?
(9)	Where do the involved see the *guarantee* that their planning will be successful? (E.g. In the theoretical competence of experts? In consensus among experts? In the validity of empirical data? In the relevance of mathematical models or computer simulations? In political support on the part of interest-groups? In the experience and intuition of the involved?, etc.) Can these assumed guarantors secure the design's success, or are they false guarantors?
(10)	Who among the involved *witnesses* represents the concerns of the affected? Who is or may be affected without being involved?
(11)	Are the affected given an oppportunity to *emancipate* themselves from the experts and to take their fate into their own hands, or do the experts determine what is right for them, what quality of life means to them, etc? That is to say, are the affected used merely as means for the purposes of others, or are they also treated as "ends in themselves" (Kant), as belonging to the client?
(12)	What *world view* is actually underlying the design of S? Is it the world view of (some of) the involved or of (some of) the affected?

no guarantee that they will be given the chance to do this. Nevertheless Ulrich sets out, in the second part of his critical heuristics methodology, to provide them with a tool which can cause the involved to reflect on a design's normative content even if they should appear less than willing to do so.

Table 9.2 The 12 critically heuristic boundary questions in the "ought" mode

(1)	Who ought to be the *client* (beneficiary) of the system S to be designed or improved?
(2)	What ought to be the *purpose* of S, i.e. what goal states ought S be able to achieve so as to serve the client?
(3)	What ought to be S's *measure of success* (or improvement)?
(4)	Who ought to be the *decision taker*, i.e. have the power to change S's measure of improvement?
(5)	What *components* (resources and constraints) of S ought to be controlled by the decision taker?
(6)	What resources and conditions ought to be part of S's *environment*, i.e. not be controlled by S's decision taker?
(7)	Who ought to be involved as *designer* of S?
(8)	What kind of *expertise* ought to flow into the design of S, i.e. who ought to be considered an expert and what should be his role?
(9)	Who ought to be the *guarantor* of S, i.e. where ought the designer seek the guarantee that his design will be implemented and will prove successful, judged by S's measure of success (or improvement)?
(10)	Who ought to belong to the *witnesses* representing the concerns of the citizens that will or might be affected by the design of S? That is to say, who among the affected ought to get involved?
(11)	to what degree and in what way ought the affected be given the chance of *emancipation* from the premises and promises of the involved?
(12)	Upon what *world views* of either the involved or the affected ought S's design be based?

9.4.3 The Polemical Employment of Boundary Judgements

The main obstacle that might seem to lie in the way of the affected challenging the systems designs of planners is their lack of expertise and their apparent lack of "rationality". However, as Ulrich has shown, this is not really such a difficulty. All designs are based on partial presuppositions, on boundary judgements incorporating justification break-offs, and these are, of course, beyond the reach of expertise to justify. Anyone who understands the concept of boundary judgements, knows that planners who justify their proposals on the basis of expertise, or "objective necessities" are in fact employing boundary judgements, whether cynically or simply unreflectively. So if planners can be made to discuss basic boundary judgements, they are put in a position where they are no better off with their knowledge and expertise than ordinary affected citizens. It becomes a matter of trading value judgements about what premises should influence plans and what consequences are desirable (or otherwise).

In order to put recalcitrant planners into a position where they have to admit their boundary judgements, Ulrich advocates the polemical employment of boundary judgements. This idea stems from Kant's discussion of the "polemical employment of reason". For Kant an argument is polemical if it is used for solely critical intent against a dogmatically asserted validity claim. Affected citizens can employ boundary judgements against planners in this sort of way. They can assert alternative boundary judgements against the planners in the full knowledge that these reflect only personal value judgements. This is quite good enough to shift the burden of proof on to the planners and to leave them floundering to prove the superiority of their own boundary judgements. Acting in this way, the affected are able to demonstrate three essential points:

- that the proposals of experts are governed by boundary judgements;
- that the knowledge and expertise of experts is insufficient to justify their own boundary judgements or to falsify those of critics;
- that experts who still seek to justify their recommendations on the basis of "knowledge" and expertise are, in fact, employing boundary judgements dogmatically or cynically and thereby disqualify themselves.

The polemical employment of reason, therefore, secures to both sides an equal position for reasonable dialogue.

The observant reader will have noticed by now that a significant difference between Ulrich's and Checkland's methodologies is Ulrich's interest in dealing with certain issues of power and domination, about which Checkland has very little to say. The limitations of even Ulrich's efforts in this highly problematic area will be dealt with in Section 9.6.

9.5 CSH IN ACTION: THE EXAMPLE OF POLICE STRATEGY TOWARDS THE CARRYING OF OFFENSIVE WEAPONS

9.5.1 Introduction

The following example documents the application of CSH to a major study area in the Metropolitan Police Force in London. Originally soft systems analysis was applied, but was found to struggle given the kind of context faced in this instance. One reason is that SSM has been almost exclusively designed to work in organisations such as companies, firms and the like. Macrosocial difficulties and the problems to which they give rise hardly influenced at all the main evolutionary phase of SSM. Further, the nature of the issues being confronted demanded an approach which was able to penetrate the contradictory positions of those involved and affected. It was simply no good in this multi-agency situation, to expect the constraint "cultural feasibility" to work positively. The actors did not form a loose coalition with basic interests in common which could be appealed to, as possible social system designs were negotiated, with some expectation of compromise. We discovered all this during the process of applying soft systems ideas to the difficulties at hand. In the spirit of TSI, we maintained an open mind about other possibilities, and how and why they might prove to be beneficial. The following account represents a reworking of the original soft systems study carried out with Chief Superintendent T. Brydges, exploring how critical systems heuristics might have better exposed and dealt with the contradictory and at least partially coercive nature of the issues.

9.5.2 Background

The primary centre of the study was Lambeth Borough in London. Essentially, 12 different actors, or agencies, were recognised as operating within the problem context: the Home Office, the police (incorporating Community Liaison Officers' and Operational Officers' viewpoints), trade organisations, shops selling offensive weapons, the media, the Crown Prosecution service, The Lambeth Consultative Group, the WHY group, carriers and assailants, youths, schools, and the magistracy. The following is a brief appraisal of the 12 viewpoints.

The Home Office represents the administrative side of law and order (the police representing the operational side). The role of the Home Office, however, extends beyond the authority of the police force, being responsible for the rights of individuals. This often leads to tension between the role of the police and the rights of the people. Two examples where this tension shines through are the 1953 Prevention of Crime Act and the 1984 Police and Criminal Evidence Act (PACE), which were deemed, especially by the police, as inadequate for tackling crime. One grey area that remains is the definition of "reasonable suspicion". An important last point is that the Home Office does not see crime as a manifestation of social factors. A consequence of this outlook is that the law can only be used as a deterrent and cannot provide an impetus for beneficial social change.

The Chief Superintendent of Kennington, in Lambeth Borough, was considered to be a key person from the policing angle. Kennington and the Metropolitan environment is reputed to have the highest incidence of crime in London. Statistics suggest that Lambeth suffers seriously from persons carrying knives. Police in the area, seeking to curb the problem, look towards tightening existing legislation but, since 1984, PACE has constrained the police by equating reasonable suspicion needed to stop and search with that needed to arrest. This obviously makes things difficult for police who are eager to get on top of the situation and erase weapon-related offences. Directives from the Chief Superintendent of Kennington sought to encourage policemen to spot possible carriers of knives. He issued a statement that effectively gave permission to policemen to confiscate offensive weapons without the need to arrest or charge.

The Association of Chief Police Officers (ACPO) has called for three changes in legislation in order to combat crimes associated with offensive weapons. First, a lowering of the standard proof required for reasonable suspicion; second, the right to trial resting with the prosecution; and third, an updating of the offensive weapons Act to include survivalist type weapons. ACPO has expressed the opinion that the courts are too lenient, readily accepting that accused offenders were defending themselves.

The Police Community Liaison Officers (Superintendents and Chief Inspectors involved with consultative groups) argue that education is the key to a long-term solution, supported by a hard line judiciary. An education that instils traditional values was advocated, aiming to eliminate the criminal classes. Methods suggested included the provision of information packs which detail laws on knife carrying.

Operational Officers (Chief Inspectors, Inspectors, Sergeants, Constables) consider that there are three distinct reasons for the apparent increase in knife use: availability and low cost, ease of concealment, and an ineffective law. When asked to describe the knife offender, the officers pointed to the following main features. Such criminals are aged between 14 and 30, are male, have previous convictions, are unemployed, are poorly housed, and are poorly educated. Another key factor identified was race. All in all there are a number of acute social factors that need to be addressed if the root of the problem is to be tackled. Consequently, and following youth consultation, it was decided that police must interact more closely with the community, gaining access to children from an early age. The aim would be to instil trust, dependence and honesty.

The trade organisations have reacted in different ways to the South-East Co-operative Society's decision to remove from stores toys that glamorise violence. The British Toy Manufacturers' Association claims that this is an overreaction. Rainbow Toys, one representative of the manufacturers, thought that a blanket ban was wrong. Other reactions to the ban included a Chief Inspector who welcomed the removal and Slough Council, near London, who were delighted. The issue that remains contentious concerns the extent to which toy weapons mould aggressive attitudes in young adults. Shops selling real offensive weapons are accused by many of being more commercially oriented than socially responsible. There are many documented records of weapons being sold to persons under the age of 18. There are no laws, however, barring the sale of many offensive weapons. Voluntary guidelines have been drawn up by the Home Office, but are generally considered to be non-influential. Working out effective legislation would be extremely difficult because there are certain vendors, such as ironmongers, who need to be able to sell knives.

The local media relates to the community, needing to reflect local views thus securing financial viability. The national media contrasts strongly with this, working around eight qualities of a "good story": immediacy, dramatisation, personification, simplification, titillation, conventionalism, structured access, and novelty (crime stories are often used to sell nationals). Both types of media are influential on people's attitudes, but each one takes a different angle.

The Crown Prosecution Service (CPS) accepts that the knife problem is prevalent, but considers action taken to be too lenient. It has also complained that the police too often provide insufficient information to support accusations of "intent to use" offensive weapons. This disparity indicates a source of antagonism when crime problems are transported from the police to the CPS.

The Lambeth Consultative Group reckons that there are five relevant issues: seeking new legislation on knife carrying, reviewing police "stop and search" powers, banning sales of offensive weapons to juveniles, controlling magazine advertising, and an education campaign in consultation with local police.

The WHY group (why helpless youngsters?) is a pressure group based in London whose main aim is to prevent young people from carrying offensive weapons. Three solutions have been put forward. First, a relaxation of reasonable suspicion criteria, thereby allowing the police to react to public demands for tougher action. Second, promotion of education programmes from the age of eight or nine years. Third, legislation to restrict sales of offensive weapons.

The views of carriers and assailants were sought, but this did pose some major difficulties. The "closest" contact available came via youth clubs, Afro-Caribbean clubs, and youth custody centres. From two clubs emerged the following justification: there is a fear of being attacked and there is a status associated with knife-carrying. Further, knives have been used to secure robberies from "rich people". Such wealth distinction is often used to justify acts of theft.

During the study, the Inner London Education Authority was approached and asked whether it was possible that discussions could be held in schools with the children. This request was rejected. The following points were revealed through less direct means. School children offered three main reasons that explained from their viewpoint why knives are frequently carried: it was fashionable, knives are available, and, in our interpretation, it accorded with a certain mythology. Schools attempt to deal with this difficulty by day, confiscating weapons when found and punishing by suspending children and informing their parents. The School Curriculum Development Committee has been considering promoting relevant rules in the school, with the hope of engendering social responsibility.

The magistracy consider themselves to be well balanced in respect of community problems, since the majority of magistrates are lay magistrates who have a direct relationship with the community. In their deliberations it is assumed that the societal implications of prosecutions are more fully appreciated. Carrying is put in more of a sociological context.

A major new initiative has been instigated in several quarters of the Metropolitan Police Force. It has been labelled a multi-agency approach. One area in which this planned social systems design has been discussed is that of the carrying of offensive weapons. Let us consider the basic ideas of the design, before subjecting it, in the context of the above discussion, to a first run through of the 12 critically heuristic questions (we will return to this example in the case study that we ask you to tackle, at the end of this chapter).

A multi-agency approach in the Lambeth context was described as being:

> "Designed to pursue an objective of identifying and locating key social agencies, with the aim of designing and implementing better community social crime prevention organisation through decentralised community services, based on the principles of self help and support neighbourhood watch schemes, geographically aligned to Ward boundaries, to be administered by the local council, for the purpose of providing a local (ground floor) multi-agency forum within a consultative and accountably controlled and monitored hierarchical structure in respect of local environmental crime community affairs."

The above account draws out the main issue areas concerning the problem of carrying offensive weapons. We shall now turn our attention to investigating how critical systems heuristics can be applied in such a context.

9.5.3 Applying the 12 Critically Heuristic Categories

In this example, we will concentrate on the first part of critical systems heuristics, employing the 12 critically heuristic categories, in the "is" mode to interrogate the proposed social system design of a multi-agency approach to the carrying of offensive weapons. We shall do this as far as our knowledge of the situation allows. In the case study we shall then ask you to carry out the same analysis in the "ought" mode, considering alternative clients, purposes, etc., and thus generating alternative social system designs. A thorough critique of the proposed strategy should then have been achieved.

At the outset we need to define S, the social system design. S relates to the Metropolitan Police Force, in particular the Lambeth Borough, as it upholds the laws relating to the carrying of offensive weapons. We are concerned with the design of police strategy, in particular through the introduction of the multi-agency approach, towards the carrying of offensive weapons. Let us begin the enquiry.

(1) Who is the actual client of S's design?

The "design" according to the stated purposes of the constitution of the Metropolitan Police Force, is to enforce the law of the land. The beneficiaries are presumed to be those living in the Metropolitan Society, including the offenders who may be reformed as defined by the legislature.

(2) What is the actual purpose of S's design?

The declared intention is given in the response to question (1) above. We are now concerned with identifying the actual consequences of the operation of this intention. This is difficult as all consequences precipitate to form further consequences. The consequences of S's design can only be understood through the responses of interested parties. We can extract some examples from the background to the situation presented above.

A main consequence of the old (pre-multi-agency) system is to frustrate the Police Officers involved in trying to implement the laws determined by the legislature. The main reason appears to be difficulty in equating reasonable suspicion needed to stop and search with that needed to arrest. It is possible that the proposed multi-agency approach may lead to some relief from the current situation. This may come either from the greater involvement of local citizens in reducing this kind of crime, or directly through pressure being brought to bear on the authorities who are responsible for producing the laws.

In contrast, carriers and assailants consider the police strategy towards the carrying of offensive weapons, crudely speaking, as either infringing their rights to self-protection in the case of some carriers, or supporting a society with class distinction between the "haves and have-nots". In Ulrich's terms, the purpose of S is either to suppress citizens' rights to self-defence, or to support the structure of a two class society. The multi-agency approach may have no effect on this conception, or may even strengthen it, being seen as a way of consolidating the current situation.

(3) What, judged by the design's consequences, is it's built-in measure of success?

A traditional measure has been the progress or regress of crime, measured according to standard statistics. These statistics have recently been accepted as highly inaccurate measures of crime and crime reduction. For example, they are based only on reported crime, leaving out what is generally agreed to be a substantial number of crimes which are not reported because of difficulties such as fear of reprisal. Consequently, a recent initiative has been to work out useful sets of performance indicators, which incorporate actors not usually explicitly considered, for example, social agencies and residents and their level of satisfaction. This is proving to be a significant challenge which, if successfully carried through, would obviously marry well with a multi-agency initiative. Another indicator is the number of crime prevention initiatives that have been implemented. Obviously, the built-in measure of success of S is by no means clear cut.

(4) Who is actually the decision taker, *that is, who can actually change the measure of success?*

We obviously have to put to one side the new initiatives for performance indicators, since these have not yet been adequately worked out. This leaves two measures of success: the volume of crime prevention schemes, and progression or regression in the number of crimes.

There is no clear definition of crime prevention schemes, but this can be inferred: the schemes relate to various agents who have an underlying interest in the crime of concern, and who formulate and implement policies or initiatives in order to prevent and reduce the crime. In this sense the decision taker is the person/group who influences/dictates the focus and adoptability of the crime prevention scheme. In the majority of cases the decision takers will be professionals, and most likely the Police Force.

Taking the second measure to be progression or regression in the kind of crime of concern, leads us to a diversity of possible decision takers.

The most obvious is the Police Force, who can make judgements about the actual, rather than reported, crimes, and who decide upon what constitutes a "clear-up".

The measure of success, however, can be changed by way of defining and redefining what actually is a crime related to offensive weapons. Whoever is able to amend existing, or create new, laws is a decision taker. Ultimately, in the United Kingdom, this is the Home Office.

One additional decision taker can be identified; the media. All forms of media have a strong influence over how the public understands and measures the success of bodies like the Police Force. Since this "measure" can become all important, the media must be identified as decision takers.

(5) What conditions *of successful planning and implementation of S are really controlled by the decision taker?*

The social design, relating to police strategy towards the carrying of offensive weapons, incorporates the idea of a multi-agency approach. Whoever administers and controls the meetings can have a strong influence over membership and hence the possible range of issues, time allocated to discuss them, etc. Primary control at this level lies in the hands of those who administer the meetings. Ultimate control according to formal channels is, however, held by the Home Office.

(6) What conditions are not *controlled by the decision taker, that is, what represents "environment" to him?*

Significant difficulties are faced when attempting to deal with macro-social issues. The nature of control over social difficulties is particularly sticky. Those such as unemployment, bad housing, unstable family life and ineffective schooling are examples. These kinds of social issue represent the environment to our decision takers.

(7) Who is actually involved as planner?

The actors involved with the multi-agency approach ideally will be offered an integral role in the consultation and decision-making process. Groups such as local agencies are planned to be involved, thus involving school groups, church groups, local councillors and planners. However, actual planning of meetings, etc., is likely to lie with the Police Force.

(8) Who is involved as "expert", of what kind is his expertise, what role does he actually play?

Many of the actors are considered to be experts in their particular field or vocation, each having a valid contribution to make within the debate. For example, a representative from the schools will be an expert in the running of schools and the kinds of issue which are of concern to those responsible for developing the character and intellect of children.

(9) Where do the involved see the guarantee *that their planning will be successful?*

The guarantee has traditionally been only with a minority, but with a multi-agency approach, those involved might see the guarantee in a form of local societal consensus.

(10) Who among the involved witnesses *represents the concerns of the affected? Who is or may be affected without being involved?*

Ideally, in a multi-agency manner of organising people around an issue, all of those affected will be involved, at least in as far as they are represented through a related agency. One of the main tasks of this kind of approach, is to search for those who may be affected without having the kind of involvement that Ulrich would demand. For example, if we were to identify rather simply two types of witness, the attacked and the attacker, we may find that it is the latter who is quite likely to be omitted from discussions about how the carrying of offensive weapons can be appropriately dealt with. The multi-agency approach is clearly supported by the kind of reasoning that is proferred in critical systems heuristics.

(11) Are the affected given an opportunity to emancipate *themselves from the experts and to take their fate into their own hands?*

One group of affected at least, the carriers and assailants, are given little chance to emancipate themselves. All resources are mobilised to improve the statistics or proposed performance indicators. Carriers and assailants can be seen, in some sense, as merely a means used to achieve this state. There is a danger that the emphasis on statistics or other hard measures will undermine the validity of the multi-agency approach. Those who are responsible for working out the measures, of whatever sort, can easily take up a position of control and dominance.

(12) What world view is actually underlying the design of S? Is it the world view of (some of) the involved or of (some of) the affected?

In the preceding 11 responses we have made several points directed at highlighting potential taken-for-granted assumptions in the development of the multi-agency approach with respect to the carrying of offensive weapons. These assumptions suggest that the world view, despite the good intentions of the designers, may be subject to dominance. It is difficult to imagine that the bias towards the Police Force, in terms of those responsible for measures of performance and, to some extent, determining the membership and functioning of the discussion groups, will not be responsible in part for setting the underlying world view, emphasis and purpose of the design.

We have considered some of the details of the proposed multi-agency approach, employing the 12 critically heuristic categories in the "is" mode. Ulrich's scheme has suggested that, although the approach is multi-agency in intent, it may be in danger of falling short of this ideal in practice. This can be further demonstrated if the 12 critically heuristic categories are used in the "ought" mode to explore alternative boundary judgements. This task we leave to the reader in the case study.

9.6 CRITIQUE OF CSH

The critical comments which follow do not at all detract from Ulrich's achievement. Rather they point to the sort of significant debate his work makes possible. This work has helped considerably to raise the standard of dialogue in the systems movement and focus that debate on the most fundamental issues. A massive debt is owed to Ulrich for his painstaking analysis of the foundations of the systems approach and for his own contribution—an emancipatory systems perspective.

Theory

(a) Critical systems heuristics is regarded as corresponding to simple–coercive problem contexts but not complex–coercive. Coercion, which is in the realist sense embedded structurally in organisations and society (giving rise to the more subtle and complex exercise of power), cannot be addressed using Ulrich's approach. Critical systems heuristics is critical in terms of the idealism of Kant, Hegel and Churchman but not in terms of the historical materialism of Marx and the Frankfurt School of sociologists. Ulrich's work allows us to reflect upon the ideas that enter into any social systems design, but it does not help us to reflect upon the material conditions that give rise to those ideas and which lead to certain ideas holding sway. Obviously an analysis conducted according to Ulrich's recommendations will help point to such material conditions. What it cannot do is provide an examination or explanation of the nature and development of those conditions. Material conditions that lead to particular ideas prevailing and to particular designs winning acceptance have to be introduced by Ulrich as "common sense" explanations of what is occurring.

(b) This same neglect of the structural aspects and development of social systems means that Ulrich's recommendations ultimately are just as Utopian as Habermas'. The question remains: "Why should the involved bother to take account of the views and interests of those who are affected but not involved?" The question of which class, group or agency has the power, the will and the interest to bring about the rational society has bothered theorists throughout the twentieth century. No consensus has been reached, but at least it has been treated as an important question. Ulrich rather neglects this type of issue.

Methodology

Although the 12 critically heuristic categories have been found penetrating when employed in a deep enquiry into finding out about social systems design, the lack of methodological guidelines for action and intervention underline the methodological immaturity of the approach. As we saw in the example of police strategy towards the carrying of offensive weapons, it is perfectly possible to employ the 12 questions in the "is" and "ought" modes to reveal the social system design and all that implies. What is not evident is how to integrate these findings in intervention. We see in critical systems heuristics an approach which is only just coming to the fore and has not matured in the way, for example, soft systems methodology has matured by way of intense use for about 20 years. This immaturity does not invalidate the basic methodological ideas, rather it poses an interesting challenge for anyone who cares to tackle issues at the leading edge of systems thinking.

Ideology

As we saw in discussing the philosophy of critical heuristics, Ulrich rails against the limitations of the machine and organismic analogies so frequently employed in systems thinking. It is the influence of the culture and coalition metaphors and especially, perhaps, of the idea that organisations can be "prisons" or coercive systems (when planners do not submit their designs to rational argumentation) that is most easily traced in his work. It is not surprising, of course, that the metaphors Ulrich uses to address the "real world" are those most relevant to his purposeful systems paradigm. The effect of all this, however (from the TSI viewpoint), is that Ulrich's criticisms of systems science and cybernetics seem somewhat overplayed and the important role that instrumental reason can offer when handled critically in planning tends, therefore, to get neglected. This is unfortunate since rational social action will depend on what it is possible to do and the choice of efficient means—matters of instrumental reason—as well as upon what we ought to do—a matter of practical reason. We would not want to labour this point—experts do have a role in Ulrich's systems approach. It may simply be a matter of emphasis. Nevertheless, the impression is conveyed that systems science approaches are more dangerous than useful when applied to questions of social systems design. A better view perhaps (which is the TSI view) is that systems science is all right in its place, and it does have a place in social systems design.

Utility

(a) Critical systems heuristics, therefore, certainly does not seek to assist with complexity management along the "systems" dimension. Its positioning towards the coercive end of the participants' dimension should, however, be taken as more of an indication of the unique contribution of the approach than of its limitations in dealing with pluralism. In particular it should not be read as suggesting that there will be few opportunities to use critical systems heuristics in the "real world". Many situations can be seen as exhibiting aspects of coercion, and most pluralistic debate could benefit from the kind of clarification Ulrich's approach provides.

It should also be mentioned that Ulrich himself has more recently suggested a "three level" concept of rational systems practice which embraces the concerns of systems science, organisational cybernetics, soft systems approaches and critically normative systems thinking. This can be seen to parallel the TSI approach in line with the complementarist integration of systems thinking advanced in this book.

(b) One consequence of labelling Ulrich's critical heuristics as simple–coercive and not complex–coercive—and this will not have escaped the observant—is that there is no systems methodology corresponding to complex–coercive problem contexts. Readers are invited to contribute such a methodology to the next edition of this book.

9.7 CASE STUDY: A CONTINUATION OF THE OFFENSIVE WEAPONS EXAMPLE

9.7.1 Introduction

In Section 9.5 we considered a first stage application of critical systems heuristics to the proposed multi-agency approach to the carrying of offensive weapons. We examined the situation using the 12 critically heuristic questions in the "is" mode. Enough information was provided in the background information to allow the reader to complete the investigation by now using the questions in the "ought" mode. Some very interesting results should be obtained.

9.7.2 Your Task

Your task is to go carefully through the 12 critically heuristic questions in the "ought" mode (see Table 9.2). Try to do this exercise drawing as many stakeholders as possible into the design, so that you produce the outline for a genuine multi-agency approach. Remember that the worked example using the "is" mode revealed the current design to be very constrained in multi-agency terms. What you are doing as you complete this task is to redraw the boundaries of the design's conception in order to challenge the original social system design.

As a hint let us consider the first question in the "ought" mode drawing in more fully a stakeholder largely excluded from the existing proposed design—the carrier/assailant.

(1) Who ought to be the client *(beneficiary) of the system S to be designed or improved?*

A very simple conception of the situation is the carrier or assailant, the attacked and those who are affected by the events bringing the above two together. In many cases the (potential) attacked are seen as the ones served by actions oriented to deal with the "problem". If we could change conception, however, and consider that the (potential) attacker is the client, then our attention might be turned towards alleviating the conditions which give rise to the attacks. For example, we might attempt to develop an interest in social responsibility, or reducing class and race differences in society. It would seem that the real danger is in labelling carriers/assailants as objects, thus ascribing an inferior position to them in the analysis and making them "the problem" rather than one of the clients. It is reasonable to suppose that if we nominate the carrier/assailant as a client, then we may find ourselves attacking the primary difficulties rather than nursing the symptoms.

The main shift in emphasis you may wish to concentrate on is that from the groups who are concerned about the potential attackers (the emphasis revealed by the "is" mode), to the actual carriers/assailants themselves. This would reflect a shift in the boundaries of the design. Despite the good intentions of the original multi-agency notion, very careful attention needs to be paid to how the design is realised. Fundamentally, as Ulrich suggests, we need to ask about the clients, purposes and designers of this system and how the purposes can be properly realised.

If you are doing this exercise in groups you could usefully seek to use the "polemical employment of boundary judgements" to challenge the proposed social system design and the proposed designs of other groups emerging from using the 12 questions in the "ought" mode.

9.7.3 Further Task

One of the criticisms that was levelled at critical systems heuristics in the previous section was that, in its very young state of development, the methodological ideas have concentrated mainly on "finding out" rather than intervention itself. You might like to consider what necessary developments could be made to critical systems heuristics in order that the methodological ideas relate as much to action and intervention, as they currently do to heuristic learning. We would be interested in learning about any significant developments along these lines in order that we may enhance this chapter for the second edition of the book.

9.8 FURTHER READING

• Critical systems heuristics is presented in detail in:

Ulrich , W. (1983). *Critical Heuristics of Social Planning*, Haupt, Berne.

• The interested reader should also consult:

Ulrich, W. (1986). Critical heuristics of social systems design, *Working Paper 10*, Department of Management Systems and Sciences, University of Hull.
Ulrich, W. (1987). Critical heuristics of social systems design, *European Journal of Operational Research*, **31**, 276–83.
Ulrich, W. (1988). Systems thinking, systems practice, and practical philosophy: A program of research, *Systems Practice*, **1**, 137–63.

Flood, R. L. and Ulrich, W. (1989). Testament to conversations on critical systems thinking between two systems practitioners, *Systems Practice*, **3**, 7–29.

• For the critique, see:

Jackson, M. C. (1985). The itinerary of a critical approach, review of Ulrich's "Critical Heuristics of Social Planning", *Journal of the Operational Research Society*, **36**, 878–81.
Wilmott, H. (1989). OR as a problem situation: From soft systems methodology to critical science, in *OR and the Social Sciences*, (eds. M. C. Jackson, P. Keys, S. A. Cropper), pp.65–78, Plenum, New York.

Chapter 10

Total Systems Intervention (TSI) Revisited

That we disavow reflection is positivism.
J. Habermas, in the Preface to *Knowledge and Human Interests*.

10.1 A BRIEF NOTE ON TSI

Throughout this book we have emphasised the importance of the logic and process of TSI for the management and systems sciences; how "creativity", "choice" and "implementation" TSI style amount to a powerful approach to "problem solving" for managers, decision makers, planners, consultants and all people engaged in social systems and attracted by the idea of changing them. This at the broadest level is "Total Systems Intervention". "Intervention", because we are advocating an activity that will inevitably bring about change, change of all sorts and right from the very beginning too, from invisible effects of learning by interjecting new creative thoughts among old stale ones, to relevant, progressive change in organisational and social order. "Systems", because we are drawing upon and critically interpreting a mass of ideas from systems thinking, ideas which promote the process of TSI itself as well as underpinning in various ways the methodologies that we consider most important for intervention. "Total", because we seek to use insights from the whole of the systems and management sciences to address the whole array of organisational and societal "problems", and because we want to be explicit that what we are ideally talking about is the involvement of all actors caught, willingly or not, in "systems" and in systems intervention activities.

This is our claim. We are confident that we have constructed a new way forward for the systems and management sciences which is theoretically coherent, practically useful and which does not involve wholesale commitment to just one body of thought or approach.

Let us now look once again at TSI, following one complete intervention driven by its logic and process. We should provide a complete run through now, anyway, because we have just finished discussions on "implementation" (the use of methodologies) which completes our presentation of the three phases of TSI. Earlier in Chapter 3, we were only able to work briefly through the three stages in a short example. But now with so many actual uses of methodologies, guided by TSI, behind us, we are in a position to be able to take the reader through a larger example in a hopefully informative way. Naturally, this then sets the scene for constructing the last piece of this book not yet in place— a critique of TSI itself.

At that point, you may wish to turn to the next case study. It will not be found on these pages. You will need to look elsewhere, to those centres of your life that demand of you the extreme challenges with which TSI tries to assist.

10.2 TSI IN ACTION: THE EXAMPLE OF A COUNCIL FOR VOLUNTARY SERVICE

10.2.1 Introduction

The study described in this section was done for "West Newton" Council for Voluntary Service. It employed the TSI approach, using SSM as the dominant methodology throughout but with viable system diagnosis in a strong supporting role. The political metaphor also helped to illuminate the nature of the problem situation, although it did not become necessary to translate this into the use of any additional systems methodology. The contribution of Mary Ashton, as student-researcher, was crucial to the success of this project.

10.2.2 Description of the Situation

Councils for Voluntary Service act as umbrella organisations for the wide variety of other voluntary bodies they have in their membership. They are local development agencies which are non-profit making and non-governmental. There are about 200 such Councils for Voluntary Service in England and Wales. Councils for Voluntary Service aim to promote more and better voluntary action in their areas by:

- providing a *focal point* for local voluntary action generally;
- *developing* new areas of voluntary activity to meet local needs;
- acting in a *liaison* capacity to link up voluntary bodies with similar concerns;
- *representing* the voluntary sector to appropriate statutory bodies;
- performing a *vanguard* or educating role for other voluntary organisations (e.g. setting exemplary standards on equal opportunities).

West Newton is a large Council for Voluntary Service (CVS). It was founded in 1980 and grew rapidly in size and influence. By the time of the study it had more than 300 voluntary and community organisations under its umbrella, employed around 80 staff (including over 60 Manpower Services Commission "Community Programme" supervisors and participants), and had a turnover of around £500 000 per annum. The CVS had a General Secretary and Deputy General Secretary and its work was divided into seven main areas, each headed by a core-staff member (e.g. Carlton Estate Voluntary Action Centre, Project Placement, Alcohol Education and Information Project).

West Newton CVS was troubled by a number of "problems", but the one on which the project came to focus concerned certain difficulties faced by its Executive Committee. This Committee was trying to oversee and control what was a rapidly expanding organisation in a turbulent environment. It continued to operate as it did when the CVS was first founded, meeting every six weeks for a programmed two hours. The Executive did not possess the flexibility or means to respond to the needs of the CVS West Newton had become, and was widely perceived to be ineffective.

The project began with the gathering of information about the Executive Committee, its structure and role, and the views held of it by both Executive Committee members themselves and the CVS staff.

The Executive Committee was subordinate to a Council in the CVS hierarchy. The Council consisted mainly of representatives of member organisations and met once a year at the Annual General Meeting of the CVS. The Executive was democratically elected by Council at the Annual General Meeting. Each member of the Executive was elected for a three-year term and one-third of the members were elected each year. Two induction sessions were held for new Executive members. Executive Committee members were, of course, unpaid. The Executive's job was to make policy by representing and refining the broad judgement of the Council and translating this into specific guidelines for action by the CVS. These relationships are shown in Figure 10.1.

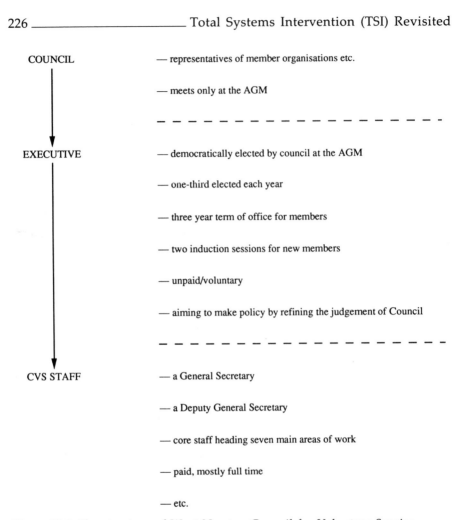

COUNCIL — representatives of member organisations etc.

— meets only at the AGM

EXECUTIVE — democratically elected by council at the AGM

— one-third elected each year

— three year term of office for members

— two induction sessions for new members

— unpaid/voluntary

— aiming to make policy by refining the judgement of Council

CVS STAFF — a General Secretary

— a Deputy General Secretary

— core staff heading seven main areas of work

— paid, mostly full time

— etc.

Figure 10.1 The structure of West Newton Council for Voluntary Service

The specific structure of the Executive is shown in Figure 10.2. The Executive consisted of a Chair, Vice-Chair, Treasurer, 18 other representatives elected by Council and four co-opted members (a City Councillor, a County Councillor and two direct from Council). The General Secretary of the CVS was minutes secretary and though he had no voting powers, he exercised a strong influence through his knowledge (as the senior full-time person on the Executive) and power of recommendation. Other CVS staff could attend but, again, had no voting rights.

The Executive was supported in its work by a Finance Committee. This had certain delegated powers, also met once every six weeks and provided reports and recommendations for the Executive to consider. It

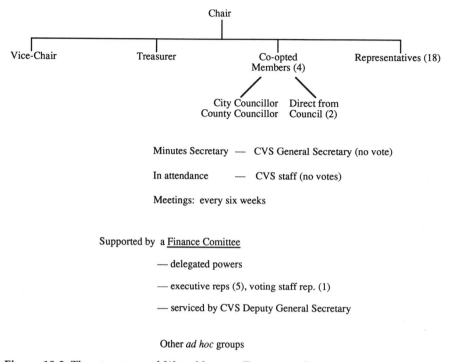

Chair

Vice-Chair   Treasurer   Co-opted Members (4)   Representatives (18)

City Councillor   Direct from
County Councillor   Council (2)

Minutes Secretary   —   CVS General Secretary (no vote)

In attendance   —   CVS staff (no votes)

Meetings: every six weeks

Supported by a Finance Comittee

— delegated powers

— executive reps (5), voting staff rep. (1)

— serviced by CVS Deputy General Secretary

Other *ad hoc* groups

Figure 10.2 The structure of West Newton Executive Committee

was serviced by the Deputy General Secretary of the CVS, and was made up of five Executive representatives and a voting staff representative. Other *ad hoc* groups were occasionally set up by the Executive to oversee and report on particular developments.

Items found their way on to the agenda of Executive Committee meetings from a variety of places. They could emerge from the General Secretary, from the Finance Committee, the *ad hoc* groups, from core-staff members heading areas of work, or simply as Executive submissions (especially from the Chair and Executive members on outside committees). There was some filtering of the items for discussion, usually by the General Secretary, but nevertheless the agenda was severely overloaded. Meetings had become lengthy and acrimonious. It was felt, by both Executive and staff, that the Committee was not providing the direction required. Two-thirds of the issues that came up for discussion concerned "management" rather than the policy matters on which the Executive was supposed to concentrate.

After Executive meetings, minutes would be circulated to all section heads for discussion. The General Secretary and Deputy General Secretary were responsible for monitoring the execution of policy as decided at the meetings.

In order to find out what people felt about the Executive, lengthy interviews were carried out with eight key Executive members and nine staff. Each of these was followed up with a second interview later in the study, with a check made that the interviewer had fully grasped the subject's meaning (the "cognitive mapping" technique developed by Eden was employed for this purpose). Anonymous questionnaires were sent to all other Executive members and to other staff who had recently attended Executive meetings (35 questionnaires in all).

Summarising massively, the views of Executive members divided into those with an "efficiency orientation" and those with a "suspicion orientation". The efficiency oriented were frustrated by the inability of the Executive to get important business done. They felt that agendas were too lengthy and not prioritised. They wanted each item to come with a clear recommendation. Meetings became bogged down, they thought, because of the massive overload of work, the chronic shortage of time for discussion, and because people attended "cold" without digesting the information. Worse, there was poor committee discipline, with sidetracking and standing orders not enforced. The "efficiency oriented" felt that the Executive was not concentrating enough on policy. It was wasting time on management issues which the staff should take care of. Unfortunately some members did not trust the key staff enough to keep their noses out of management issues.

The "suspicion oriented" were generally distrustful of key figures on the Executive and of the Executive's role. They wanted to promote more debate to find out what was going on. They felt that key officers had too much power and that agenda filtering was preventing important issues reaching the Executive. Executive meetings were too formal and hierarchical and this suppressed participation and creativity from ordinary members. The "suspicion oriented" wanted to know more about what was actually going on in the CVS.

Staff views could also be characterised as falling into two broad types. One group saw Executive shortcomings as having developed as a natural result of the rapid growth in activities of the CVS. They felt that the CVS had grown too rapidly and it was now time to apply the brakes. The Executive was overloaded and could not give enough consideration to staff views. Further, because of bad filtering, staff views did not get through to the Executive. For these reasons it was not surprising if some Executive members felt out of touch. There was a need for more contact between Executive and staff. This could provide learning for the Executive and support for staff. The second group was much more critical of the Executive and saw its shortcomings as self-inflicted. They thought that the Executive had not adapted to change and was, therefore, a stumbling block to getting things done. It was largely cut off from the reality of CVS work on the ground. More contact with staff was needed to wake up Executive members.

From the interviews and other gathering of information, therefore, it seemed that the following were very significant issues that had to be addressed:

- providing more time for the Executive to deal with policy issues;
- increasing the professionalism of the Executive's handling of management issues;
- improving the handling of Executive business;
- generating mutual respect between Executive members and staff;
- making the Executive more aware of staff work;
- increasing Executive contact with staff;
- increasing staff confidence in the Executive.

10.2.3 TSI Analysis

On the basis of what was found out about West Newton CVS, it would have been easy to think of it in terms of an organism trying to grow at the same time as adapt in a highly turbulent environment. Our attention had, however, become focused on the brain of that organism—the Executive did not possess the "variety" to manage the organisation. It had somehow to be equipped with the various functions of management exhibited by Beer's VSM. As will be seen, this proved a particularly useful metaphor.

Presenting a report based upon viable system diagnosis might well, therefore, have provided some useful solutions to the Executive Committee's problems. It would probably, however, have ignored other very significant aspects of the problem context. For the CVS was nothing if it was not a coalition of different groups, all with somewhat different interests and ways of perceiving the situation. A way had to be found to generate a consensus for change among the elements of this coalition. And what was surely needed was a change in the culture of the organisation, so that it was ready to accept change and particularly to rethink the way the Executive functioned. If these matters were not tackled then any "rationalistic" report might fail to achieve improvements because of the opposition it generated or because it failed to gain the commitment and enthusiasm of the most involved agents. There had, in fact, been previous internally generated suggestions for improving the performance of the Executive. These were sound enough and we were unlikely, as outsiders, to discover any magical solutions that had not occurred to those already living in the situation.

The role of the project, therefore, had to be seen as generating a "culture" for change in the organisation; and change which did not offend any of the groups in the "coalition". At the same time, of course, the eventual design had to meet cybernetic criteria of viability. The Executive had to become an effective "brain". This led to the choice of SSM as the dominant methodology. SSM rests upon "complex–pluralist" assumptions and articulates particularly well the concerns of the culture and coalition metaphors in its procedures. There was also likely to be a role for VSD as a supporting methodology, backing up SSM in dealing with complexity because of its uniquely explicit understanding of brain-related issues (learning, forward thinking, etc.).

Finally, it seemed as well to be aware of the significant political aspects to the problem context. These, at times, threatened to take the situation beyond the pluralistic, towards the conflict and coercion end of the "participants" dimension. There was conflict between some on the Executive and some staff, and on the Executive, between those happy to leave responsibility for "running the show" to the staff and those who tended to suspect the motives of the key officers. The General Secretary's position as an important "broker" between Executive Committee and staff could clearly be threatened by any suggested redesign of the Executive. Particular attention had to be paid to the most influential individuals associated with the various interest groups in order to gain their support and trust. However, in this case, the political aspect could be handled informally within the bounds of SSM.

10.2.4 The Project Itself

Embarking on the project using SSM, the first task was to build a "rich picture" of the problem situation. In this case it was deemed sufficient to work with the verbal rich picture already presented in Section 10.2.2. In that, the structures and processes impinging on the Executive Committee are set out and the viewpoints of key actors detailed. The next step, therefore, was to consider all this information and to choose some "relevant systems": some insightful ways of looking at the work of the Executive and the difficulties it faced. Six relevant systems were, in fact, proposed:

(a) A *policy processing* system: handling policy so that other bodies can execute it or be guided by it.
(b) A *need-seeking and idea-generating* system: helping the organisation to seek and develop new initiatives.

(c) A *representative* system: expanding the voluntary sector's voice and other crucial decision-making bodies.
(d) A *monitoring and controlling* system: embracing the classical role of a management committee.
(e) An *accounting* system: ensuring that the organisation is seen to conduct its affairs competently in the eyes of those to whom it is accountable.
(f) A *staff support* system: practically demonstrating support towards those appointed to manage the organisation.

During the course of the work on relevant systems, it occurred to the analysts that much of our thinking was being guided by the roles any management or "meta-system" would have to perform in seeking to control a highly complex set of operations. In other words, we were thinking in "cybernetic" terms. It was decided to make this explicit and to see whether our relevant systems "covered the ground" in terms of the functions a meta-system has to fulfil. This was done by locating the function of each relevant system on Beer's VSM. Relevant system (a), *policy processing*, was clearly at System 5 level; relevant systems (b) and (c), *need-seeking* and *representation*, were at System 4 level. Relevant systems (d) and (e) *monitoring and controlling* and *accountability*, were System 3 and System 3* audit functions, respectively. While relevant system (f), *staff support*, operated at the System 3 and System 1 levels. This information is captured in Figure 10.3.

The fact that our choice of relevant systems had this additional cybernetic legitimacy gave us confidence. We were clearly thinking along the right lines if we wanted to provide the Executive with the "requisite variety" to manage the organisation. Throughout the study we continued to employ this cybernetic rationality in a subordinate role, thinking about what functions had to be carried out in West Newton CVS. From the outside, indeed, it might look as though we could have taken a short cut through all the information gathering, interviews and questionnaire survey, by using Beer's VSM directly to pin-point cybernetic faults. This, though, would be a mistake. We had to engender change in the culture of the organisation to create a momentum for "redesign", and we had to hold together the various factions in the coalition, securing the support of each for the proposals. At the same time we had to sidestep and manage the political problems. Only constant working with the people in the organisation, so that they were fully involved in generating proposals and came to own the suggested solutions, could address these issues. SSM had to remain dominant if anything was going to change in West Newton CVS. At no time was the "brain" driven logic allowed

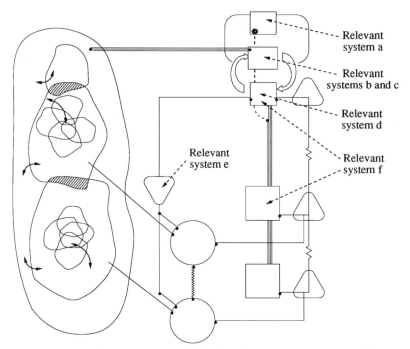

Figure 10.3 The six relevant systems related to functions in Beer's viable system model for the Council for Voluntary Service example

to take over from the "culture" and "coalition" emphasis supplied by SSM.

Although all six chosen systems were relevant to improving the overall effectiveness of the CVS, it became clear that only four related specifically to the main area of concern—the ability of the Executive to control the organisation. The "need-seeking" and "representative" systems (the System 4 roles) were taken a little further in the study and then dropped. They will not be discussed again here.

The next stage was to build "root definitions" and "conceptual models" of the relevant systems. The root definitions and the CATWOE checks are supplied below. For reference purposes the systems retain the original letters by which they were identified above. Figures 10.4 and 10.5 are the conceptual models developed respectively from root definition (a) and root definition (d), and are supplied as examples.

Root Definition (a): A Policy Processing System

"A West Newton CVS owned policy processing system which aims to represent the broad judgement of the Council and is thus able to create,

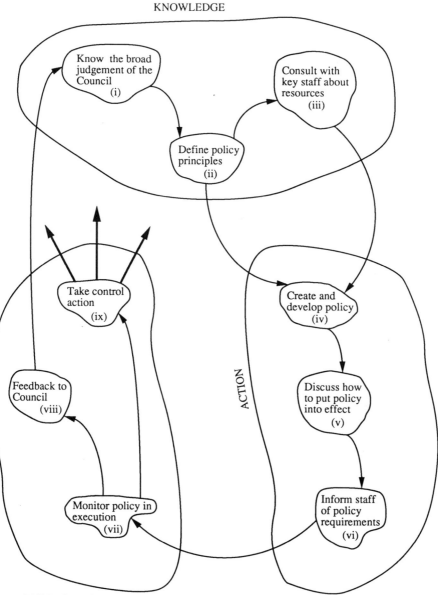

Figure 10.4 Conceptual model of the policy processing system (RDa) for the Council for Voluntary Service example

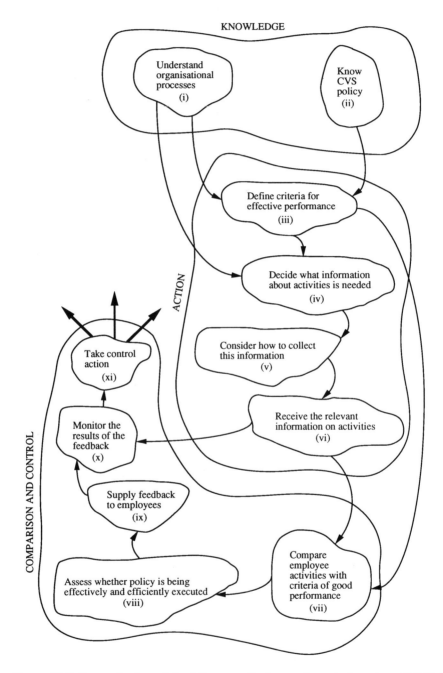

Figure 10.5 Conceptual model of the monitoring and control system (RDd) for the Council for Voluntary Service example

develop and put into effect execution of CVS policy on its behalf; within the constraints of time and resources available to Executive Committee members and the organisation."

C = CVS employees, the Council.
A = The Executive Committee.
T =

Broad judgement of the Council → Created, developed and "put into effect" CVS policy

W = The Executive Committee carries the ultimate responsibility for committing the CVS to a particular course of action.
O = West Newton CVS, that is, The Council (the Membership).
E = Time and resources available to the Executive Committee members and the organisation.

Root Definition (d): A Monitoring and Controlling System

"A West Newton CVS elected system for monitoring and controlling the complex organisational processes in which CVS employees are involved day to day, to ensure that policy is being implemented effectively and efficiently within the limitations of time and experience available to Executive Committee members."

C = CVS employees, the CVS.
A = The Executive Committee.
T =

Situation where Executive Committee doesn't know how effectively and efficiently policy is being implemented → Situation where they do

W = The Executive Committee in their role as company directors should be aware how well the policy they make is being implemented.
O = West Newton CVS.
E = Time and experience available to Executive Committee members.

Root Definition (e): An Accountability System

"A West Newton CVS owned collective responsibility system which impartially safeguards the organisation's accountability to the Membership and the various bodies who enable its existence as a centrally and locally government funded Charitable Body, and Company Limited by Guarantee; within the capacity of the resources currently available."

C = West Newton CVS, CVS employees, the "various bodies".

A = The Executive Committee, the relevant staff.

T =
| Organisational accountability potentially at risk | → | Organisational accountability safeguarded |

W = The organisation must be able to handle its affairs with competence to survive in its present form.

O = West Newton CVS, the various bodies.

E = Resources currently available.

Root Definition (f): A Staff Support System

"A West Newton CVS elected organisational support system which can build and maintain a flexible mutually helpful, and supportive working relationship between the Executive body and the key staff - so raising levels of knowledge, respect and understanding; and improving the overall "health" of the organisation, within the time and resources available to both parties."

C = Executive Committee, the key staff.

A = The Executive Committee, the key staff.

T =
| Less than satisfactory supportive relationship between the Executive Committee and key staff | → | Mutually helpful and supportive relationship |

W = Each party needs knowledge and understanding of the other to perform their respective organisational functions well.

O = West Newton CVS, The Executive Committee, key staff.

E = Time and resources available to both parties.

The implications of the conceptual models were then fully discussed with the most important members of the Executive and the staff. Using a set of guiding questions, a comparison was drawn up between the conceptual models and the "real world situation". The Executive was asked whether the activities in the conceptual models existed in the "real world" or not; if they did exist, "How are they done at present and are they done well?" and if they did not exist, or were done badly, "Are they feasible and how might they be carried out effectively in the 'real-world' situation of West Newton CVS?" From the comparisons, an agenda for further and wider debate was drawn up. This focused on the following requirements.

From conceptual model (a), *policy processing*:

- the need for more time for the Executive to consider major policy issues and to review implementation;
- the need for a better way of consulting core-staff about basic matters of policy implementation;
- the need for a sub-structure within which the Executive could improve its knowledge and understanding of the organisation they make policy for;
- requirements for a method by which the Executive could more closely monitor the execution of that policy and be aware of any necessary control action.

From conceptual model (d), *monitoring and controlling*:

- the need for a sub-structure within the Executive body that can become better informed about the organisation being monitored and controlled;
- the need for a body which can specifically "predigest" issues relating to management, with the assistance of the General Secretary and core-staff, and on behalf of the full Executive.

From conceptual model (e), *accountability*:

- the need for a way of strengthening and giving credibility to the Finance Committee, so that it can better support and represent the financial management of the organisation to the full Executive body;
- the need for a system whereby the Finance Committee may better fulfil its Executive responsibilities for overall financial monitoring and control;
- the need for a way of identifying the training needs of the staff thus involved.

From conceptual model (f), *staff support*:

- the need for a structure which will provide more than one official point of contact for Executive and key staff members;
- the need for a system whereby joint consultation on needs and expectations, and joint monitoring of the relationship can take place.

On the basis of this agenda we, the analysts, began to think about possible changes which we felt would help alleviate the difficulties. Most of these came from suggestions made by various CVS officers in discussion with us. We would then bring these up in meetings with other personnel to gauge their reaction. This was particularly the case with specific suggestions for change, such as the controversial idea of setting up a "management committee" to aid the Executive. We were acting as "brokers" between the interested parties, and moving forward only with ideas which seemed to attract general assent or, at least, failed to provoke severe disagreement. The political situation made it simply impossible to bring all the significant actors together, at one time and place, to hammer out an agreed set of proposals. The likelihood of such a meeting breaking up in disarray, and taking the proposals down with it, was too great. We also had our own "hidden", cybernetic, agenda which contained a set of minimum specifications we felt any changes should meet in order to make the organisation "viable". Top of this agenda was to see management issues handled "lower down", thus reducing the "variety" flooding up to the Executive and exhausting its capacity to handle significant policy issues.

Eventually, through a long drawn out and time-consuming process of going back and forth between important Executive members and staff, and constantly modifying the recommendations, we arrived at proposals we believed had general support and met the cybernetic criteria. We were rewarded for this hard work when the recommendations were presented at an Executive meeting. The significant actors had come to own them as their own, and there was no opposition to the setting up of a sub-committee charged to oversee their implementation. The recommendations are set out in the next sub-section.

10.2.5 Recommendations

The report detailed recommendations in three areas: structural, procedural and attitudinal.

Structural

In order to bring Executive members closer to the organisation it was suggested that five *support groups* be set up in the five main areas of the CVS's work. Each support group would consist of six to eight people. Three to four (including the Chair) would be Executive Committee members. In addition there would be the relevant core-staff member and one or two senior staff from that area of work. Each support group would be serviced by the relevant core-staff member and represented on a general management committee by the Chair.

To improve Executive Committee control of management issues, to relieve overload, and to support the General Secretary and Deputy General Secretary, it was recommended that there should be a *general management committee* and *a strengthened finance committee*.

The general management committee would consist of about ten people; being the General Secretary, four or five from the Executive and the support group Chairs. Its role was to support the work of the General Secretary. It should help shift "supervisory" management issues away from the main Executive and thus cut overload. It could also pre-digest management issues for the Executive. Of course, it was also the focus for the support groups.

The strengthened finance committee should comprise the General Secretary, Deputy General Secretary, five or six Executive representatives and, perhaps, a financial adviser—around eight people in all. Its role was to support the Deputy General Secretary. Executive members on this committee should possess some financial acumen, and thought should be given to involving an external adviser. It was recommended that both these committees be delegated strong powers by the main Executive to deal with management and finance issues, thus freeing the Executive for policy discussions.

Procedural

The three tier system (set out in Figure 10.6) was to operate on a nine week cycle.

The *support groups* would meet during weeks one and two, with important issues being taken to the general management committee by the Chairs.

The *general management committee* and *finance committee* would meet sometime during weeks four to six. Decisions taken upon items under their discretion would be minuted and the minutes passed on to the core managers. Other items could go up to the full *Executive* at the discretion of the General Secretary and Deputy General Secretary. The Executive would meet during week eight or nine of the cycle.

Attitudinal

To prevent factions developing, with different Executive members getting attached to particular aspects of the organisation's work, it was suggested that Executive members rotate around the support groups. They would then begin to gain an overall appreciation of the CVS's work. The Chair of each support group should also rotate.

Initially to allocate Executive members to support groups, it was suggested that they be asked to provide a "1,2,3" preference ordering of the groups in which they were most interested.

New Executive members, elected by the Council at the Annual General Meeting, should be provided with an induction booklet setting out the new structure of the CVS, and their responsibilities with regard to the support groups.

In addition, the report set out the ways in which the recommendations would help correct what everybody saw as obvious difficulties with the Executive's current mode of functioning.

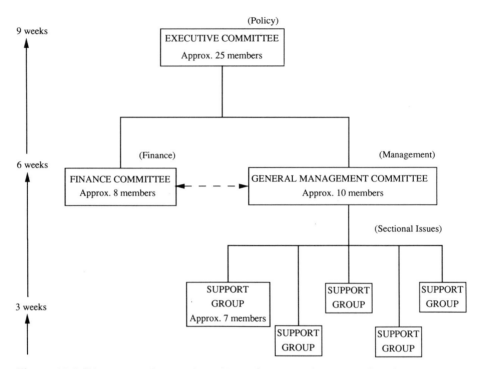

Figure 10.6 Diagrammatic representation of proposed structural and procedural changes for the Council for Voluntary Service example

The support groups would improve Executive contact with the staff and help the Executive become better informed. This communication should encourage mutual respect and increase core-staff motivation and effectiveness, since they would see an interest being taken in their area of work and receive valuable support.

The general management committee should leave the full Executive freer to debate significant policy issues. It would support the General Secretary in his management tasks and provide the Executive with more informed feedback on management. In addition, it was to be the focus for support group matters.

The strengthened finance committee would be able to provide the full Executive with better presented and more reliable information. It would help the professional image of the organisation.

Thus, guided by TSI, a deep intervention was achieved by using a variety of systems ideas to address the total problem situation faced by the Executive Committee of West Newton CVS.

10.3 CRITIQUE OF TSI

We shall present some criticisms that we suspect might be levelled against TSI and seek to address them. In due course other criticisms will emerge and those will have to be answered at that time.

Theory

(a) It might be argued that we have massively over elaborated. We have subjected the reader to many different metaphors and methodologies and, on top of that, we insist that he or she becomes familiar with the logic and process of TSI. Furthermore, we suggest that the five main metaphors presented in Chapter 1 can easily be supplemented with others, for more sophisticated users of TSI. And there are, of course, other systems methodologies which could be included in the TSI schema.

If we had to answer this with respect to the metaphors we would state that we are in fact simplifying the task for the reader by making sophisticated use of some basic understandings that each one of us already possesses. What we would suggest is that loosely organised ideas relating to scientific knowledge are already there in our world. We regularly refer to organisations, societies, etc., as operating like machines, or teams, as evolving like species, as learning like brains, as acting as one or many cultures, or even as imprisoning our existence. At times, each of these, and other perceptions, represents a meaningful way of considering a situation. All we have done with the metaphors is to step back and to recognise a pattern underlying these thoughts, one that in fact reflects at a very general level the whole of management and organisation theory, and indeed systems-based "problem solving". In seeing this we realised that we could propose a relatively easy way of accessing and harnessing that knowledge. We have come up with five systemic metaphors that give an overview of a variety of managerially oriented disciplines, and suggest that all readers can make something of the knowledge that they inevitably have in this area, no matter how little that is. Of course, becoming a more sophisticated user of TSI requires accepting the challenge of boosting the knowledge base you have. The basic framework of TSI, starting with the metaphors, is not difficult to comprehend and becomes no more difficult in the process of further knowledge acquisition.

With respect to the systems methodologies we believe we have done a similar simplifying job. The variety of systems methodologies around makes "systems" look incoherent as a discipline and is off-putting for would be users of systems approaches. By showing the relationships between different systems methodologies, by exposing their fundamental assumptions, we have been able to re-establish "systems" as a unified discipline of thought which can readily be grasped by managers and decision makers.

(b) TSI could be accused of being very much centred on human beings and the pursuance of human well-being. We have followed Habermas in seeking to promote the three human interests in control, communication and emancipation. Perhaps this is assuming a superior position over other orders of life and over all inanimate things. The approach of TSI, for example, does not properly deal with environmental issues. In a sense its monolithic discourse is concerned only with the achievement of human well-being in the longer term.

To this charge we have to plead, to some extent, guilty. The question is, it seems to us, "How can we introduce the environment, or certain relevant aspects of it, as a kind of stakeholder in our analysis?" A good start is being sympathetic to the idea, an even better conclusion would be the development within the logic and process of TSI, of explicit guidelines that address environmental issues.

No doubt, too, we have neglected feminist and non-Western ideas. We hope to learn enough so that TSI can one day pay proper respect to these other perspectives.

Methodology

(a) One angle of attack on the methodology of TSI could be directed at the "system of systems methodologies". A successful assault here would be damaging indeed, because the "system of systems methodologies" not only reflects our interest in metaphors, but shows how we can organise systems-based "problem-solving" approaches. It is also a framework that can be linked to the complementary interests of human beings: the technical, practical and emancipatory interests set out by Habermas. We would also argue that it helps to satisfy the original intent of systems thinking—that of comprehensiveness. Destroy the "system of systems methodologies" and the rest of TSI might crumble.

One obvious argument is that the "system of systems methodologies" amounts to little more than trivial pigeon-holing—that it recommends methodologies in boxes, choosing an appropriate one when a particular problem context has been identified, and then popping it back in again when the problem has been solved.

Our answer is that the "system of systems methodologies" should not be interpreted literally as it physically appears in the figures in Chapter 2. These are merely diagrammatic representations of what are termed in sociology "ideal types". An ideal type is constructed to inform debate by drawing out some key features of an area of concern. In our case we use ideal-type representations of problem contexts. We do not expect any "real world" appreciation of a problem context to fit exactly any one box. We do, however, expect those having to deal with difficult management and planning issues to be informed by the ideas of Chapter 2, and the ideal-type frameworks developed therein. This is because the frameworks point to the assumptions different systems methodologies make about problem contexts. We should be aware when we use a particular systems approach what assumptions it is making.

(b) Although on the one hand TSI offers clear guidelines which is appealing, it could be argued on the other hand that it is too structured and actually closes down on creativity, dictating a particular bias. We would argue that we are helping everyone to think within the very wide boundaries of knowledge in the managerial sciences and hence helping to avoid biases arising from limitations in knowledge. We are encouraging all users of TSI to expand their knowledge and broaden their horizons. It seems eminently sensible to help people to put together their ideas in a synergistic (but not closed) whole—ideas that would otherwise be used in an incoherent and unorganised, even confusing fashion.

A further point is that not only do we provide very broad structures but we remain critically self-reflective about them. In TSI we decided to give good clear guidance about how to think creatively at the outset, through the metaphors, but have also dealt critically with the implications of any partial conception so produced in terms of legitimacies and limitations.

(c) Another criticism might be that TSI is simply pragmatic at the methodological level and, in an approach that has more than a whiff of contingency about it, TSI is merely eclectic. We maintain that this criticism can be refuted by considering our theoretical base, which is critical systems thinking (see Chapter 3). In critical systems thinking contingency is replaced by critical self-reflection. Eclecticism is the enemy of critical systems thinking.

Ideology

Our ideology is revealed in critical systems thinking. The interesting thing is that the systems idea logically builds to a view where human well-being and emancipation is implied. As with *any* position it is ideologically oriented, however. Hard, cybernetic and soft systems approaches tend to be ideologically conservative. We are happy if our approach turns out to be a socially conscious and caring system of thought. Critical systems thinking is a politically conscious and self-reflective approach, distinguished by an openly declared emancipatory interest in an equal distribution of power and chances to satisfy personal needs, and in liberating people from dominance by other people and forces they do not currently control.

The critic might come back, of course, and ask if we are not simply liberal minded consultants, but when the coercive crunch comes whether we would not simply have to avoid the issues. We agree, this does raise a major dilemma. What should we do as managers, planners, decision makers or consultants when all the evidence we have highlights coercive forces at work? Obviously this would be a matter of strategy and conscience. We could refuse the work since we might be obliged to concede our interests to those in power. On the other hand we might take on the job in the hope that some progress can be made towards our ideals, and that something is better than nothing.

Utility

It might be argued that we are more philosophically than practically oriented, always looking into the black box for some new intangible. On the contrary, we would argue that we are more practically oriented than most managers. We are only being realistic about the nature of organisational and societal difficulties, or complexities if you like. The "manager" searches for the tangible problem, "finds it" and then "grabs hold of it", "takes it away" and "solves it". The TSI analyst, being more realistic, recognises that under the folds and other dark and usually unexplored areas, the black box we could say, we can find a host of other issues, issues that will confound the "manager" with his/her solution. TSI analysts seek ways of managing these issues using a range of appropriate methodologies. The "manager", the one the critic implies is practical, is in an impoverished position unable to handle sufficiently competently the realities—he/she is not properly practically oriented. The TSI analyst, the one the critic accuses of being philosophical, is in a stronger position to handle the realities in a relevant way—he/she is much more practically oriented.

10.4 CONCLUSION

This volume, *Creative Problem Solving: Total Systems Intervention*, amounts to the bringing together of ·a huge human effort in the area of the management sciences. Our part in this has been a major contribution to the development of critical systems thinking, and the pragmatisation of this in the logic and process of Total Systems Intervention. This effort has taken many years, which includes substantial amounts of time applying the worked out ideas in the practical world. The nature of our employment, being currently based at Hull University, has allowed us to employ the ideas at both competitive consultancy rates for commercial enterprises and free of charge for voluntary and charitable organisations. Through this we have been able to analyse our ideas at work across a whole spectrum of contexts.

The part played by others in this huge human effort is vast. Each particular methodology that we have presented in this book is the realisation of years of work by many people, and the management and organisation theory to which we refer goes back nearly a century and has employed armies of researchers. We rest, with TSI, on the very top of this mountain, able to experience an overview of the management-oriented disciplines and able to help managers and decision makers gain a command over how to employ them as a whole.

10.5 CASE STUDY

Now it is time for you, the reader, to tackle your next case study, and that is to be found in your own work or social domain, wherever that may be.

10.6 FURTHER READING

- For "cognitive mapping" mentioned in this chapter see:

Eden, C., Jones, S. and Sims, D. (1983). *Messing About in Problems*, Pergamon, Oxford.

- For the rest of the chapter consult those references mentioned in the further reading section of Chapter 3.

Index

Action concepts, 170
Actuality, 93
Algedonic signal, 92, 109
Attitudinal change, 184, 239
Autocratic management, 97, 104, 112

Boundary judgements, 204–5, 207–8

Capability, 93
Coalition metaphor, 14, 39
Coercive relationships, 13, 34–5, 158, 159, 161, 168, 188, 198, 217–18, 244
Coffee Selling Organisation ("Hull Far East"), 162–5
Communicative competence, 189, 199, 201, 202
Complementarism, 47–8, 219
Complexity, 34, 89
Conflict, 158–9, 188
Constitutive meaning, 170
Construction Industry in Singapore, 22–8
    Development Board, of, 22–8
Contingency theory, 37
Control, 89
Co-operative Development Agency ("Winterton"), 128–33, 178–86
Council for Voluntary Service ("West Newton"), 224–40
Critical systems heuristics (CSH), 36, 40, 53, 197–8
    critique of, 217–20
        ideology, 218–19
        methodology, 218
        theory, 217–18
        utility, 219–20
    in action, 208–17
    methodology of, 204–8

polemical employment of boundary judgements in, 207–8
    12 critically heuristic categories in, 204–7, 213–17, 220–1
    philosophy of, 199–202
    principles of, 202–4
Critical systems thinking, 46–9
Cultural feasibility, 171, 209
Culture metaphor, 11–12, 20, 39
Cybernetics, 87, 88, 89–90, 110, 112, 187, 238

Democratic management, 109, 111, 113
Devil's advocate approach (to planning), 127–8, 135
Dialectical approach (to planning), 127–8, 134–5
Dissolving problems, 147
Distorted communication, 189
DYNAMO, 70, 78

"Electronics Components Distributors", 190–4
Emancipatory interest, 49, 187, 244
Emergent properties, 6
Entertainments Group ("XY"), 114–17
Environmental issues, 242
Expert approach (to planning), 127–8
Experts (in the systems approach), 121, 149

False consciousness, 159, 161, 188
Feedback, 5
Feminist ideas, 242
Frankfurt School of sociologists, 217

General system theory, 37

Hard (systems) paradigm, 170
Heroic mood, 122
Hierarchy, 6–7
Homeostasis, 4, 6, 105
Human relations theory, 9
Human well-being and emancipation,
    49

Ideal-seeking system, 151, 152
Ideal-types, 243
Idealism, 187, 188, 217
Idealised design, 150–2, 155–6
Ill-structured problems, 119–20, 135
Imperialism (in management science),
    47, 48, 187
Inactivist planning, 146
Industrial democracy, 131
Instrumental reason, 198, 200, 219
INTERACT, 153, 167
Interactive planning (IP), 39, 53,
    143–4, 147
  critique of, 157–61
    ideology, 160–1
    methodology, 159–60
    theory, 157–9
    utility, 161
  in action, 153–7
  methodology of, 150–3
    design of implementation and
        control, 153
    ends planning, 150–2, 155
    formulating the mess, 150, 154
    means planning, 152–3
    resource planning, 153
  philosophy of, 144–8
  principles of, 148–9
    continuity, 149
    holistic, 149
    participative, 148–9
Interpretive theory, 186–7, 188
Isolationism (in management science),
    47, 48, 83, 187, 188

Law of requisite variety, 90, 112
Learning system, 171, 177–8

Machine age, 145
Machine metaphor, 8–9
Management theory, 2, 8, 9, 241, 245
Materialism, 187, 217–18
Means-end thinking, 169
Mechanism, 3

Messes, 122, 147, 179
Meta-paradigmatic net, 60
Meta-system, 90, 231
Metaphor, 14–15
  dependent, 51
  dominant, 51
Model formulation 64–7
Model validation, 65–7

Neuro-cybernetic metaphor, 10–11, 38,
    40, 98

Objectivity, 121, 122, 144–5, 160
Operational research, 36
Organic metaphor, 9–10, 18, 38, 40

Participation, 133–4, 148–9, 156,
    159–60, 171, 189, 202
Pluralist relationships, 13, 34, 168
Polemical employment of reason, 208
Police strategy on offensive weapons,
    208–17
Political metaphor, 12–14
Potentiality, 93
Power, 12, 13, 40, 41, 49, 112, 134, 159,
    188, 189
Practical interest, 49, 187
Practical reason, 198, 199, 200, 219
  dialectical approach to, 199
  scientistic approach to, 199
Pragmatism (in management science),
    47
Preactivist planning, 146
Printing Company ("Thornton"),
    136–40
Prison metaphor, 14, 40, 41
Problem contexts, 32
  complex–coercive, 41, 219–20
  complex–pluralist, 39–40, 144, 168
  complex–unitary, 37–8
  ideal-type classification of, 33–5
  participants dimension of, 33–5
  simple–coercive, 40–1, 198
  simple–pluralist, 38–9, 135
  simple–unitary, 36–7
  systems dimension of, 33–4
Procedural change, 185–6, 239
Project management, 83–5
Purposeful systems, 146, 157
Purposeful systems paradigm, 203
Purposefulness, 202–3

Quality management (*see also* Total
    Quality Management), 124, 136–40
Quality of Work Life, 155, 156

Rationality, 145
Reactivist planning, 146
Recursion, 89–90, 98, 100
    triple recursive-level, 98
Reductionism, 3
Reference scenario, 150, 152
Relativism, 189
Resolving problems, 147

Signed digraph, 67
Social dynamics, 170
Social systems design, 38
Sociological awareness, 48
Sociotechnical systems thinking, 37
Soft systems methodology (SSM), 39,
    53, 57, 168, 230
    critique of, 186–90
        ideology, 189–90
        methodology, 188–9
        theory, 186–8
        utility, 190
    in action, 178–86
    methodology of, 172–8
        Analysis, 1, 2, 3 in, 174
        CATWOE, 175, 181, 232, 235–6
        comparison stage, 176–7, 181–4,
            236–8
        conceptual models, 176, 181–3,
            232, 233, 234, 236
        defining changes, 177, 184
        finding out, 172–5, 180
        Mode 1 use, 172, 179
        Mode 2 use, 172
        relevant systems, 174, 180, 230–1
        rich pictures, 173–4, 230
        root definitions, 175, 180–1, 232,
            235–6
        taking action, 177, 184–6, 238–40
    philosophy of, 168–71
    principles of, 171–2
Soft (systems) paradigm, 170
Soft systems thinking, 167–8
Solving problems, 147
Stakeholders, 122, 146
STELLA, 70, 76, 78
Stock control, 68–9, 70–3, 75–8
Strategic assumption surfacing and

testing (SAST), 38, 39, 53, 58,
    119–20
    critique of, 133–35
        ideology, 134
        methodology, 134
        theory, 133–4
        utility, 134–5
    in action, 128–33
    methodology of 124–8
        assumption rating, 126, 130
        assumption specification, 126, 130
        assumption surfacing, 125–6,
            129–30
        dialectical debate, 127, 130–2
        group formation, 124–5, 129
        stakeholder analysis, 125, 129–30
        synthesis, 127–8, 132
    philosophy of 120–3
    principles of, 123–4
        adversarial, 123
        integrative, 123
        managerial mind supporting,
            123–4
        participative, 123
Structural change, 185, 238–9
Subjectivity, 121
System (general conception of), 5–7
System diagnosis, 94–5
System dynamics (SD), 36, 53, 61–2
    critique of, 78–83
        ideology, 81
        methodology, 80–1
        theory, 79–80
        utility, 81–2
    in action, 75–8
    model and methodology of, 64–75
        auxiliaries, 69
        flows, 69
        levels, 67, 68
        loop analysis, 74–5
        model conceptualisation, 67–73
        rates, 67, 68
    philosophy of, 62–3
        feedback, 62
        feedforward, 63
        structure, 62–3
    principles of, 63–4
System identification, 94
System of systems methodologies, 22,
    32, 41–3, 48, 51–2, 57, 119, 120,
    242–3

Systemic metaphors, 1, 2, 4, 7–15, 18,
    21, 50–1, 56, 58, 241
Systems, 2
  closed, 4, 10
  complex, 33–4
  open, 4, 10
  simple, 33
Systems Age, 145
Systems analysis, 36, 37
Systems engineering, 36
Systems methodologies, 14, 15, 21,
    52–3, 59, 241–2
  dependent, 52
  dominant, 52, 179
Systems science, 198
Systems thinking, 3, 5

Team metaphor, 14, 21, 37, 38
Technical interest, 49, 62, 187
Total Quality Management (TQM) (see
    also Quality Management), 15–21,
    54, 57
  communication in, 16, 18
  control in, 16–17, 18
  implementation of, 17–18, 21
Total Systems Intervention (TSI),
    xi–xiii, 15, 45, 46, 82, 178, 203–4,
    245
  critique of, 241–4
    ideology, 243–4
    methodology, 242–3
    theory, 241–2
    utility, 244
  in action, 54–8, 224–40
  methodology of, 50–4
    choice phase, 51–2
    creativity phase, 50–1
    implementation phase, 52–4

    iteration in, 53–4, 58–9
    philosophy of, 46–9
    principles of, 50
Tourism Services Group ("Zania"),
    96–110

Undistorted communication, 199, 200
Unitary relationships, 13, 34
Utopia, 151, 218

Variety, 105
Viable system diagnosis (VSD), 36, 37,
    38, 53, 88, 229
  critique of, 110–13
    ideology, 112–13
    methodology, 111–12
    theory, 110–11
    utility, 113
  frequent faults discovered by, 95–6
  in action, 96–110
  methodology of, 93–5
  philosophy of, 89
  principles of, 89–90
Viable system model, 58, 87–8, 231–2
  audit channels in, 104
  information flows in, 92–3
  System 1 of, 90, 94, 100–3
  System 2 of, 92, 94, 96, 103
  System 3 of, 92, 94–5, 96, 103–5
  System 4 of, 92, 95, 96, 105, 108
  System 5 of, 92, 95, 96, 109
  Using the model, 93–5
Vitalism, 3

Weltanschauung, 175, 187
Whole systems judgements, 205
Wicked problems, 122
Witnesses, 204, 205